''OUR FATHER''

"OUR FATHER"

An Introduction to the Lord's Prayer

ERNST LOHMEYER

TRANSLATED BY JOHN BOWDEN

Harper & Row, PUBLISHERS

NEW YORK

First published in Germany under the title
Das Vater-Unser by Vandenhoeck & Ruprecht, 1952

242.722
LOO

Published in Great Britain under the title *"The Lord's Prayer"*

FIRST EDITION

LIBRARY OF CONGRESS CATALOG CARD NUMBER: *66-10228*

Foreword

Ernst Lohmeyer was born in Westphalia in 1890, and in 1920 became Professor of the New Testament in the university of Breslau. In 1936 he was sent for political reasons to Greifswald, where he remained. In 1945 he was appointed Rector of Greifswald, but during the night before the official re-opening of the university after the war he disappeared. Nothing certain is known of his fate, but it is assumed that his life was ended somewhere in Russia in September 1946.

These brief facts conceal a lifetime devoted to the scholarly interpretation of the New Testament and the Church struggle in Germany. His great commentaries in the series of critical-exegetical commentaries established in 1832 by H. A. W. Meyer, especially those on Mark and Matthew, as well as his many other distinguished contributions to the study of the New Testament and of the Primitive Church, have long been cherished by students of German. In these works there may be found a remarkable conjunction of critical acumen and scholarly judgment with a strong sense of the compelling reality of the material under investigation.

These qualities may be seen in the present work on the Lord's Prayer, which is the first of Lohmeyer's works to appear in English. Studies of the Lord's Prayer are so plentiful that a word of apology might seem in place. In fact, Lohmeyer's standards of scholarship are such, and his feeling for the life of the Christian in present-day circumstances is so deep and so authentic, that this work will readily be recognized as one of the great studies of the sources, the milieu, the uniqueness and the living reality of the teaching of the Lord's Prayer. It may be recommended to the faithful perusal of both the scholar and the patient layman.

R. GREGOR SMITH

Contents

Translator's Preface

The text of the Revised Standard Version has been used throughout for the biblical quotations. In a few instances, individual words have been changed (e.g. 'hallow' for 'sanctify', 'consecrate') to bring out the parallels between the Lord's Prayer and other parts of the New Testament. The changes are sufficiently obvious to make a special note in each case unnecessary. The Pseudepigrapha are quoted in the collection edited by R. H. Charles. English versions of Jewish texts are taken from the *Soncino Talmud*, edited by Dr. I. Epstein, and from the *Authorized Daily Prayer Book*, translated by the Rev. S. Singer. For the convenience of the reader a translation of the Eighteen Benedictions from the prayer book has been included in an appendix. The translations of Babylonian texts in chapter VII are those in J. B. Pritchard, *Ancient Near Eastern Texts*. Because the value of this book lies in the author's own writing rather than in the reference he makes to other authorities, no attempt has been made to bring the few footnotes up to date. One fault in the German edition is that there is in several cases no indication of where the footnotes should be placed in relationship to the text. The numerals indicating the footnotes have been omitted from the latter. I have supplied them in the English text where they seemed to belong, but there have sometimes been several possibilities to choose from.

I am most grateful to Mrs. Pauline Miller for her help in preparing the typescript for the press.

J.S.B.

Abbreviations

CIL	*Corpus Inscriptionum Latinarum*
CSEL	*Corpus Scriptorum Ecclesiasticorum Latinorum*
GCS	*Griechischen Christlichen Schriftsteller der ersten drei Jahrhunderte*
HTR	*Harvard Theological Review*
JBL	*Journal of Biblical Literature*
LXX	Septuagint. The Greek translation of the Old Testament
PG	Migne, *Patrologia Graeca*
PL	Migne, *Patrologia Latina*
TWNT	*Theologisches Wörterbuch zum Neuen Testament*, ed. G. Kittel
ZNW	*Zeitschrift für die Neutestamentliche Wissenschaft*

I Preliminary Questions

1. Is there any need to devote a whole book to the Lord's Prayer? For centuries it has been a living influence in Christendom, and no one anywhere has failed to understand it. Wherever it has spread, the differences of countries and peoples, languages and nations, time and place, class and status have ceased to matter. All have been taken up together, through its utter simplicity, into a deeper, all-embracing unity. And yet new explanations of this short and easily understood prayer have been given continually ever since the beginnings of Christianity. At every turning point of Christian history the Lord's Prayer itself has seemed to need new interpretation.

When the Christian Faith allied itself with late-Hellenistic philosophy and culture, the ascetic and philosophical spirit of Origen, in an exposition of the Lord's Prayer which is one of the finest and most mature of his works, indicated the approach that Greek theology was to follow for centuries. Gregory of Nyssa and Maximus the Confessor moved in this direction, and even Cyril of Jerusalem and Chrysostom, despite all their independence, allowed themselves to come under the same influence. Tertullian and Cyprian expounded the Lord's Prayer for the African Church, and at the fateful end of the fourth century, when a distinctive Latin Christianity was taking shape, Augustine interpreted the Lord's Prayer afresh for the Latin West, an interpretation by which the Middle Ages lived. When they in turn began to turn towards new forms and new aims, it was again in an interpretation of the Lord's Prayer that Meister

13

Eckhart summed up the content of scholastic theology, and a century and a half later Nicholas of Cusa felt after new foundations for faith and thought in wide-ranging meditations on it. The significance of the Lord's Prayer for the Reformation is shown by the countless expositions given by Luther, which from 1519 onwards accompany and explain its course.

These are only a few examples, and they can be interpreted in different ways, but they nevertheless show quite clearly that in all the commentaries of past centuries there have been so to speak two sides to the influence of the Lord's Prayer: everyone can understand it, yet it always calls for a new understanding; it continues to reveal new depths of meaning, and still transcends all explanations by the mystery of its transparent simplicity. These two aspects merely reflect the fact that in fixed and perfectly-chosen words the Lord's Prayer offers an inexhaustible content, which can always be grasped and repeated by the prayers of heart and mouth, yet never fathomed in the thoughts of the mind. For this reason Tertullian already called the prayer a *breviarium totius evangelii*, and for this reason it is continually in need of a new explanation, so that no generation is so poor as to be incapable of appropriating its inheritance. And again, because the Lord's Prayer is put in these clear and simple words, it needs no special explanation other than a heart which will receive it and go out to it, so that no generation is so rich that it would not benefit still further from these words. From these two aspects, however, as they have been experienced over the centuries, there continually arises the question of its historical origin and its objective content.

Of course this question has often been put in recent decades. Every catechism touches on it, and every commentary on the First or the Third Gospel seeks an answer. But since Jacob Wettstein declared (on *Matt.* 6.9), *Tota haec oratio ex formulis Hebraeorum concinnata est tam apte, ut omnia contineat quae a Deo peti possunt cum agnitione majestatis divinae et subjectionis nostrae,* the concrete historical questions have always stood in the foreground. How firm and how close is the connection with Jewish prayers and ideas? To put it bluntly, just how much of the Lord's Prayer is still Jewish, and how much is already Christian? Adolf Harnack, in his work on the Lord's Prayer, sought to discover a basic form of the prayer; the expositions by Dalman and Fiebig demonstrate the close relationship between its words and ideas and Jewish views. But sometimes these investigations seem to obscure the second part of Wettstein's sentence, namely that the Lord's Prayer contains all that a man could ask of God. He is asking what the objective content of the prayer adds up to, seeking its character and the context in which it stands. And if all this is only to be explained from the totality of the Gospel message, then each single detail of this message needs to be defined, however slight and familiar the word concerned may be. True, much has happened, and has happened in the last two centuries, to explain the historical background and significance of the individual words; but the number of questions which still remain can be shown most clearly by the fact that the word ἐπιούσιος in the fourth petition still remains to be explained, and probably never will be. The aim of our investigation is thus clearly defined: it will attempt to determine on a historical and objective basis the original content of the Lord's Prayer, both in its individual details and as a whole.

2. The Lord's Prayer has been handed down to us in two places in the New Testament and in two versions. The first and most important form, indeed, quite simply, *the* Lord's Prayer, has been preserved by St. Matthew's Gospel in the Sermon on the Mount (6.9-13). It consists of the full address, 'Our Father who art in heaven', and six or—according to another way of counting—seven brief petitions. In some ancient manuscripts a concise doxology and a simple 'Amen' have also been transmitted as a conclusion to the prayer, but they are not included in the important and reliable ones. Instead of this solemn conclusion, Matthew attaches a saying of the Lord which twice formulates as a rule what is stated by the fifth petition as an acknowledgment.

It seems to underline what this Matthaean tradition regarded as the most important and conspicuous petition in the framework of the prayer. This version is supported by the tradition of the Didache, individual elements of which are hardly any later than some parts of the First Gospel. Between instructions about Baptism (ch. 7) and the Eucharist (chs. 9, 10), it has a section on fasting and prayer (Matthew too puts the sayings about prayer after those about fasting), and in this section it gives the text of the Lord's Prayer. This follows the Matthaean wording quite closely, and diverges only in three almost insignificant points: the address has the singular form instead of the plural for 'heaven'; the fifth petition speaks in the apodosis of 'our debt' with the present tense, and not of 'our debts' with the aorist. Finally, a two-membered doxology (without an Amen) is added and the whole prayer is concluded with the remark, 'Pray thus three times a day' (8.3). These peculiarities probably indicate that the Didache took over its text not from St. Matthew's Gospel, but from an oral tradition which may well have come from the same district and the same group of communities as that of Matthew. So this evidence provides independent support to that of the First Gospel.

A second form of the Lord's Prayer has been transmitted by St. Luke's Gospel in a special piece of its tradition (11.1-4). The disciples ask the Master to teach them to pray, as John taught his disciples, and Jesus gives them the Lord's Prayer. The address here is brief, 'Father', without any addition, and the third and seventh petitions of Matthew are completely absent. This Lucan form does not have a doxology, and in the fourth and fifth petitions it has some peculiarities of language and content which will be discussed in more detail later. It is significant for the relationship between these two forms that only a few manuscripts, and not many Church witnesses, but nevertheless some important ones, attest this shorter Lucan form of the Lord's Prayer. The broader and more solemn Matthaean form has found its way into most of the manuscripts of the Third Gospel and has suppressed the briefer and simpler form, although, as we

16

shall soon see, the latter moulds itself more flexibly to the needs of the community and the individual. In addition to this Lucan version of the Lord's Prayer there is evidence of a second version of the second petition in some minuscule manuscripts and in some of the Fathers. It runs: May thy holy Spirit come upon us and cleanse us! Its position also varies: the earliest witness, Marcion, has the petition first and puts the usual form of the second petition 'Thy kingdom come' after it. All the rest begin with the petition 'Hallowed be thy name' and replace the request for the kingdom with the new one for the holy Spirit. The question of what is ancient and what is later in this version will be investigated in due course.

3. 'Lord, teach us to pray', begins Luke, 'Pray then like this', says Matthew, in introducing the words of the prayer. The two introductions show how significant the Lord's Prayer was for the first Christians. It may seem remarkable that the Second and Fourth Gospels do not give the words of the Lord's Prayer. Nor do they appear elsewhere in the New Testament, either in Paul, or in the Catholic Epistles, or in the other Johannine writings. They are not even in the Apostolic Fathers and the Apologists. And yet they were at hand and well known, for the Didache appoints them as a prayer to be said three times a day. Another, though not completely certain, sign of their use is the *Rotas-Opera* Word Square which has been discovered at Pompeii, i.e. to be dated at the latest A.D. 78, and in Dura on the Euphrates, i.e. no later than the third century A.D. If it is correct, as the independent investigations of Pastor F. Grosser and G. Agrell, a Slavonic scholar from Lund, have ascertained, that the letters of this square, taken apart and reassembled, produce *Pater noster* twice and AO twice, then we have here further testimony to the currency and significance of the prayer and perhaps also an indication why we do not find its full wording quoted more often. For it is hardly by chance that it is concealed from the pagan public in a magic square; its words therefore

only seem to have been used in the prayers of individuals or in the liturgy of the community, just as the Didache transmits it within the directions for the sacred actions of Baptism and the Eucharist.

But if the Lord's Prayer was so widespread in the congregations of the ancient world, we might expect that there would be at least allusions to its words and phrases in the Christian literature of the first and second centuries. This expectation is not disappointed. In instructions about faith and prayer Mark already hands on the saying (11.25): 'And whenever you stand praying, forgive, if you have anything against any one; so that your Father also who is in heaven may forgive you your trespasses.' The saying is certainly first and foremost a variant of the rule which Matthew, too, has handed down in connection with the Lord's Prayer, but it differs from it by the addition, 'and whenever you stand praying', and the phrase, 'your Father also who is in heaven', which occurs only there in St. Mark's Gospel. Still, if the duty to forgive is understood as a part or even as a prerequisite of prayer, if God is spoken of only here as 'your Father who is in heaven', then we can probably trace in this verse the influence not only of the fifth petition, but also of the whole prayer. We might perhaps also find an indication of this in the fact that some old manuscripts have inserted the Matthaean rule at this point in the Marcan text (11.26).

The traces of the Lord's Prayer in the Fourth Gospel are not so clear. The fact that here the address 'Father' (never 'Our Father who art in heaven') is always put on the lips of Jesus when he prays, merely corresponds to a more general custom of prayer which Jesus perhaps initiated and certainly filled with new meaning and life. Both the thanksgiving (*Matt.* 11.25) and the prayer of the agony in Gethsemane testify to this. More plainly, the first petition occurs once in the form 'Glorify thy name' (12.28); but it is also plain that its wording derives from Old Testament formulations. The seventh petition probably lies behind the words of the High-Priestly Prayer (17.15): 'I do not pray that thou shouldst take them out of the world, but that

thou shouldst keep them from evil.' Both the terminology and
the sense suggest that this is a Johannine exegesis of the last
Matthaean petition, but this precise thought is so often attested
in Primitive Christian writings, as well as earlier in the Old
Testament, that it, too, cannot be derived with certainty from
the Matthaean conclusion to the Lord's Prayer.

In no place do the Pauline Epistles display a knowledge of
the individual petitions of the Lord's Prayer. This is even true
of the great prayer of the Epistle to the Ephesians (3.14-21). True,
it has been called the 'Apostolic Our Father', but the relationship
does not go beyond the quite general parallelism in the address,
'Father', which it shares with almost all Primitive Christian
prayers. Apart from the Gethsemane narrative, there is one
variation on the petition 'Thy will be done', in the Acts of the
Apostles (21.14). The conclusion of II Timothy seems to allude
to the end of the Lord's Prayer, which it perhaps knew with
the doxology (4.18): 'The Lord will rescue me from every evil
and save me for his heavenly kingdom. To him be the glory
for ever and ever. Amen.' In his letter to the Philippians,
Polycarp of Smyrna admonishes them to beseech the all-seeing
God to 'lead us not into temptation', and in the account of his
martyrdom the petition 'the will of God be done' is put into his
mouth (7.1). Alongside the testimony of the first great episcopal
figure stands the testimony, already mentioned, of his great
opponent Marcion, and to this twofold witness from the beginning and the middle of the second Christian century there
corresponds at the end that of Clement of Alexandria, who was
the first person to reverence the words of the Lord's Prayer as
the vessel of an infinite knowledge.

Perhaps we may not consider this evidence to be very strong
or even in some respects remarkable, but it is enough to testify
that the Lord's Prayer is one of the most ancient pieces of the
Gospel tradition. And this testimony reaches from the East of
Syria to Rome, from the north of Asia Minor to Egypt, thereby
so to speak marking out the area within which the Gospel, and
with it the Lord's Prayer, flourished. At the same time it also

lets us guess at the often obscure ways by which the Gospel travelled through the whole of the Mediterranean world. It is only important for us here that a firm chain of tradition links the first occurrence of the prayer in the Gospels with its first interpretation by Clement of Alexandria.

4. The motives for which Matthew and Luke give the words of the Lord's Prayer are different, and therefore the light which falls on the prayer from these motives is different too.

In Matthew, the Lord's Prayer stands in a context which is distinguished by similarity of form and affinities of content. The instructions about giving alms, prayer and fasting (6.1-18) are not commands, but admonitions; they are to be fulfilled like traditional exercises of piety. Nowhere is there an explanation of these exercises or the reason for them; it is simply said how they are to be carried out. The way in which this is to be done is determined by the eschatological opposition of hiddenness and openness; all these exercises are to be done in secret because God will reward them openly. For now is already the time when the signs of God's eschatological works are beginning to appear; therefore those who recognize these signs live and work in secret even from themselves, so that the left hand does not know what the right hand is doing.

This basic thought is made clear in the section on prayer in three different ways. From a literary point of view it probably comes from different traditions, as is already shown by the change from the second person singular to the second person plural; we must therefore beware of associating the words of the Lord's Prayer too closely with the two warnings which precede it. Above all, the Lord's Prayer should not be regarded as the pattern of a brief prayer to be taken in opposition to the 'vain repetitions' of the Gentiles. For, precisely at this point, the inner difference between the two parts becomes particularly clear. After the words, 'Your Father knows what you need before you ask him', which perhaps show words of prayer in general to be superfluous, and surely show their character to be a matter of indifference, one would not expect instruction in the specific wording of a prayer. But if the Lord's Prayer comes from a tradition different from that of the context in which it is placed, the introductory words are no more than an external transition. But even this transition does not follow the basic thought of the whole section, for the injunction is to 'pray like this', not to 'pray *this*'; it speaks of the way to pray, not of these particular words of prayer; the emphatic 'you' then also introduces into these thoughts a mark of distinction from the 'Pharisees' and Gentiles mentioned earlier, the ones as hypocrites, the others a babblers.

A further standpoint for assessing the Lord's Prayer is given by its position in the Sermon on the Mount. The Lord's Prayer, like the whole of the Sermon, is directed towards 'the people'. Of course, the concept of this people must not be taken in an external, historical sense, as though it meant the chance crowds of hearers from all the districts of Palestine which are depicted by Matthew. 'People' here designates that group to whom it is said, 'You are the salt of the earth; you are the light of the world', the community of disciples distinct both from the Gentiles and the Jews (5.20,46,47) who in this sermon receive the basic law for their conduct in the eschatological time, which is now still hidden, and with this basic law also the basic prayer. The prayer involves the whole man, just as the whole sermon involves him in thought and action, and just as the sermon gives him the freedom of his being and his will only in this involvement, so too does the prayer. So for the Gospel according to St. Matthew the Lord's Prayer is the basic prayer for the eschatological community of the disciples, not a prayer for individuals, but for the community, not for the necessities of human life but for the requirements of the life of a disciple, life in this eschatological time, which will presently emerge from its hiddenness into the eternal light of the eschatological day of God.

Luke's tradition is different. Here, a brief narrative gives the framework and introduces the subject; Jesus has been praying;

when he ceases, a disciple asks him, 'Teach us to pray.' He asks
not as an individual but as a spokesman for the disciples who share
Jesus' life and teaching; and this link between the pupils and
their teacher is further underlined by the reason attached to the
request, 'as John taught his disciples'. In answer to this request,
Jesus gives the disciples the Lord's Prayer. Here is a *hieros logos*
which explains where the Lord's Prayer derives from and how it
was given. It says nothing of the significance that the prayer has
or is to have in the group of the disciples; in this account the
prayer is a holy heritage from a holy past. Even the comparison
with John the Baptist is more a historical reminiscence than a
permanent distinction, at least it is not a distinction which makes
inward demands on the disciples like the saying in Matthew about
hypocrites and babblers. Here Luke only explains the fact which
has left its mark right up to the present, namely why the disciples
of Jesus and the disciples of John, who have such close affinities
in their origins, customs and aims, should nevertheless differ in
their prayers. Whether this narrative is historically accurate
we can neither ask nor say, because there is no possibility of
proof or of comparison. The difference between these two
accounts of Matthew and Luke is not to be explained from this
one piece of tradition, but is connected with the material and
historical differences which characterize both Gospels all the
way through.

Behind these differences, there is, however, a common question: what is the significance of the instruction of a group of
disciples in a prayer as the norm and pattern of their praying?
For the suggestion that John, too, taught his disciples a prayer
does not explain why Jesus should have done the same. Why
was not the prayer of John's disciples taken over, like his baptism?
Why not a prayer from the Psalter or from other synagogue
traditions? And if a new and different prayer was, in fact, given,
then this was certainly not to distinguish the disciples from other
historical groups; for a man prays to join himself to God, not
to distinguish himself from other men.

If, then, a traditional prayer is not chosen, but a new one is given, the underlying thought is that this prayer brings the person who prays it closer to God than earlier ones, that it is more acceptable to God and will be heard by him in preference to another. And it can only be given if the one who gives it knows God's will more deeply and more truly and is therefore the person to point the way to God. For, 'Lord, teach us to pray', in the end, means, 'Lord, teach us to believe rightly'. Now some not unimportant presuppositions underlie these thoughts.

Judaism, too, knows patterns of, and norms for, prayers. The Eighteen Benedictions, composed by men from the Great Synagogue, as the Talmudic tradition tells us, and perhaps reaching back in its most ancient elements to the time of Jesus, is such a pattern of how men should pray. These men could give it to their people because they themselves belonged to the people of God and were grounded in his revelation in the Old Testament. The people designates the sphere, the revelation the norm and the power, and often even the words, which determine what is right prayer and the way in which it is to be made. Moreover, the work of these men is legitimate, for the Word of God, once sent forth, requires an appropriate answer of each and in each generation; so whoever teaches how to pray rightly can only do so with the support of the Word and in the community which is supported by it. For this reason the rabbinic prayers refer again and again to the words and actions of God, which were once performed for the Fathers; and even in some New Testament prayers these reminiscences of the Old Testament revelations recur: 'As he spoke to our fathers' (*Luke* 1.55,69). So, too, each pious Jew is able and empowered to teach right prayer from the Torah for his people. For John and Jesus however, these foundations, unshakable for both the individual and for the people, are no longer present in the same way. They teach not from the Torah, but on their own authority, and teach not for the people, but for a clearly distinguished group of disciples. So wherever there are community and revelation in Judaism, for the disciples of Jesus there is the Master who embodies both in his person, himself the foundation and the pattern of the community which he creates, himself the norm and the power of the revelation which it receives. It is not even enough to say that he is a prophet who teaches a group of men to pray rightly. For a prophet does not make a community in proclaiming a revelation; he works in a community which is already there, the community of which he is a prophet. It would also be too much to say that he is the final eschatological figure who teaches men to pray rightly, for while this figure indeed creates a community, he teaches neither God's Word nor man's answer—he himself is the perfect truth and reality of all revelation. Here, then, is a man who teaches prayer, who stands midway between the prophet and the final eschatological figure. With the former he has in common a life and work among the people of God, like a prophet he preaches the Word of God in his time and associates it with earlier revelations in whose strength he lives and which he makes his own. With the final eschatological figure, on the other hand, he stands aside from tradition and begins something new, which leads his elect on a straight and sure path to God. Both these elements are contained in the great sentence, 'You have heard that it was said to the men of old, but I say to you', preservation and annihilation leading to a new creation, continuity and disjunction, affirmation and negation.

From this eternal centre there comes the possibility of an eschatological revelation such as pervades the whole of the Sermon on the Mount and with it the Lord's Prayer. From here, too, there comes the simple doctrine of the Word of God in revelation and man's answer in prayer, as it is possible in principle to anyone who reads holy Scripture. This unique intermediate position is passed on from the giver of the prayer to those who receive it. The disciples who pray the prayer of their master are on the one hand simply members of the people of God, among whom God's Word has been alive since the time of the patriarchs and the prophets, while on the other hand they are members of the eschatological community which is only created by the final eschatological figure. In that case, this dual standpoint must be true to a special degree of the prayer which is taught here. It is, in fact, 'only' a prayer, such as pious Jews of the time of Jesus would pray and teach, steeped in the words and thoughts of the Old Testament and suffused with its spirit, and it is equally and precisely in being this an eschatological *novum*, the way to the eternal life that the Master brings.

All this only hints at the relationships within which a prayer stands which disciples ask from their master or the master gives to his disciples, and these relationships are more open questions than clear answers. Nevertheless, they do show some standpoints from which the Lord's Prayer has been and must be regarded. They also make superfluous the dispute whether the wording of this prayer is a binding norm or a variable pattern. The prayer is both at the same time, and yet neither of the two; it is as binding as all the words which come from the mouth of the Master in this eschatological time, and it gives as much freedom and responsibility as everything that is still on the way to the final eschatological revelation.

5. From ancient times, the petitions of the Lord's Prayer have been divided in various ways to match their content. The first three are taken together, relating to God, and the last four relating to men; or the first four, asking for good things which God is to give, and the last three, praying to him to avert ill. Or, finally, the first three are taken together as petitions for God, the fourth as a petition for man's bodily well-being, and the last three as petitions for his spiritual well-being. All such divisions are influenced, implicitly or explicitly, by the model of the Decalogue, which is usually divided into two parts: duties towards God and duties towards one's neighbour. So in the Lord's Prayer, too, the first three petitions have also been distinguished as *pia vota* from the other four as *petitiones* proper (Grotius). All such distinctions are only justified if they can be supported by the content of the prayer; thus they anticipate what can only be demonstrated later. It is more important here that the very form of the prayer seems to disclose a definite arrangement.

The Lord's Prayer consists of a number of brief clauses, which in turn are composed of very few words; even where, as in the third, fourth and fifth petitions, the sentences become fuller and longer, the additions conform to this rule. The Matthaean form suggests a sequence of five pairs of lines which are prefaced by an address of the same form and nature. This can be seen most clearly from the following arrangement:

πάτερ ἡμῶν ὁ ἐν τοῖς οὐρανοῖς
ἁγιασθήτω τὸ ὄνομά σου
ἐλθάτω ἡ βασιλεία σου
γενηθήτω τὸ θέλημά σου
ὡς ἐν οὐρανῷ καὶ ἐπὶ γῆς
τὸν ἄρτον ἡμῶν τὸν ἐπιούσιον
δὸς ἡμῖν σήμερον
καὶ ἄφες ἡμῖν τὰ ὀφειλήματα ἡμῶν
ὡς καὶ ἡμεῖς ἀφήκαμεν τοῖς ὀφειλέταις ἡμῶν
καὶ μὴ εἰσενέγκῃς ἡμᾶς εἰς πειρασμόν,
ἀλλὰ ῥῦσαι ἡμᾶς ἀπὸ τοῦ πονηροῦ.

Our Father who art in heaven,
Hallowed be thy name.
Thy kingdom come,
Thy will be done,
On earth as it is in heaven.
Our (daily*) bread
Give us this day;
And forgive us our debts,
As we also have forgiven our debtors;
And lead us not into temptation,
But deliver us from (the) evil (one)†.

In this sequence, the first pair of lines corresponds with the fifth, and the second with the fourth, as in the former case each pair has two predicates and in the latter a comparative 'as', which holds together heaven and earth, God and 'us'. In between, differing from the other form and nevertheless approximating

* See ch. VI.   † See ch. IX.

to its pattern, there stands the third pair of lines; it is also the
only case in which the two lines form a whole. Each line, however, seems to revolve round two concepts or to consist of two
words which are either joined together or separated from each
other as though by a slight caesura.

This pattern obtains up to and including the address, and here
it has often been stressed that there is a certain interval and tension
between 'Our Father' and 'who art in heaven'. All the double
lines begin with the verb—only the third once more is a significant
exception; this is a characteristic of the style of prayers not only
in Aramaic, but in all languages. The verbs are put side by side
in asyndeton in the first two clauses, where they speak of the
things of God, but where they speak of human things they are
joined by conjunctions. This distinction is still further stressed
by the threefold σου ('thy') of the first two pairs and the
ἡμεῖς ('us') of the last three. Here and there we have the
beginnings of assonance in the Greek translation, though in this
case it may sometimes be a matter of chance. But is it really
accidental that the beginnings of the first two pairs of lines sound
just the same, that in the third the ends of the lines have the stress
on the antepenultimate syllable, that the fourth, whose two
members correspond word for word, has a sort of rhyme, or that
the fifth, again formed in exactly the same way in each line,
twice ends with an oxytone accent?

But perhaps this Greek form is merely a faded reflection of
another one, which was plainer in Aramaic. If we try to translate
the Lord's Prayer back into Jesus' mother-tongue, in which it
was given and first handed down, Matthew's version would run
approximately as follows:

'ᵃbūnan dᵉbišmayyā
yitqaddaš šᵉmāk
tētē malkūtāk
yit'ᵃbēd re'ūtāk
kᵉbišmayyā kibᵉ'ar'ā
laḥman dᵉyōmā
hab lan yōmā dēn

27

> *ūš^ebōq lan ḥōbēn*
> *k^edišbaqnan l^eḥayyābēn*
> *w^elā taʿlīnan l^enisyōnā*
> *'ellā paṣṣīnan min bīšā*

This retro-translation closely follows that given by C. F. Burney (in *The Poetry of our Lord*, 1925, p. 113): it differs only in two points: Burney included the address in the strophes and consequently had to divide the third petition into two pairs of lines—as a result the merely explanatory phrase 'in earth as it is in heaven' occupies a whole pair of lines. He translates its first half *t^ehē ṣibyōnāk*, but the *t^ehē* does not correspond with the meaning of γενηθήτω, which is here made the passive of ποιεῖν. True, in this way Burney manages to find in the prayer two strophes, each with three four-stress lines, but this is at the expense of the third petition, which loses its weight and its compactness.

The metre which we find here, a series of five pairs of clauses, each of which is arranged in two two-stress lines, is a familiar one in the Old Testament. The number of double lines is already variable in the Old Testament; the Gospel according to St. Matthew is also fond of taking five lines together in other passages of the Sermon on the Mount. The language is expressly a Galilaean Aramaic; the beginnings of a rhyme, which could already be noticed in the Greek translation, here become somewhat clearer. Burney already noticed that this metre is not to be applied to the Lucan form of the prayer which is as follows:

Father,
Hallowed be thy name.
Thy kingdom come
Our (daily*) bread
Give us each day;
And forgive us our sins,
For we ourselves forgive every one who is indebted to us;
And lead us not into temptation.

* See ch. VI.

If it, too, is translated back into Aramaic, the result, strikingly enough, is another metric and rhythmical structure:

Abbā
yitkaddaš šūmā dīlāk
tētē malkūtā dīlāk
laḥmānā dī sorkēnan
hab lānā yōmā b^eyōmā
uš^ebōq lānā ḥōbēnā
k^edišbaqnan l^eḥayyābēnā
w^elā ta'līnan l^enisyōnā

This rhythmical structure has been produced by C. Torrey (*Zeitschrift für Assyriologie* 1914, pp. 312-17) on the basis of a letter from Enno Littmann; Littmann himself took up the attempt and improved it twenty years later (znw 34, 1935, pp. 29*f.*). Torrey, too, includes the address in the first line, thereby destroying the parallel construction of the first and second lines. He translates the fourth petition *laḥmā t^edīrā hab lānā*, whereas Littmann here inserts the two-lined Matthaean text *laḥmānā dī hū limḥar/hab lānā yōmā hādēn*. But it is always hazardous to conflate texts in such investigations. So, in the version above, the fourth petition has been translated back into Aramaic as literally as possible, without using such force as Torrey, who, following the example of the Curetonian, takes Luke's ἐπιούσιον and τὸ καθ' ἡμέραν together as 'constant' bread. Torrey, like Burney from his standpoint, has established that it is impossible to obtain similar verses from a retro-translation of Matthew's Greek.

Another metre and another rhythm predominate in this form; there are seven lines, each of seven syllables, a metre which is not only customary in Aramaic literature, but is in fact, *the* syllabic metre *par excellence*, widely attested from the fifth century B.C. to the poems of the Syrian Church Father Ephraem. Though the rhyme is not so plain, it is nevertheless clearly there. The language is a western Aramaic, such as was commonly spoken in Palestine, without Galilaean peculiarities of dialect.

Both in details and as a whole, these retro-translations are surrounded with considerable uncertainty, but we should not fail to recognize—to use E. Littmann's careful words (zNW 34, 1935, p. 30)—'that there may be some degree of truth in these observations'. This element of 'truth' permits some careful conclusions. The Lord's Prayer is primarily a poetic creation; its form and its unity are clear. Little is said in it arbitrarily, or by chance, but everything suggests an entity which is clearly more than a formal one.

The fact that there were two different poetic forms of the Lord's Prayer serves as a warning against any assumption that one form arose from the other as a result of abbreviation or expansion. Such a view destroys rather more than just the discovery of a poetic form. For Matthew follows a familiar metre, hallowed by prophets and psalter, and Luke one which is not attested in the Bible; the former remains in Galilaean, the latter in Palestinian Aramaic. It would be presumptuous and unjustified to argue from these peculiarities, say to the greater originality of one or the other form, or to transfer it from Jesus' authorship to that of the community. We are justified only in concluding the character and home of the traditions or communities which handed down these versions. The Matthaean tradition, therefore, flourished in that so to speak separate area where the Galilean dialect predominated, and rests on the forms and therefore also on the book of the Old Testament. The Lucan tradition seems more closely related to the life of contemporary Judaism, as its language can be spoken all over Palestine, and above all, of course, in its chief city.

Some of these details are, and must remain, uncertain, but in both instances we cannot mistake the liturgical stamp of the poetical forms. The Lord's Prayer is the prayer of a community, with a marked rhythm and also a partial rhyme, like many Eastern prayers up to the present day; it is far removed from the immediate, formless expression of personal concerns; despite the urgency of its language and thought, the prayer here is never made in the first person singular, but in the measured form of the first person plural, giving clear and firm expression to its inner compactness.

The poetic structure is also not without significance for the inner character of the prayer. In either version the fourth petition stands clearly in the centre, at the same time forming the transition from the measured solemnity displayed by the language of the first half to the greater and more living richness of the second half. The former breathes the transcendent atmosphere of the Word of God, which dissolves all normal links, even to the extent of linguistic asyndeton; the latter has the familiarity of human speech, which is held together both through the common bond of need and through the formal link of conjunctions. Of course, all these formal indications are only given their proper significance in that they reflect the objective content of the petitions and the way in which they are joined together. But the principle of method which is to be adopted in interpreting their content comes through even more strongly: even if there be just a possibility of a metrical structure of this kind, then no clause occurs by chance in these petitions and no word is simply 'taken over'; each and every one is chosen and formed from the whole of the Gospel message. In that case it is also necessary to interpret the history and content of each word in the light of this totality, for Tertullian's saying that the Lord's Prayer is a *breviarium totius evangelii* also holds in respect of method.

II   Our Father

1. Since ancient times it has been customary to use the first two words of its address as a short title for Jesus' prayer, as though the whole message of the prayer before God was already expressed in this designation. The custom is first attested by the *Rotas-Opera* Word Square, already mentioned, on a Pompeian wall, and probably derives from the Jewish custom of quoting passages of holy Scripture according to their opening words. Thus the passage which stands at the heart of the Jewish faith, *Deut.* 6.4-9, is called in brief the *shema*, after its first word, just as the Lord's Prayer is called the 'Our Father'. We therefore should not infer that these opening words have any special significance.

The New Testament often speaks of God as Father; whether this is a designation of him or an address to him does not make any difference. The way in which the address or the designation is used, in which individuals are also said to be children or sons of the Father, does, however, vary so much in the individual writings that we must look more closely at these additional differences.

'The Father', without any further addition, is not often used as a title of God in the first three Gospels. The instances are limited to two sayings of the Lord with a sound tradition (*Matt.* 11. 27= *Luke* 10.21 and *Matt.* 24.26=*Mark* 3.32); only Jesus speaks in this way, and the absolute title is heard on the lips of no one else. We may infer from this that 'the Father' was understood to be not a name of God but a name used in addressing him. This difference can be seen particularly clearly if a comparison is made

32

THE NAME 'FATHER' IN THE N.T.

with the terminology of the Johannine writings: the Fourth
Gospel speaks of the 'Father' seventy-five times, almost always
in sayings of the Lord, and the First Epistle twelve times, where
it is an expression of the writer; here, then, the word 'Father' is
really used as a name. The position with the address 'Father' is
rather different. In Luke, Jesus uses the address 'Father' five
times, in Matthew he uses 'Father' twice and 'my Father' three
times; this, however, merely reflects Aramaic word usage,
where a personal suffix 'my' is never added to the 'Abba', but
is tacitly implied. Only once are men found praying 'Father',
in the Lucan version of the Lord's Prayer; this is all the more
remarkable, since the primitive community, as Paul testifies, has
handed down the Graeco-Aramaic double address, 'Abba,
Father' as the correct expression of its prayer and its confession.

The designation 'my Father' is far more frequent than the
address. Luke indeed uses it only four times, but Matthew has it
fourteen times, ten of these with the addition 'heavenly' or 'in
heaven', which Luke never has; but even this expression occurs
only on Jesus' lips. Both are once again put in the shade by the
Fourth Gospel, which makes Jesus speak thus twenty-five times.
With the expression 'your Father' the position is again different:
it occurs in John only once, in a saying which he has taken over
(20.17); it is in Luke three times; but twelve times in Matthew,
and here too, with the exception of four passages, it includes the
addition of 'heavenly' or 'in heaven'. Perhaps it is not wholly
insignificant that 'your Father in heaven' occurs only in the
Sermon on the Mount, which also contains the Lord's Prayer,
and that 'my Father in heaven' never occurs. With regard to
the other personal pronouns we need only mention that Matthew
alone uses the second person singular three times in ch. 6, 'his'
and 'their' once each. 'Our Father' is as singular in the Gospels
as the address 'Father' is in the prayers of anyone but Jesus; here,
too, the earliest community testifies through the blessing transmitted by Paul, 'Grace to you and peace from God our Father',
that the designation 'our Father' is quite familiar to it.

At the same time this formula draws attention to a further

point: whereas the apostolic writings of the New Testament (with the exception of the Johannines) rarely use the name 'Father' by itself, but most often speak of 'God our Father', the Gospels never have 'Father' in addition to 'God', but use other designations of God in addition to 'Father' (cf. *Matt.* 11.25 *par.*). In one case, 'Father' replaces the name of God, in the other it defines it.

The addition 'in heaven', which is also replaced by the adjective 'heavenly', calls for brief comment. This variant is of course without linguistic or interpretative significance, as there is no such adjective in Aramaic. The Greek 'heavenly' is therefore merely an alternative translation. The fact that Matthew puts the plural in this phrase seems merely to indicate his nearness to the Aramaic language, for which the word 'heaven' exists only in the plural. Luke has this plural twice, Mark six times (of which two in 11.25 reflect the address of the Lord's Prayer), Paul, too, only six times (in Philippians, Colossians and I Thessalonians—Ephesians, on the other hand, has only the plural); the Johannine writings have the plural only in the Old Testament quotations in *Rev.* 12.12. But even Matthew sometimes has the singular, as in this prayer: 'In earth as it is in heaven'. The difference in usage seems to have the following basis: Matthew uses the singular wherever the stress is on the relationship of heaven to earth and to men, and the plural wherever he is trying to describe God's world in its infinite difference from that of mankind. So the two phrases, 'Father in heaven' and 'kingdom of heaven'—both peculiar to St. Matthew's Gospel—are full of references to each other, and in putting together the name, 'Father', and the place, 'in heaven', the address stresses two things: the nearness of God and the 'distance' of his world infinitely removed from mankind.

'Our Father in heaven' has been translated: *'abūnan dᵉbišmayyā*. But would not *abba*, the usual word in the vernacular, and attested for primitive Christianity, fit better? True, *abba* simply means 'Father', but just as it is used for 'my Father' (cf. *Matt.* 26.39 with *Mark* 14.36) so too it can occasionally stand for 'Our Father' (e.g. *Sheb.* vii 7). The religious language of Judaism does not, however, know the word *abba*, which is limited to everyday usage; for greater sanctity it prefers the obsolete Hebrew forms. Thus the Eighteen Benedictions twice address God as *ābīnū*, the beginning of a much-used New Year prayer runs: *ābīnū malkēnū*, and that of the daily morning prayer: *ābīnū šebbaššāmayīm*. There could be a simple *abba* at the root of Matthew's petition precisely because its familiarity would heighten the inner tension with the addition 'in heaven'. But as he expressly paraphrases the *abba* in Mark in the Gethsemane narrative as 'my Father', it is more probable that the expression *ᵃbūnan*, fuller and more solemn in Aramaic, is to be put here.

The addition 'in heaven' brings the address nearer to the language of Jewish piety. Thus a saying of R. Akiba has been transmitted which celebrates the sacrifice on the Day of Atonement: 'Happy are you Israel! Who is it before whom you become clean? And who is it that makes you clean? Your Father which is in heaven' (*Yoma* viii 9, fol. 85b). But the Matthaean address does not completely correspond to the customary language of Jewish prayers, as this does not usually add 'in heaven' when speaking to God. It is unnecessary to distinguish God the Father from earthly fathers because it is self-evident that in prayers only the one Father can be meant. Matthew goes against this Jewish custom and even against the Lord's saying (*Matt.* 23.9), 'And call no man your father on earth'; his addition therefore has a special sense and overtone.

It is instructive to compare the use of 'Father' as a designation of God with the correlative term 'son' or 'child of God'; it sheds still more light on the changes in the use of the name 'Father'. The 'Son' is used in the absolute only when 'the Father' is used similarly (*Matt.* 11.27; *Mark* 13.32); in that case, the expression simply means Jesus. 'My son' occurs only in quotations of or allusions to Old Testament sayings; the first three Gospels speak far more often of the Son of God—once again, this means Jesus. Now if we nowhere have either 'Son of the Father' or 'of God the Father', this again shows that

'Father' is not a name of God but a closer description of God which speaks of his relationship with men. As this relationship is already designated in the term 'Son', there is no need of the title 'Father' in this connection. It is never said of the disciples that they are 'sons of God', but twice in Matthew we have, 'that you may be sons of your Father who is in heaven' (5.9, 45), and the same thing in the same sense and context once in Luke (6.35).

The expression 'children of God' does not occur anywhere in the first three Gospels, and once again the difference from the Johannine writings is clear. For the Fourth Gospel gives Jesus the title 'Son of God' twelve times, and I John has it equally frequently; other men are never given the title. The absolute 'the Son' occurs sixteen times in the Gospel and ten times in I John. Those who believe in Jesus are never called 'sons of God'; instead, the closely related and more intimate 'children of God', embracing all the fullness of salvation, occurs three times in the Gospel, and four times in I John. Again, this distinction in the Gospels is most remarkable, for in the well-known words of Paul (*Rom.* 8.14; *Gal.* 3.26; 4.6,7) the prayer 'Abba, Father' also carries with it the comforting designation 'children' or 'sons of God' for the believers.

This pattern of linguistic usage has some not unimportant consequences and raises some new questions: in the First and the Third Gospels, the stress lies on the designation of God as Father. The conclusion that those too who call on God as the Father are or may be called the children of God is not itself a fact of the present, but a promise of the eschatological future, and it is given only rarely. Nevertheless, the primitive community lived in the consciousness of already belonging among the 'children of God' in this present, which is grounded in the prayer 'Abba, Father'. But only Paul and John speak of it, and in so doing show that for them the idea of being a child of God is something rooted in the ground of their eschatological belief, of which they speak with words which they have inherited. 'Our Father' also occurs frequently in the witnesses of the apostolic period, always of course in the form 'God of our

Father'; even more frequent, however, is the almost indirect form 'Father of Jesus Christ' or something similar.

The different attitudes of the First and Third Gospels are connected, so it seems, with another difference. The evangelists frequently compare the relationship between God and the believers with that of a Father to his children; in the well-known story of the Blessing of the Children (*Mark* 10.13-16 *par.*) or in kindred sayings of the Lord they promise the kingdom of God even to children. This 'for theirs is the kingdom of heaven' embraces what Paul and John, who in fact let the concept of the kingdom fade into the background, understand by the words 'children of God'. The difference also holds in the wider sense that in Paul and John God acts as the Father and reveals himself with the miracle of his immediacy, whereas in the Gospels there is no hint that God or his ambassador is bringing this kingdom through men. Here, then, we seem to have an expression of the peculiarities of the Gospel tradition: the First and Third Gospels speak of the Fatherhood of God that is now in process of being revealed; but it is familiar and needs no justification or description. What it means for men or even for the Jewish people is expressed more fully and more urgently by the message of the kingdom of God, which does not have the correlative that God or 'his Son' is the eschatological king, just as the name of Father does not mean that men are children of God. This side of the Gospel tradition which is lacking in Matthew and Luke was preserved by the primitive community in the prayer 'Abba, Father', and from it comes the comforting thought of being children of God, which both Paul and John have received, presumably independently of each other. Both sides, then, seem to have their firm place and foundation in the original preaching of Jesus. But this is a point which we must go on to discuss in rather more detail.

2. When it is said, as it is so often, that the address 'Father' already contains all that is new and all that is comprised in Jesus' preaching,

we should not conclude that the word 'Father' was rarely, or hardly ever, used of God at an earlier date. Quite the opposite. The designation 'Father' occurs abundantly in the surrounding world of Jesus, in Judaism and in paganism, in the East and in the West. It is not new; it has had a place in religion from primeval times and almost seems to belong among the original designations, even of primitive religion, whether it merely means the God of the tribe or is a title of that hidden deity of the universe who rules unseen above every difference of tribes and peoples.[1] Ancient Christendom also knew this, for Clement of Alexandria says at one point (*Strom.* vi 17 §151.4*f*., Stählin): 'We should not look so much at the expression as at what it means. Even Homer said "Father of men and Gods" without knowing who the Father is and how he is Father.' So we must ask whether the ancient name has been given a new meaning in the preaching of Jesus and thus in the address of the Lord's Prayer, and if so, what this meaning is.

In the ancient world, the idea of the father is always accompanied by that of the lord; indeed the one often defines the other. 'Father Zeus, who rules over the gods and mortal men,' said Homer, and Aristotle explains: 'Paternal rule over children is like that of a king over his subjects. The male parent is in a position of authority both in virtue of the affection to which he is entitled and by right of his seniority: and his position is thus in the nature of royal authority. Homer, therefore, was right and proper in using the invocation "Father of Gods and of men" to address Zeus, who is king of them all.' So the name 'father' first of all simply means the same as the word 'lord', namely that there is an unconditional and mutual bond between father and children which on the one side has the character of a sovereign will and on the other that of a necessary obedience. But this bond is based on the idea of physical paternity and thus of possession, and makes the Father responsible for the care and nurture both of the human race and of each individual. 'Should not the fact that we have God as Father and Creator and Provider rid us of fear and sorrow?' Perhaps this view, because it seems to derive from Homer and Hesiod, remained a philosopher's view in the Greek and Hellenistic world, as it is completely absent from the comedies, which reflect more of the language of every-day life, and from the Hellenistic papyri. Perhaps it only reached a wider audience of educated people through the Stoa, an early head of which, Cleanthes, uses it in his well-known Hymn to Zeus. For although Servius at a late date still testifies that the name 'Father' is common to all the gods, it does not seem to have become the foundation and the strength of an idea to shape human lives; instead, it has turned into a broad outlook in which 'men and gods' come together under the warm, glorifying rays of a divine will and care which considerately illuminates the course of their life to happiness and good fortune.

In contrast to such breadth, the Old Testament knows and uses the word 'Father' as a designation of God with a narrow reference to tribe and people, although it belongs to the most ancient elements of the faith. The idea that God is the father 'of men and gods' is attested, say, in Josephus and Philo under the influence of Hellenistic philosophy, but it is not a part of authentic Old Testament or Jewish thought. From earliest times, the people of Israel is rather 'the firstborn Son of God', as we are first told in the narrative of the Exodus from Egypt (*Ex.* 4.22f.) and such a title probably lies behind the view later formulated in the Song of Moses (*Deut.* 32.6; cf. also *Num.* 11.12; *Isa.* 63.16; 64.8; *Mal.* 2.10):

> *Is not he your father, who created you,*
> *who made you and established you?*

The idea of God's lordship and his kingship is necessarily bound up with his fatherhood. We read still later (in *Mal.* 1.6): 'A son honours his father, and a servant his master. If then I am a father, where is my honour? And if I am a master, where is my fear?' An ancient synagogue prayer, which perhaps goes back to the time of Jesus, begins, 'Our Father, our King', and even Jesus prays, 'I thank thee, Father, Lord of heaven and earth' (*Matt.* 11.25=*Luke* 10.21).

These ideas of God may indissolubly connect the idea of the

father with that of the lord as in classical antiquity. But there is another invariable accent and emphasis which pervades this context. For the idea of natural paternity has completely vanished from this idea of fatherhood, or faded to an obvious analogy, and its place has been taken by the idea of historical, i.e. moral, guidance—in religious terms, of creation in power and holiness. Thus *Isa.* 64.8 runs: 'Yet, O Lord, thou art our Father; we are the clay, and thou art the potter.' Or *Isa.* 63.16; 'Thou, O Lord, art our Father, our Redeemer from of old is thy name,' or *Jer.* 3.4: 'My Father, thou art the friend of my youth.' This idea of creation is intimately associated with that of the love which cares for the work of its hands (*Job* 10.8*ff.*; 14.15) and deals with it like a father with his son (*Prov.* 3.12), punishes it and nurtures it (*Deut.* 8.5; *Ps.* 118.18; *Jer.* 30.11; *Job* 5.17), has mercy on its own and graciously regards it (*Deut.* 1.31; *Ps.* 103.13; *Isa.* 49.5). But all this special colouring and definition arises from the fact that this fatherhood relates solely to the chosen people. On God's side it gives the relationship between God and people the character of immutable fidelity, and on the people's side that of a fickle unfaithfulness. The whole pattern of salvation and ruin which makes the history of the people such a clear pattern of his guidance, as the prophets from first to last never tire of proclaiming, can be included in this father-child relationship.

The concept 'father of the people' does, however, also reveal the limitations of this Old Testament approach: the two parts of the phrase are as it were joined together from different spheres. The idea of the people perhaps requires the concept of patriarchs or fathers as the foundation and guarantee of its existence in time, but not that of a father who is its God. So nowhere is there in the Old Testament the direct address, 'my' or 'our Father'. In this respect, too, the people has destroyed God's ideas: 'And I thought you would call me, my Father, and would not turn from following me. But . . . you have been faithless to me, O House of Israel.' The idea of the people needs to be expanded by that of the lord and the king; these forms of address abound throughout the psalms and the prophets, and at the climaxes of their sayings grow more profound, to become the image and word 'father', because here the people knows itself or is known of God as his child and possession. Only at a late date, when political and religious developments after the Babylonian exile begin more and more to change the idea of 'the people', when the people no longer has a law, but the law a 'people', can the individual believer say, 'Lord, thou art my Father, my God and my mighty deliverer' (*Ecclus.* 51.5-10, similarly *Wisdom* 2.16; 14. 3; 3. *Macc.* 5.7; 6.3,8). Then, too, God is addressed in prayer as often in the Greek and Roman world, 'O Lord, Father and Ruler of my life' (*Ecclus.* 23.1,4). From this point onwards this form of address sometimes finds its way into Jewish prayers, though we can only rarely demonstrate that these prayers belong to the time of Jesus. The other form of address, 'Lord', or 'King', remains far more frequent.[2]

3. 'Father' as a form of address to God and the idea behind it are anticipated elsewhere. But even if it has not been newly minted in the Lord's Prayer, but taken over from a Jewish pattern, the question arises whether there is still something special in the address, and in what this consists. 'Abba, Father,' a cry preserved both in Aramaic and in Greek, and, according to *Mark* 14.36, already used by Jesus, shows that Primitive Christianity knew and believed that the name Father was its special possession with a special significance. It is a cry not of the man who prays but of the holy Spirit (*Rom.* 8.15; *Gal.* 4.6), and this very cry shows the complete change which has been achieved in the world among men and peoples by the gospel of Jesus Christ. But precisely because of a believer's verdict like this, the question of the special element in this prayer of Jesus becomes all the more urgent. Even in the Gospels, we have no other prayer of Jesus which does not have this name Father in the first and often the only place. (*Matt.* 11.25; 26.39, 42; *Luke* 23.34; *John* 11.41;

12.27*f*.; 17.1, 5, 11, 21, 24, 25)—the cry of desolation on the cross, 'My God, my God', is the exception, grounded in the Old Testament and fulfilled on the cross, which proves the rule. The Primitive community already shared the blessing which introduces St. Paul's letters and has clearly been taken over by him: 'Grace to you and peace / from God our Father!' There is no evidence of the 'newness' of such a designation; it is there as the act which governs the whole life and faith of Primitive Christianity, as the one miracle which calls believers from all nations and men simply as 'children' to their 'Father' . . . So we are not to infer any special sense and content of the name 'Father' to distinguish Primitive Christian usage from that of Judaism and paganism; it is used just as in the Old Testament, and as it has been known and revealed since earliest times, becoming a pillar of the faith in Judaism as well.

The one basic fact, however, that has not hitherto been included is that God reveals and will reveal himself as the Father in what happens and is proclaimed here and now, and will soon come to pass. The eschatological reality and presence of this one action and this one fact, the Fatherhood of God, is the new element which is contained in the address 'Our Father'. Just as the Spirit of God, through whom alone the faithful can cry 'Abba, Father', is a means and a way towards guaranteeing the beginnings of the eschatological consummation, so too the Fatherhood of God reveals itself as its ground and destiny. Wherever and whenever believers can pray, there God is 'the Father', who will give 'good things'—*Luke* 11.13 says 'the holy Spirit'—'to those who ask him' (*Matt.* 7.11). Therefore prayer to the Father, too, is now sure of that hearing; it is, so to speak, a part of that eschatological reality which he is bringing to perfection here and now, in part and as a whole, in things both small and great.

But what is the significance of calling the Fatherhood of God an eschatological fact? We may feel, first, that it expresses the idea of a fulfilment of the Old Testament prophecies, and indeed there are some prophetic sayings which have been understood in an eschatological sense not only in the New Testament but also by the later rabbis, like *Ps.* 89.26:

> He shall cry to me, 'Thou art my Father,
> my God, and the Rock of my Salvation.'

It is mentioned in the New Testament at *I Peter* 1.17; *Rev.* 1.5; 17.18; 21.7,24; rabbinic instances are collected in Billerbeck (III 673*f.*) In Judaism, the promise to David (*II Sam.* 7.14): 'I will be his father, and he shall be my son,' and the saying of Jeremiah quoted above have also been referred to the eschatological consummation of the people.

But is a reference to Old Testament prophecies sufficient to explain the special character of this address 'Our Father' or 'Abba, Father'? The New Testament has usually interpreted these Old Testament sayings as referring to the final eschatological figure, and not to the fact of its own community, and even then one or other saying confirms a given fact with the authority of holy Scripture, rather than being spoken on the basis of it. Moreover, Judaism unshakably continued to believe that God's Fatherhood of his people at the end of its history would simply be and prove itself to be what it had been shown to be at the beginning and during the course of this history. If the relationship was sometimes destroyed, perhaps even seemed to have ended for the whole world-age, it was still never ended from God's point of view. The 'sons', the people, have caused the Father to exile them (*Berak.* 3a); hence the Father laments over his children, 'What is the father to do who has banished his sons?' Whatever the disobedience and wrongdoing, he maintains in words and deeds that he is the Father of his children through time and eternity. R. Juda can teach, 'If you behave as children, you are called children; if not, you are not called children,' and R. Meir can contradict such teaching sharply: 'Whatever you do, you are always called children' (Billerbeck I, 371*ff.*). But this very dispute merely confirms that God is and will be the 'Father', just as he was the Father, and from this standpoint it is no longer possible to believe that in the name 'Father' an eschatological promise should have become a long-awaited

43

and hitherto unheard-of reality—as the 'Abba, Father' shows us.

So another view seems to underlie this strange state of affairs in Primitive Christianity. It has often been said that Jesus replaced the Old Testament proper name Yahweh by the address, 'Father', and this alternation has been taken as a symbol of the transition from Judaism to Primitive Christianity. There is an element of truth here, but it is put in a crude and inaccurate way. The Tetragrammaton can at most be regarded as a 'proper name' of God because the Old Testament uses it in an exclusive sense and to an exclusive degree of the God of the people of Israel; for the people, however, the name is a meaningful form of address, the significance of which is not 'explained', but recognized and grasped in countless places. In the time of Jesus, it has become for the individual a holy symbol which is spoken only in the Temple by the priests, and is replaced in everyday language by the name 'Adonai', 'Lord'. But this symbol, too, was understood; it is still a living influence in the Revelation of St. John, where its sense is paraphrased, 'Who is and who was and who is to come' (1.4). But if the ancient name is still a living influence, this is no explanation to say that it has been replaced by the more intimate name Father, especially as the reasons for such a change are hardly ever given. And yet there is a still deeper element in this contrast with the Tetragrammaton.

In some Old Testament passages, an eschatological prophecy is bound up with the holy name of Yahweh, and the knowledge of it marks the transition from the present world-age to the consummation: 'Therefore my people shall know my name; therefore in that day they shall know that it is I who speak; here am I.' (Isa. 52.6f.) The ground and content even of the name Father is, then, what is promised eschatologically in the name of Yahweh, namely, the presence of God. The story of the Burning Bush understood it in this way (Ex. 3.14). God is there, he is among his own, as the Father of those who pray to him. So in the idea of the eschatological presence of God, the Old Testament promise and the New Testament experience and fulfilment meet. We may perhaps even say in historical terms that it was the achievement of Jesus to have included in the name Father whatever could have been concealed in the secret name of Yahweh, only to be revealed at the last time. And then it would also be most significant, as we have already suggested, that Jesus 'replaced' the mystery of the inexpressible name with the ordinary everyday word 'Abba'. But even then the decisive question has still not been answered. What is the decisive element which led to the eschatological understanding of the name Father? This answer can be found only in what Jesus' own words say about this 'Father'.

What is said about the 'Father' there, points to a number of directions. We hear most often the demands: Do the will of my Father in heaven (*Matt.* 7.21; 12.50); be perfect as your heavenly Father (*Matt.* 5.48); forgive as your Father forgives (*Matt.* 6.14; 18.35). Whoever feeds the hungry and gives drink to the thirsty is called 'Blessed of my Father' (*Matt.* 25.34); those who love their enemies are called 'sons of your Father who is in heaven' (*Matt.* 5.45). 'Your Father in heaven' will judge anyone who does not forgive his brother, as the king judged the unmerciful servant. All such commandments and promises do not give a reason for the name Father, but they presuppose it as the common ground of an ultimate bond, an extreme demand and a supreme hope; it is significant that both 'My Father' and 'Your Father' are here used interchangeably. The picture of the Old Testament's lord and father who has absolute power over his own possessions has hardly been altered in these numerous sayings.

Alongside the Father who commands and promises, we have in other sayings the Father who cares and loves. No one is to worry about clothing and nourishment, for 'Your heavenly Father' even feeds the birds of the air (6.26). No sparrow falls to the ground without 'Your Father' (10.29); it is also 'Your Father's will' that none of these little ones should perish (18.10, 14); he gives good things to those who ask him (7.11). The loving care of the Father in heaven is shown by the fact that he hears all prayers, that there is no seeking without finding and no knocking without opening. Here we no longer have 'My Father', but 'Your Father', who directly cares for those who need him, the meek and the sorrowful, the poor and the persecuted. So it is in prayer above all that the 'Our Father' is pressed on the lips of 'these little ones' as the innermost expression of the community between God and those who pray; prayer becomes a conversation between father and child, made by man to God in sorrow or joy, despair or thankfulness. Here, too, we touch on a deeper thought, which brings us nearer to the eschatological idea of this Fatherhood. For what it describes is the onset of the eschatological age, when the poor and the persecuted will be blessed, and those who have hitherto been excluded from it will receive salvation. This certainty is, then, simply a consequence of the eschatological Fatherhood of God.

Three other sayings, however, speak of the basis of this Fatherhood, and in them the form used is characteristically no longer 'Your Father', but 'My Father'. The first, *Matt.* 15.13, is still negative in form: 'Every plant which my heavenly Father has not planted will be rooted up.' The image is sometimes already used in the Old Testament (*Jer.* 1.10; also *Ps. Sol.* 14.3*ff.*, *Jubil.* 1.16); it also occurs elsewhere in the parables of Jesus (*Matt.* 13.29; *Luke* 13.7) and is therefore a firm element in the tradition, even if only Matthew has handed it down. The thought which it expresses is also characteristic of the Old Testament: because God has 'created, made and established' the people, in *Deut.* 32.6 he is called 'Father'; because he has planted men, here, too, he is called 'Father in heaven'. But in that case it is strange that we have 'my' and not 'your' Father, as though the fatherly love of God to his messenger was demonstrated in this planting, as though to speak of the Father meant first to speak of '*His* Father' and only then to go on to speak of '*Your* Father.' If this were so, the eschatological character of the idea of the Father would also be clear: because he has sent the final eschatological figure with words and works of eschatological power,

God has become 'the Father' who has mercy on the poor and therefore makes on them the supreme demand: 'You must be perfect, as your heavenly Father is perfect.'

The saying to Peter puts the same point in a positive way and at the same time enlarges on it. Again it has been handed down only in Matthew. When Peter confesses, 'You are the Son of the living God,' Jesus replies, 'Flesh and blood has not revealed this to you, but my Father who is in heaven' (16.17). Might we not expect here that the God who has given Peter the eschatological revelation of his 'Son' would also be called 'your Father'? If Jesus still says 'My Father', we may rightly conclude that the acknowledgment of 'the Son' also means the acknowledgment of 'the Father'; because he is 'My Father', he is in consequence therefore also 'Your Father'. Jesus' thanksgiving clearly confirms the necessity and correctness of this conclusion: 'I thank thee, Father . . . that thou hast revealed this . . . to babes' (11.25). The circle of thought is here closed. Jesus calls God 'Father' because he has given 'this' knowledge to babes; whatever we may understand by the 'this', which does not refer plainly to anything, it is certain that it also means the nearness of the eschatological age and the actions that accompany it. In the eschatological event which is taking place here and now, in the election of the 'babes', the eschatological Fatherhood of God is being revealed: because God is 'His Father' he may speak to these babes of 'Your Father', and they may therefore pray, 'Our Father who art in heaven'.

But it would be one-sided and incorrect to see only this one reference, which joins the disciples to God as 'their Father' by means of 'the Son'. Beside this personal connection there is also an objective one. There is a saying about 'My Father's kingdom' (*Matt.* 26.29); Matthew also speaks of the righteous who will 'shine like the sun in the kingdom of their Father' (13.43), and Luke hands down the saying (22.29): 'As my Father appointed a kingdom for me, so do I appoint for you.' This suggests that the proclamation of the kingdom of God is the act of God which makes it possible for him to be known as the Father of those who accept this message, just as he is the Father of the one who proclaims it. This is also to be inferred from the countless commands which are associated with the Father's name, for they give the conditions under which the disciples of Jesus are to enter into the Father's kingdom (*Matt.* 5.22). Thus we may say: God's eschatological Fatherhood is revealed in the fact that he now begins the eschatological work and sends the person of the final eschatological figure; both are present in a preparatory and hidden way, which can be known only through revelation, in the person and work of Jesus. So God is called 'Our Father', because he is the Father of Jesus.

4. It may perhaps be objected that this conclusion is based on words which are suspected of being a later creation of the community. We cannot investigate here the methodological justification for such an objection, which is questionable precisely as a result of this approach. Nor will we go more closely into the fact that the problem of the idea of the Father as it was understood particularly in Primitive Christianity has not been solved, indeed cannot be solved, if we rule out the solutions which the Gospels offer. We will content ourselves here with confirming the result from another direction.

The idea of the Fatherhood of God is so closely bound up with the other one, that the disciples of Jesus are children of God, that what is true of one also confirms the other. Now at this point the evidence of the New Testament is quite remarkable. Although the Gospels often speak of 'your Father' and the apostolic writings of 'God our Father', the disciples are rarely described as 'children' or 'sons' of God. Mark never uses the expression; while sayings of Jesus in both Matthew and Luke speak of 'sons of God' (*Matt.* 5.9, 45; *Luke* 6.35; 20.36) this is only in the sense of a promise of what the disciples will be or will be called on the last day, and not in the sense of an eschatological fact already given here and now. Nor can we increase these few passages by bringing in the parables which speak of happenings between father and children; for in the first place they are only analogies which, while preparing for believers to be called children of God, do not say this outright, and secondly, there are others besides this pure picture of Father and children, of the master and his servants, the host and his guests, and so on. We cannot even add the sayings of the Lord about children, for it is here that the expression 'children of God' is missing. Within the first three Gospels, then, evidence is rare and questionable. The Fourth Gospel, on the other hand, with impressive clarity makes the name 'children of God', which the other Gospels do not have, the embodiment of eschatological salvation and the expression of the fatherly love of God (*John* 1.12; 11.52; cf. also *I John* 3.1,2,10), just as it uses the name 'Father' for God to an overwhelming extent and further strengthens this testimony by the other equivalent expression 'be born of God' (*John* 1.13; 3.3,5,6-8; cf. also *I John* 2.29; 3.9; 4.7; 5.1,4,18). The well known Pauline passages (*Gal.* 4.6-8; *Rom.* 8.15-17,21) which link the 'sons of God' or 'children of God' with the cry 'Abba, Father' show that this is an early heritage of Primitive Christianity and not a late Johannine idea.

This evidence suggests two things; first, the idea of being children of God is not based on the synoptic words of Jesus but is a consequence which the disciples of Jesus drew from their Master's message of the eschatological Fatherhood of God. Thus the disciples do not know that they are children of God because God has shown himself to them as Father and has chosen them to be his children. Because he has shown himself to be Father in the eschatological event which is bound up with their master, they may call him their 'Father' and go on to draw the same conclusions as St. Paul: 'We are children of God' (*Rom.* 8.16). So the Fatherhood of God is the primary element and remains quite apart from the relationship between him and the disciples; this is a secondary element. One more conclusion follows from this linguistic usage: the First and Third Gospels have the idea of being children of God only as a promise, and not as a present eschatological possession, although both often speak of 'your Father'. This means that the disciples here already know themselves to be the eschatological elect, although this general early Christian experience is rare in Paul—his title of honour is 'servant of Jesus Christ'—and is attested more widely and strongly in the Johannine writings. The latter, then, have preserved an original idea which goes with the Fatherhood of God.

In that case, how has God shown himself to be 'Father'? The question leads to another group of sayings and ideas according to which it is the final eschatological figure who is himself 'the Son' in name and nature. Wherever this title may come from, it is not late, as has often been assumed, but is an ancient and early concept which already occurs in the words of Jesus. It also occurs in the triad Father, Son and Angel, deriving from the Son of Man tradition, which has been taken over from Judaism and transformed.[3] This is an expression of the heavenly court which according to *Dan.* 7 and *I Enoch* 39.5-7; 51.3,4; 61.8-10 consists of God, the Son of Man and the angels. We also find the same idea in the form 'Father, Son, Angel' in the words of Jesus (*Mark* 8.38): 'Whoever is ashamed of me and of my words ... of him will the Son of Man also be ashamed, when he comes in the glory of his Father with the holy angels' (similarly, and identical in the crucial words, also in *Matt.* 16.27 and *Luke* 9.26). To the positive expansion of this saying, 'everyone who acknowledges me before men ...' *Luke* 12.8f. adds, 'the Son of Man also will acknowledge before the angels of God' and *Matt.* 10.32f., 'also will acknowledge before my Father who is in heaven'. In the Synoptic Apocalypse we have the great saying, 'But of that day or that hour no one knows, not even the angels in heaven, nor the Son, but only the Father' (*Mark* 13.32= *Matt.* 24.36). There is no reason for critics to be suspicious of these words, as it is hard to see why the Primitive Christian tradition should have excluded its Lord from knowledge of the last hour, as happens here. We may therefore say that the titles 'Father' and 'Son' belong not only to the oldest tradition but also to the original preaching of Jesus.[4] At the same time the historical and objective basis for them becomes clear: they are connected with the name of the Son of Man, which Jesus took for himself. In that case, God has shown himself to be 'the Father' in the 'coming' of the 'Son' or the Son of Man, and so those who recognize in their master the 'Son' of his Father can and may call God 'Our Father'.

If we see these connections rightly, we may draw some not unimportant consequences. First, we can understand the striking language which makes a firm distinction between 'my' Father and 'your' Father: 'I am ascending to my Father and your Father, to my God and your God' (*John* 20.17). For this distinction and conjunction reflects the relationship between the disciples and their Master and Lord. The address 'Our Father' is possible only because God is the Father of him who teaches his disciples to 'pray like this'. More important still are some objective consequences. Two sentences and events are combined in the idea of the eschatological Fatherhood of God which sum up the life and work of Jesus: 'The kingdom of heaven is at hand' and 'the Son of Man has come'. Both imply that God is present and that he is here and now bringing men and the world, country and people, to their eschatological consummation. No reason in substantiation of these two statements is ever given, and the same is true of the statement about the Fatherhood of God; just as the two former statements are neither capable of, nor in need of, substantiation, but present themselves to the open gaze of the disciples as a fact and an event, so too the latter statement has become and will become an event in the here and now.

The name Father, then, first of all has nothing to do with the question of God's relationship with the individual or the community or of the individual's relationship with God, much less with the question whether God is imagined more as the strict judge or the majestic lord or the loving father. The Father, too, judges the unmerciful strictly and demands that his will shall be done; he dwells in that 'glory' with which he has directed the world since the beginning and in which he will judge the world at the end. He blesses and rewards, he punishes and he condemns

—in all this the idea of the Father is not distinguished from the manifold witness of the Old Testament. He is Father because he is now beginning to complete what he has made and to fulfil what he has promised. Just as the message of the kingdom of God proclaims an event which is coming and is present, whether men see it or not, so too the idea of the Father has a place in the strict objectivity of the eschatological event. It is revealed to men, but it exists and pervades the age which is moving towards its end with that still, immutable force with which day follows night. But precisely this quality of 'event', which can be seen everywhere, in the lilies of the field, the sparrow on the rooftop, the hairs on the head, does alter its familiar, imagined aspect. For it does not clothe this event with the strange grandeur of dark and obscure names, nor with the glory of an infinite majesty, but with the common simplicity of the work and rule of a 'father' in his house. And here we may recall once again that the Aramaic 'Abba' is not a hallowed word, but is one of the first that a child learns to say at home. What the 'Father' now does is, therefore, despite all its eschatological power and significance, an earthly event. But what is the relationship between this Fatherhood of God and the message of the kingdom of God and the work of the 'Son of Man'?

The one common foundation is this: the Fatherhood of God is revealed in the fact that 'the kingdom of Heaven' is at hand and that the pronouncement of this nearness is now made clear. But there is no direct path from the idea of Fatherhood to the idea of the kingdom of God. The two concepts derive from different spheres, one from the natural family, the other from the sphere of people and state which is governed by human action. But both are equally common in the East and particularly closely connected in the Old Testament tradition. An ancient Jewish New Year Prayer begins 'Our Father, our King', and the Old Testament is always speaking of God as the Father of the people, thereby joining the two spheres in a unity which has become traditional. So we can see and understand the reason for the connection between God's eschatological fatherhood and his eschatological kingdom; it is all the more plain because this kingdom is often imagined as God's house and his fatherhood as a rule and reign. Nevertheless, there remains the question why the far more familiar title 'Lord' or 'king' has been abandoned almost everywhere in favour of that of Father, which Judaism uses far more rarely. One answer is easily given: the kingdom of God is proclaimed and promised to the poor, the hungry, the suffering, and to those who seem to be excluded from temporal and eschatological salvation this is a sign of the all-powerful 'fatherly' care of God. But important as this connection may be, clearly as it may be realized in the works of the Master, it is formulated explicitly nowhere in the Gospels. As we have seen, they do not call the poor 'children of the heavenly Father', but simply promise twice that they will become so. They do, however, know all the more clearly that this acceptance of the poor and the sick follows from the powerful words and works of the Master. We may therefore conclude that the name 'Father' owes its objective origin not to this message of the kingdom of God, but to another source.

Now as well as the message of the coming of the kingdom of God, there is the other one: 'The Son of Man' has come. He is also called 'the Son', in short. We cannot now look for the historical reasons for the abbreviation of the Danielic title 'like a son of man' to the simple dignity of the name 'the Son'; let it suffice here that there is evidence for a close connection between the two names. Although the title is rare even in the Synoptic Gospels, it makes the meaning of the Fatherhood of God clear and direct: because 'the Son' has come, the eschatological 'Fatherhood' of God has been revealed in him. That is not to say that this Fatherhood is limited to the relationship between God and the Son of Man—for it is not a matter here of a substantial being, but of an eschatological function—; its significance may be put in this way: because God acts eschatologically here and now through the Son of Man, it is clear that the one is 'the Son' and the other 'the Father'. So the latter also becomes

Father to all those who know the hour and the manner, the way and the means—or even the mediator—of this eschatological action.

Only this view, supported by the idea of the Son of Man, makes the name 'Father' plain and understandable. But it also helps us to see that one side of this eschatological view, which is little in evidence in the Synoptic Gospels and frequent only much later, particularly in the Johannine writings, belongs to the original material of the oldest proclamation, probably even to the preaching of Jesus: God's eschatological action is not directed solely towards the cause of the kingdom of God, but also towards the person of the Master and so to those who become his disciples. The way on which they have to go, which is revealed to them by 'my Father in Heaven', leads through the one 'Son' to the one 'Father'; in this almost personal association they have an already present, yet still future, share in salvation. 'The kingdom' is simply the place, 'the house of my Father', where there are many mansions, to use an ancient saying taken by the Fourth Gospel.

This view, then, is orientated on the person of the final eschatological figure and does not need the idea of an order working itself out in the heavenly kingdom. It also knows a relationship based solely on the will of the 'Father', orientated on the existence of 'children', and mediated through the still hidden eschatological presence of the 'Son'. It is therefore simply and naturally connected with the one pattern and the one reality of eschatological fulfilment for world and people, that dispenses with heaven and earth, people and country and all suprapersonal powers and spheres, finding in the association of father and children the initial foundation and the final destiny of God's world. So it clearly answers more originally to the name 'Father' and the content of this name than the concept of the kingdom of God. For the latter concept, as it is to be found in the Synoptic Gospels, is distinguished in a peculiar way from the idea of the Father: it has no other name for the ruler of this kingdom than that of God or once, in another context, the traditional title 'the great king'; nor does it have any name for the subjects of this kingdom (the word 'citizen of the kingdom' is quite late and grew up only in the West); it is simply the idea of the eternal order which the 'perfecter' is appointing for the 'perfect' and it is silent about the things or persons which go to make it up.

So once again we are faced with the same question. What are the distinguishing features of the notion of the eschatological Fatherhood of God? For does what has just been said show more than that God reveals himself in the works of Jesus, as he did earlier in the history of the people through other prophets and servants of God? In putting such a question we recognize that the revelation which Jesus proclaims and embodies is not a historical revelation like those that preceded it. It is the eschatological revelation of the Son of Man. Wherever the Son of Man works and preaches, 'all things are made new; the old have passed away.' So even the Fatherhood of God, which is revealed in his works, 'is made new', it is already filled with the power of the coming aeon, proclaimed and brought in by the Son of Man. But while the Son of Man is there, he is still hidden, to be seen only by the eyes which have been opened and to be heard only by the ears which have been unstopped; and because he is hidden, his preaching is basically the same as that of the Old Testament prophets. And just as the 'Son' stands in a twofold relationship, end and beginning, heir and creator at the same time, so too does the Father. He is what he has shown himself to be in the history of his people; he clothes the lilies of the field and feeds the birds of the air. Yet at the same time his Fatherhood is completely new and unheard of, because it is already the source of the powers of the final age. What is it, then, that is new? It is the historical uniqueness of the actions of this 'Son' on earth. Whomever he draws to himself in his words and actions, the sick and the possessed, the publicans and the harlots, the beggars and the sinners, the 'Father' too has drawn to himself. This 'Son', as the teaching and healing Rabbi, this Rabbi, as the 'Son' who is now made manifest, is the pattern of the 'Fatherhood of God' which is at the same time both hidden and revealed in him. Now we can understand how the primitive community saw a plain and unadulterated expression of its new faith in the cry 'Abba, Father'.

Now all this has a definite historical value. For it has become clear that the Synoptic tradition of the kingdom of God is only one side of the greater and richer proclamation which is contained in Jesus' words. Here, in fact, the message of the kingdom of God is the centre and the nucleus, and from it the preaching turns to what men must do to enter the kingdom and what God will do to set up the kingdom; here the all-important thing is an objective view of the eschatological work and its final result, and as a result the person of him who proclaims this kingdom of God here and now falls back before the greatness of his cause, and becomes its mouthpiece and its instrument. But however deeply this message may be rooted in fact and in history, there is another idea in giving the title of 'the Father' to God; that of the very bond now made between God and man (or God and the 'people') in which the Father guarantees to define what order he will and may give to this bond. Only the Fourth Gospel speaks plainly and frequently of this association of 'Father and children'; and it speaks of it in a way which substantiates the words of Jesus, particularly in the first Gospel. God is called 'Your Father' because he is 'My Father'. In accordance with this pattern, the Fourth Gospel seldom speaks of the 'kingdom' and therefore concentrates all the more on 'the Son', making him the centre of all salvation. So we may say that the origin of both the Synoptic and the Johannine ideas and traditions is to be found in the plain addressing of God as 'the Father', and these two streams now show themselves to have sprung from the one source, the original preaching of Jesus. Perhaps we might be allowed a slight exaggeration: The 'Our Father' in the Lord's Prayer contains in germ both the so-called Synoptic and the Johannine preaching of Jesus. We will find still more indications of the way in which these two trends belong together in the individual petitions.

5. We must now say something about the Matthaean additions to the address 'Father' which do not occur in the Lucan version; there are two of them: 'our' and 'who art in heaven'.

It already follows from the origin and significance of the title 'Father' that this 'our' is not meant to unite the disciples who pray with the Master who teaches them this prayer; the language of the Gospels always distinguishes between Jesus and the disciples, as it does between 'my Father' and 'your Father'. Because God can be addressed as 'Father' only through him, he does not say 'Father' in the same sense as his disciples. As a result, the earliest community already put the 'Lord Jesus Christ' beside 'God our Father' in its form of grace, thereby referring the 'our' to the community asking for God's blessing. This sense is still clearer in the only evidence from the first century A.D. in which 'Our Father' occurs once again as a prayer: the prayers of thanksgiving in the Didache, which the community is to say over the bread and wine at the beginning of the Eucharist, begin 'We give thanks to thee, Our Father' and end with 'through Jesus thy Servant', thereby showing how strongly the earliest Christians felt this 'our' to express their new and unbreakable fellowship, founded by God.

This helps us to avoid yet another misunderstanding. The 'our' does not include anyone who lifts his eyes to heaven knowing that 'Brothers, over the starry sky a loving Father must dwell'. The 'our' does not take in the wide world of men; it is limited to the small circle of disciples. They are as different from 'men' as the people of Israel, whose God was similarly called 'Father', was once different from the nations. But the form of address is not simply a familiar Jewish heritage, although Jewish prayers also address God in this way. For if the exclusiveness of the 'Our Father' expresses the knowledge of those who pray, that they are the eschatological elect of the Father—as he once revealed himself as Father of the people through the election of Israel—then as a group they are both distinct from the people and at the same time bound up with them, just as the eschatological community is distinct from, and for just this reason also bound up with the Old Testament people of God. In their prayer, this group is in an analogous position to that once, indeed hitherto, occupied by the people of God; it has taken the place of this people simply because it is a community of the eschatological elect, while the Jewish nation is not only founded on revelation but is also united by its ancestry and its native land. In this case, all historical links, blood and soil, glory and affliction, the splendour and the anguish of history, have ceased; the only bond remaining to hold together those who pray is 'Our Father who art in heaven'. He is addressed in all personal care and need and guilt, but also in the knowledge that he has given his eschatological blessing. Now this raises two questions: what objective justification is there for this 'our', and what are the historical characteristics of a group which prays so humbly and yet so proudly to 'Our Father'?

If God is called 'Father' because he 'has hidden these things from the wise and understanding and revealed them to babes' (*Matt.* 11.25), then these people who speak as 'we' are those mentioned in the Beatitudes, the poor and those who mourn, the meek and the hungry, the merciful and the peacemakers, those who are reviled and persecuted, in short, all who seek refuge from the anxieties of life in the love of the Father and here find blessing. The Lord's Prayer itself tells us of the need and the salvation of these people in more detail. They pray for bread, as though they were the poor and hungry, for forgiveness of the sins which separate them from the Father, for deliverance from evil and from all the temptations under which they suffer. And these features are all so bound up in the communion with 'Our Father' that it does not matter what the historical and human situation is of those who pray. We can see the absence of these details more clearly if we compare related Jewish prayers like the Eighteen Benedictions or the Kaddish. The latter never leave the concrete historical situation of the people, and however much they pray for what belongs to God, they also pray for what is due to men, for freedom from strife and feud, disease and calamity, for blessing on the harvest and the produce of the land, for law and righteousness, grace to friends, for mercy on city and temple and throne, for peace and blessing everywhere.

In the Lord's Prayer, however, there is no mention of any features of the life of a concrete historical community or an individual human existence. To explain this omission it has sometimes been said that the Lord's Prayer is more markedly an individual prayer than related Jewish prayers and so it may leave aside the great concerns which unite men's common life. We shall have to ask in the case of each single petition whether this is the prayer of a human soul or of a community, and it will be impossible to give an answer before the end of the prayer; the mode of address, however, already shows the direction in which this answer is to be sought. While the psalter, the prayer book of the Jewish community, utters its prayers in the person of an 'I', the Lord's Prayer speaks equally clearly of a 'we'. True, this follows a late rabbinic instruction that no one is to say a prayer for himself alone. R. Abbaye (died 338-9) said: 'A man should always include himself in a community. How then should he speak? May it please thee, O Lord our God, to rule us in peace. Only special men are worthy to take the name of God to themselves' (in Billerbeck, I 410f.). But the language of the Gospel tradition is more instructive than this late rule. It knows of only one 'I' which can stand beside God's name 'Father', the 'I' which the Master speaks; all the rest are summed up in the almost summary 'your', which corresponds with the 'our' of this address. And even this 'our' or 'your' becomes increasingly rare in the Primitive Christian tradition.

As a result, we are led to the conclusion that this 'our', too, primarily denotes a community and not a sum of individuals. The significant thing about it is that we have hardly any concrete features of the community which it indicates in this way. It is a community of people who pray, or, rather: the community constitutes itself praying to 'Our Father', just as it is itself constituted through him. So we can also see why those who pray are justified in using the word 'our' to associate themselves with the Father. The justification for it in Jewish prayers is that each person knows himself to be the member of a people which God has made and led throughout its history. In the Lord's Prayer, however, we can no longer recognize the basis of a people to make possible the existence of 'children of God'; the way in which the name 'Father' is used shows that only those can and may say 'Father' who by a revelation recognize his eschatological working in the here and now. So this 'our' implies that those who pray thus to God may know themselves as the eschatological elect, despite all the distress of their human life. Just as the people 'Israel' was once founded and chosen in history by its 'Father', so too those who now pray are eschatologically founded and chosen through this very 'Father', who is the Father of their Master. At the same time we can see how closely these disciples are bound up with the people of God and yet how far they are separated from them; this is why all the concrete historical features of their life fade into the background. For the eschatological Fatherhood of God more powerfully than any historical force binds them in a still-hidden community.

The other addition, 'who art in heaven', does not seem to need much understanding, as it occurs so often in other sayings of Jesus that it has apparently been introduced into this prayer because it is so familiar. But does it not go without saying that when a pious Jew prays to the one Father he prays to the Father in heaven? And does this commonplace not also correspond with the Jewish custom of leaving out this otherwise customary addition? So this 'who art in heaven' has a special sense. What is it?

In the first place, it was not all that obvious to the Judaism of the time of Jesus that God dwells 'in heaven'. He also dwells in Sion and his holy temple, and for the Samaritans he also dwells on Gerizim and in his temple there. In the Old Testament, 'God calls from Seir' and thunders from Sinai; Elijah travels to Horeb to hear his voice. Even in the New Testament, the absolute use of 'the mountain' in the First Gospel shows that there is a particular place where God is revealed.

This sort of geographical association is not a myth from a distant past, it is a living force and a contemporary view, which guarantees God's presence in Jerusalem or on Sion, in his house, his city, his land; and this close presence does not contradict his boundless distance and the omnipotence with which he rules heaven and earth. God's self-limitation and his omnipotence are interrelated; he would not be on Sion were he not Lord of heaven and earth, and as this almighty ruler he has also pledged himself to be king in Sion, thereby manifesting his grace.

The controversy between the Jews and the Samaritans over the holiness of their mountains, and in Primitive Christianity the Johannine conversation between Jesus and the woman at the well of Sychar, show that such questions were vigorously discussed and disputed in the Judaism of Jesus' day. To all such questions the address gives a clear and simple answer: God is the Father 'in heaven', and if he once pledged himself to dwell on Sion or on Sinai, on mountains or in deserts, this pledge no longer holds. The confines within which a people so to speak lives and dwells with its God are broken open and replaced by the immensity 'of heaven', not so that God is lost in it, but so that he can find his people there. For this heaven is not distant, removed from human sight; the kingdom 'of heaven' is at hand, it is at the door, or rather: those who pray are at the door and the door need only open for them to go before their Father's face. God is no longer bound to one place, and the feeling of security given by the holy seat of God in his own land is taken up into the deeper security which children know to be assured by their father. Behind this addition, then, there stands the idea which the Fourth Gospel has expressed in the great sentence: 'God is spirit, and those who worship him must worship in spirit and in truth' (4.24). Wherever the Father who is in heaven reveals himself, the suppliant too is near to him and before his heaven.

Perhaps a second contrast is alluded to in this addition, as it does not simply refer to a place but also shows clearly why Matthew speaks both of the Father in heaven and the heavenly Father. For beside all the pride and the humility with which a Jew can speak of God as the Father of Israel, there is also his pride in the fathers whom God once chose to be the ancestors of his people. Because of this abiding human ancestry, with its commands and promises, which is at the same time a historical and a religious intermediary between the people and the God of Abraham, Isaac and Jacob, guaranteeing to the children the grace of election in which their fathers shared, the idea of the Fatherhood of God has become more an improving picture than a sustaining reality in the Old Testament and in Judaism. The address, 'Our Father who art in heaven', does away with this limited form of mediation and its end is expressly confirmed in a saying of the Lord: 'You have one Father, who is in heaven' (*Matt.* 23.9).

This reliance on human ancestry is ended in two respects: a community which prays to the one and only Father in heaven no longer refers back to an historical past to sustain and guarantee its life; it stands so to speak without history before its God, divorced from the past, seeking and finding its support only in the eschatological Fatherhood of God, this unbelievable and unimaginable relationship which is here and yet is still to come: those who pray abandon human security and stake their all on an eschatological assurance. This means the end of something else, for if the address is taken literally, as the saying in *Matt.* 23.9 demands, this one Fatherhood of God comes before all human fatherhood. It says that a man can be and is a father only because God 'who is in heaven' is the one and only Father, and this statement can be maintained because it does not speak of an individual man but of the community who speak as 'we', standing without forbears or descendants before the face of God the Father, revealed in this eschatological age.

III   Hallowed be thy Name

1. The form of the language of the first petition does not seem to raise any special questions.[5] The verb in the passive, placed at the beginning, is sometimes noted as an indication of Aramaic origin, but the positioning is a stylistic rule throughout the prayer, which is also observed often in other ancient prayers, and the passive formulation is a Jewish way of paraphrasing the divine name. Nor is there any question of what the two words mean. The word ἁγιάζειν, as the Greek Bible has it almost in isolation—the *koine* uses ἁγίζειν in a technical, cultic sense—means 'to make holy in some way' (from the root ἁγι- and the inchoative ending -αζειν). It is, however, striking that the two words occur relatively seldom in the New Testament.

Matthew speaks of 'hallowing' only in two passages dealing with questions from the cultic sphere (23.17,19): Which is greater, the gold or the temple that has hallowed the gold, the gift or the altar that hallows the gift? To 'hallow' here means to make something suitable for cultic use. Mark does not use the word at all, Paul and Luke speak only of the congregation or of Christians who 'are hallowed', either through Baptism (*I Cor.* 6.11) or the Spirit (*Rom.* 15.16) or the blood of Christ (also *Heb.* 13.12; *Acts* 20.32; 26.18). In these instances, which are the most frequent, God gives men the gift of holiness, but this carries with it the task of hallowing (*Rev.* 22.11). Only in one passage is Christ the one whom the faithful are to hallow, and this is an almost literal quotation of an Old Testament prophecy (*I Pet.* 3.15=*Isa.* 8. 13*f.*): 'In your hearts hallow Christ

63

as Lord.' No other passage in the New Testament speaks of a hallowing of God or of his name.

The same is true of the expression 'the name of God'. Old Testament quotations account for most of the passages in which it occurs. One of them has a firm place in a Gospel story: 'Blessed (hallowed) be he who comes in the name of the Lord' (*Ps.* 118.26=*Mark* 11.9. *par.*). The familiar pilgrim's saying marks the climax of the story of Jesus' entry into Jerusalem and the temple. Paul and the Epistle to the Hebrews speak only occasionally of the name of God and then only with phrases from the Old Testament. Only one group of writings, the Johannines, not only has the concept of the name of God but also, in many places, that of hallowing it. Perhaps it is not surprising that the Revelation of St. John often speaks of both, as it is steeped in the language and thought of the Old Testament more deeply than any other New Testament writing. Here Christ is called 'the holy One' (3.7), a new *trishagion* rings out to God (4.8) and he is called the holy One and the True, and here too there is the name of God in abundance. It is feared (11.18; 15.4) and praised (15.4); the elect bear it on their foreheads as a sign of victory and martyrdom (3.12; 14.1; 22.4). But the Fourth Gospel also speaks sometimes in decisive terms of the name of God. The fact that the Word became flesh and dwelt among us, that the Son of Man has come down from heaven, can also be put in this way: 'I have come in my Father's name' (5.43). We may recall that 'to come in the name of someone' is a Semitic way of speaking which can mean 'to bring the name of someone'.[6] For the Fourth Gospel says just this: 'I have manifested thy name' (17.6,26). Jesus does works in the name of the Father (10.25), he prays, 'Holy Father, keep them in thy name which thou hast given me' (17.11), his work is based on the fact that God has given him his name, and is directed towards God's glorifying his name (12.28).

The Fourth Gospel speaks in just as many ways of hallowing and being holy. Unlike the Revelation, it does not call prophets or apostles holy, but reserves this adjective for God and Christ.

It does, however, speak of the work of hallowing (of sanctification) even more often: 'Sanctify them in thy truth' (17.17), as
Jesus 'is consecrated' by the Father (10.36) and consecrates himself
(17.19). Similarly, we once have, 'Glorify (δόξασον) thy name'
(12.28). Over and against this frequent and independent use of
the two terms, the other occurrences in the New Testament
(like *Luke* 1.49) seem comparatively insignificant. They keep
more to the paths shown by the Old Testament. But even they
are not unimportant.

In the first place, there is the formula 'who call on the name
of God', taken from the Old Testament, which describes those
who have become faithful followers of the Gospel. In this
phrase, the 'call' is an element of 'hallowing', so that the aim
of God's eschatological action in this age can be said 'to take out
of the nations a people for his name' (*Acts* 15.14) in whom will
be fulfilled the prophetic saying, 'I will rebuild the dwelling of
David, which has fallen, . . . that the rest of men may seek the
Lord, and all the nations who are called by my name' (*Acts* 15.16f.)
This is true not only of the Gentile nations but also of the one
Jewish people, for the result of the vision which transformed
Saul into the apostle Paul before Damascus was for him, too,
'to call on God's name' (*Acts* 22.16). So Paul, too, can say that
'Christ became a servant to the circumcised . . . in order that the
nations might glorify God for his mercy. As it is written,
"And I will sing praise to thy name" ' (*Rom.* 15.8f.). Similarly,
Heb. 2.11 says of Christ: 'For he who sanctifies and those who
are sanctified have all one origin. That is why he is not ashamed
to call them brethren, saying, "I will proclaim thy name to my
brethren." ' To sanctify and to proclaim God's name are thus
interchangeable here, and that is why the sanctified are above all
exhorted: 'Through him then let us continually offer up a
sacrifice of praise to God, that is the fruit of lips that acknowledge
his name' (*Heb.* 13.15), and their love is regarded as 'showing
forth the name of God' (*Heb.* 6.10).

So all Christian life begins and ends in acknowledging and
praising the name of God in word and deed. This is confirmed

so to speak from God's side when it is also said of the believers that God's name has been named over them (*James* 2.10 etc.). Where the Gospel is defamed by word or deed, God's name is blasphemed; this is the exact opposite to the sanctification of God's name (*Rom.* 2.24; *I Tim.* 6.1; *Rev.* 13.6; 16.9).

Their close connection with Old Testament words and ideas is the common factor of all these examples, and makes the kaleidoscopic variety of the expressions seem to be variations on a single theme. Here in the Old Testament, as in Jewish writings and rabbinic witnesses, what is said in the first petition and alluded to only rarely elsewhere in the New Testament is expressed frequently and almost word for word. Well-known prophetic sayings enjoin men to 'sanctify' the name of God (e.g. *Isa.* 29.23); others are full of anger that his name is so often profaned, whether through idolatry (*Lev.* 18.21; 20.3) or through the transgressing of cultic precepts (*Lev.* 21.6; 22.2, 32) or through any kind of illegal action (*Jer.* 34. 16; *Ezek.* 36.20ff.; *Amos* 2.7). But it is not only men who sanctify or profane the name of God; God himself sanctifies it through word and deed, and this sanctification is spoken of far more frequently and emphatically. The 'sanctification' is accomplished in many ways; God does not completely destroy the people, although they have sinned so much against him, but leaves a remnant; or he punishes the heathen who oppress his people (cf. *Ex.* 32.12f.; *Num.* 14.6; *Deut.* 9.28; 32.17f.; *Isa.* 48.11; *Ezek.* 20.9,14,22; 39.23). God's promise to purify the people and to give them a new Spirit and a new heart means that, 'I will sanctify my great name' (*Ezek.* 36.22). So Jesus Sirach prays, 'As in us thou hast been sanctified before foreign nations, so in them be thou magnified before us' (36.3).

Similar petitions are often repeated in Jewish prayers. The so-called Kaddish prays, among other things, 'Magnified and sanctified be his great name in the world which he hath created according to his will'. A sabbath prayer runs, 'Thy name, O Lord our God, shall be hallowed and thy remembrance, O our King, shall be glorified in heaven above and on the earth beneath.'

Another prayer which is to be said after the *shema* runs, 'Sanctify thy name upon them that sanctify it, yea, sanctify thy name throughout thy world; and through thy salvation let our horn be exalted and raised on high.' The words of some of the prayers may be considerably later than the petition of the Lord's Prayer, but the almost unbroken chain of witness which reaches from the earliest times to the latest suggests that we should regard the first petition as a reflection of Old Testament prophecies and Jewish prayers. This is also true of its external form, with the verb in the passive and at the most important point in the sentence. At the same time, however, this raises a question. Why has the thought and expression of this Old Testament tradition found a place in the New Testament only here in the Lord's Prayer, and at the same time in the Johannine writings?

2. The Septuagint has used the Greek word ἁγιάζειν principally as a rendering of the Hebrew *qādaš*. While the root meaning 'sanctify' remains, it has taken over a considerable amount of colouring and many overtones from the basic Hebrew word. In the *piel* form this means 'to hallow something originally profane', 'to continue to hallow what is holy'; in the *hiphil* it means 'to see that something is kept holy or recognized to be holy'; in the *niphal* and *hithpael* forms, 'to reveal oneself as the holy One', but also 'to be kept or made holy'. The richness of these last colourings is also taken over by the middle and passive of ἁγιάζειν; it therefore means 'to reveal oneself as the holy One', as well as (of others) 'to be made or kept holy', or 'to be recognized as holy'. Only the *hithpael* form is likely to have been used in the Aramaic petition, just as the analogous Jewish prayers use this form; so it is probable that the prayer here is for what God's name may do in itself and for itself, namely that it shall reveal itself to be holy.

In the Old Testament both God and men are said to be sanctified, or rather, God and his people, viz. those who believe in him. The 'nations' cannot sanctify him; they would have to have been called by God beforehand, since this sanctification, through which his people acknowledges him, is, like all cultic action, only a *re-actio* to God's *actio*, an answer to God's call. This is authoritatively put in the great sentence, 'You shall therefore be holy, for I am holy' (*Lev.* 11.45). So it is plain why God is said to be 'sanctified' more often than men in the Old Testament: 'I will manifest my holiness in her' (*Ezek.* 38.23), to which is opposed the expectation, 'They will sanctify my name; they will sanctify the Holy One of Jacob' (*Isa.* 29.23). Men sanctify themselves by sanctifying God and his name; they sanctify God because and in that God sanctifies himself in them, and thereby sanctifies them also. R. Akiba spoke in kindred terms of the sacrifice on the Day of Atonement: 'Happy are you, Israel! Who is it before whom you become clean? And who is it that makes you clean? Your Father which is in heaven!' (*Yoma* viii 9).

Among the variety of senses which are still only variations on the basic meaning, 'sanctify', one shade of colouring has a special significance. It is already clearly present in the Old Testament, but it appears to predominate more and more in Jewish writings and rabbinic instances. The principal synonyms for 'sanctify' are 'magnify' (μεγαλύνειν) and 'glorify' (δοξάζειν). *Lev.* 10.3 runs: 'I will show myself holy among those who are near me, and before all the people I will be glorified'; similarly, *Ezek.* 28.22 (cf. also 29.43; 38.23) reads: 'I will manifest my glory in the midst of you . . . and manifest my holiness in her.' So in *Tobit* 8.5, and very frequently later, we find mention of 'God's holy and glorious name'; the prayer of Jesus Sirach (36.3) which we have already quoted therefore asks for God to be magnified in the nations, as he has been sanctified in his people before them. No wonder, then, that the LXX renders a fundamental Old Testament statement like *Isa.* 5.16 as, 'The holy God will be glorified in righteousness' (Heb. *niqdaš*). The same sense is also present in the rare passages where the word ἁγιάζειν occurs outside the Greek Bible, though hardly independently of it: in the great Paris magical papyrus we have mention of 'the holy name that is glorified (τὸ καθηγιασμένον) by all the angels' (in Preisendanz, *Papyri Graecae Magicae* i 4, lines 1190f., cf. also 1, line 206). This assimilation, moreover, has taken place not only in the *koine*, but even in the Semitic languages. Only a few of the Jewish prayers already quoted refrain from defining the idea of 'sanctifying' more closely by the expressions, 'glorify, exalt, raise'. We may therefore say that in the time of Jesus, too, 'to be hallowed' is to all intents and purposes synonymous with 'to be glorified'; this is the way in which commentators of the Greek and Latin Churches have always interpreted the words of this petition of the Lord's Prayer.[7]

If this is so, it is important that in the Fourth Gospel we hear from Jesus' lips the petition, 'Father, glorify (δόξασον) thy name,' and that a voice from heaven replies, 'I have glorified it, and I will glorify it again' (12.28f). We may call the first sentence the Johannine form of the first petition of the Lord's Prayer; it is not an isolated instance in the Gospel, but finds a place in the wide range of passages in the Johannine writings which have the words 'sanctify' and 'glorify' alongside the concept of the name of God, thereby distinguishing these writings from the rest of the New Testament. The close relationship between this petition and the Johannine statements thus becomes still clearer, and it of course calls for an even stricter investigation of the objective significance of the relevant terms.

The concept of the 'holy' in the Old and New Testaments is usually defined in accordance with the sphere in which it is most fully attested and used, that of the cult. Whatever belongs to, or is owed to, the cult is holy, and so 'to make holy' means 'to make fit for the cult'. Anything that has any kind of relationship with this sphere, men or objects, places or times, means or ends, actions or customs, finally and above all, God himself, the subject of this infinitely divided cult, can be called holy and can be hallowed. The word 'holy' takes whatever is so designated out of its usual surroundings, sets it apart, and makes it participate in the character of the ultimate ground of all hallowing and holiness, God, the one for whom something is holy, the one who makes something holy. In such a sense, the altar 'hallows' the gift and the temple the gold (*Matt.* 23.17,19). It is also noted, however, that while the equation holy=fit for the cult is perhaps historically the oldest, it is not in fact the original one, but is derived from the one to whom the cult is offered. And even if some religions of earlier or later times and characteristics may express this idea of separation so strongly that it seems to be the root of all that is involved in the cult, in the Old Testament this is not the case. For only in the earliest period does the holy ark represent the cult-pattern of other religions, enclosed in a circle of separation. At a very early stage, the name of God takes its place, raising the ark to the external sign of a deeper holiness. The name is on the one hand so to speak the cultic image of the Israelite faith, and simply by being this it is, on the other hand, the sign and mark of its lack of imagery. As a result, it now raises the concept of 'holiness' into the realm related to the earlier pattern as the concept to the analogy, the word to the image. The name of God separates everything over which 'it is spoken' from any other event or existence, while still at the same time having a basic and general significance through which everything outside it is at the same time determined.

The Old and New Testament understanding of 'hallowing' is already clear in the writings of the first Isaiah. He is to an exceptional degree the prophet of the holiness of God, and the basic lines which he lays down are never altered. The first theme is 'Holiness is morality'; the holy God is the 'righteous' God and therefore to 'hallow' means 'to act rightly' or, in the New Testament phrase, 'to bring forth good fruit'. This connection is already stressed in Isaiah's great statement (5.16): 'The holy God shows himself holy in righteousness'. The same demand resounds in the New Testament: 'Be pure and blameless for the day of Christ, filled with the fruits of righteousness' (*Phil.* 1.11, cf. also *I Peter* 3.13). The saying which stands over the life and history of the Israelite and Jewish people almost from the beginning, 'You shall be holy, for I am holy', has virtually the same content, and it is echoed in the words of the Sermon on the

70

Mount: 'You must be perfect, as your heavenly Father is perfect.' This is the essential thing about the concept of holiness, that it binds God and man together in one communion. It is not a principle of separation but of conjunction, not the idea of a basic distinction but the establishment of a basic communion. The only difference between God's holiness and man's holiness is that God *is* holy, whereas men and nations *become* holy. In the case of God, the word 'holy' defines his being or, more exactly, the mode and character of his action; only through his holiness is he the revealer of his will for men and nations, the giver of his laws and the guide of their destiny. His actions may vary, but they all have the one aim of holiness. For man, on the other hand, the word 'holy' poses an infinite task which separates him from God as much as it provides an access to him. Man is infinitely separated from God through the certainty that he *is* not holy, but is to *become* holy.

The degree of this separation can be defined in different ways, and the way from the Old to the New Testament can be described as a gradual deepening of the task of sanctification until it becomes the ground of human life and existence. Even Isaiah says in the sight of the 'holy One of Israel' (6.5), 'I am a man of unclean lips', and is forgiven his sins by an angel before he is sent. If sanctification there stops at the lips, in the Sermon on the Mount it reaches right to the depths of the heart. Here, however, it is more important that the separation between God and man is seen as a fact and the ending of it understood as a task. Precisely by virtue of this, an infinite bond between God and his world, or his people, has become both possible and necessary. For if sanctification is the task of all human life and all national history or at least of the history of this one nation, if this task has been appointed by God himself, then the end that he has set for mankind is his own being and action; God himself becomes the end of human life. According to his idea of God, man's thoughts and deeds are a way to such an end, a way from the profane to the holy, from wrong to right, from evil to good. Once again, the extent of this sanctification differs, and the way in which it

is continually made broader and more profound is again reflected
in the transition from the Old to the New Testament, a transition
from the individual act or even the individual object of sanctification to the purity of the heart in which men are perfect as their
Father in heaven is perfect.

A second theme is closely associated with this first one;
whereas the first was implied by the idea of the divine action,
the second is bound up with the idea of the divine being. God
is holy; here there is also the element of a pure power or a
powerful purity which determines God's nature and activity.
It separates him from all that lives and exists, though he is still
united to it by the holiness of his action; it sets him in a realm
of unapproachable light and surrounds him with the awe of
worship, the realization of the nothingness of human existence
and the failure of human action. Holiness here is what makes
God God, the incomprehensible ground of his being, the hidden
essence of which no one even begins to be aware, which he
reveals only as it pleases him. There is no rest here; even this
final essence is action in the twofold sense of activity and actuality,
and whatever he does is a revelation of what is hidden. Both
Old and New Testaments have a special name for this revelation:
God's revealed holiness is his glory, his holiness is his hidden
glory.[4] So the cry of the seraphim runs:

> Holy, holy, holy is the Lord of hosts;
> the whole earth is full of his glory. (Isa. 6.3).

We have the same thing in *Ps.* 99 and it underlies the interrelation
which has been established between 'holy' and 'glorious'. From
this standpoint, to 'hallow' means to change God's hidden holiness
into manifest glory. This change simply describes the course
taken by the world from its creation through God to its consummation, a course directed by God. The destiny of the world
is therefore both in general and in all particulars 'to the glory
of God', and the Old and New Testaments speak of this in many
ways.

These two themes, however, merely describe what in God
is an indissoluble unity. For it is a characteristic of God, which

marks his holiness, that his acts and his nature are in a perpetual equilibrium. God's being is not something objectively or, so to speak, temporally prior, which is needed to make his acts possible; thus in God's case the actions are not accidents of his permanent being. All action is and marks his being, his whole being is and marks his action. 'For he spoke, and it came to be; he commanded, and it stood forth' (Ps. 33.9). This, in turn, means one last thing: in so far as God is holy, his being is far beyond the sensory realm, for it is itself the ground of the whole creation of this sensory realm. As creator of the world God is infinitely separated from it by his holy action, yet 'the whole earth is full of his glory' and so is necessarily bound up with him. Thus to 'hallow' here is no longer any single action; it is the transformation of all that is into a new 'holy' existence as God wills. It is the course of the world and of each individual life from creation to consummation. Here, then, history, whether of the individual or the people, the nations or the world, is the true field of God's action; it is God's act of sanctification in the world and among men that holds the world together in its innermost elements and directs its inward and outward course.

This sanctification is both positive and negative; first, it means the abolition of everything in the sensory realm contradictory to God's holiness—for the only one who is holy in his being and his actions is the one who, like the angels in the service of God, matches his actions with his being and his being with his actions. So, secondly, it means the elevation and therefore the consummation of all human and historical being in the holiness of God: 'You must be perfect as your heavenly Father is perfect.' This process of sanctification also leads beyond itself, for its ultimate end is not the sanctification of the world through God, but the sanctification of God through the world. Even the world and mankind are only elements in the process of sanctification in which God sanctifies himself. And this process leads from his hidden holiness through creation and consummation to his manifest holiness. As he is served by the life of individuals and the history of peoples, so too he is served by the creation of the world and its consummation. All is simply 'to the glory of God.' So even in the Old Testament the last of the works of God is said to be that the earth will be filled with the knowledge of the glory of the Lord, as the waters cover the sea (*Hab.* 2.14; *Num.* 14.21; *Isa.* 11.9).

3. These great areas into which the concept of hallowing leads are defined still more closely and more profoundly by the concept of the name of God. What is meant by this name of God? An ancient answer runs: *nomen Dei est Deus ipse*—put in these words by Calov (*Biblia Novi Testamenti Illustrata* (1676) 1, 231)—and all the expressions in the Old and New Testaments substantiate this judgment. How else could *Isa.* 30.27 say, 'Behold, the name of the Lord comes from far, burning with his anger . . . his lips are full of indignation', or *Isa.* 59.19, 'So they shall fear the name of the Lord from the west, and his glory from the rising of the sun', or *Heb.* 6.10, 'He does not overlook your work and the love which you showed to his name', or even *Pirke Aboth* ii 16, 'Let all thy actions be to the name of heaven'? A man fears and praises the name as he fears and praises God; if his name dwells among men or among his people, God is present among them. And it is the glory and the power of the holy mountain and the holy temple in Jerusalem that it has pleased God to make his name dwell there. In principle, therefore, there is nothing in heaven or on earth which is not dependent on God's name because it is dependent on God. God's name speaks of him as the ever-present, the manifest God. Nor can anyone ask which name is God's due, as though there were a hundred names to choose from. A choice is possible among human things, but God's name is not a human thing; a choice is perhaps also possible among the heathen gods, but what has God in common with idols? Just as there is only one God, so too there is only one name, even though men may give God a hundred names. In other words, just as one cannot ask what God there is, so one cannot ask what name of God there is. The fact that the name *is*—and that means

74

manifests and is made manifest—is as important as the fact that God *is*.

The assertion that in both the Old and the New Testament God's name and God himself mean and are the same thing may be clear and well founded. But there are still a number of questions which call for brief consideration. If God's name is God himself, then he does not exist without this name; it belongs as inseparably to him as the word to the object or the concept to its subject. God is conceivable only in his name; God's name is embodied in him alone. People have often been inclined to put the concept of the name of God with others which make a link between God and his creation, such as the spirit of God, the will of God, the word or even the kingdom of God, the arm of God, the power of God; even the Magnificat does this (*Luke* 1.49,50). But all these concepts describe directions of his action or elements of his being: God's name describes him in the totality, the uniqueness of his being and action. Whoever therefore knows God's name stands at the door of unspeakable mysteries and light unutterable; in later words, on the threshold leading from the *Deus revelatus* to the *Deus absconditus*, from the glory of God to his holiness. So an aura of reverence and adoration surrounds the name, and all the glory of the heavenly world, which never grows weary of praising God's name.

Among the functions exercised by the concept of the name of God, the first is that the name characterizes God as person, as an immeasurable and infinite 'I'; it keeps him from floating off into the lofty heights of the 'Godhead' or from dissolving into the incomprehensible expanses of pantheism. This infinite 'I' of God demands a 'Thou' or countless 'Thous'; it acts and wills, plans and creates. So the name of God also offers the possibility and the necessity of a world which he creates and directs, and therefore the idea of a process from creation to con-summation. Only then is the problem of this name rightly seen, that in signifying God, the name at the same time includes the idea of a world, and in presupposing this, still in so doing speaks only of God. So the name of God denotes a threshold in an

75

even wider sense: it is a threshold from God's conception of the world to the creation of the world, from God's nature to his revelation, from his unity to the multiplicity of created things and beings, from his holiness to the world.

Of course it has never been characteristic of biblical thought to meditate on this so to speak pre-worldly function of the name of God; 'the hidden name' is discussed only in later rabbinic writings. But wherever God's name is called or rejected, loved or hated, feared or despised, it has this double reference by means of which it mediates between God's nature and God's world. For the name is on the one hand God himself in all the incomprehensibility of his majesty and his presence, while on the other hand it is still a name, and that means that it can be grasped by human thought, uttered by human speech, assigned a place in human ideas and accepted or rejected, affirmed or denied by human hearts. In face of this present significance, the question of the independent significance of the name for God, when he named himself so to speak before all worlds, falls into the background. The fact that in giving this name from eternity God's dialogue with himself has continued from eternity also remains hidden; the name of God takes its place among those concepts or forms which, like wisdom or the word, have been in the counsel of God from the very beginning and accomplish his work.

So the name of God stands not only over the beginning of the world but also over every detail of its course. It accompanies and directs the passage of an individual life as it does the history of a nation or nations; it stands over their fulfilments and their defeats, their joy and their anguish: 'The Lord gave and the Lord has taken away; blessed be the name of the Lord' (*Job* 1.21). Just as the name stands over the course of all earthly life, so too it stands over its end and its consummation. It is the destiny and the meaning, the truth and the reality of all creation; for God's name, like God himself, is greater than his creation, and just as the name of God was before the creation, so too it will be after the consummation—indeed creation and consummation are only incidents in the being and activity of the name, as of God himself.

Once again, then, its dual character is illuminated: mirror of God's eternal nature and mirror of things temporal, after him as so to speak the ground of all realities, before him and after him the multiplicity of all grounds and realities, itself Lord of all creation and yet still created, itself unique and holy like God and yet something else beside and below him.

So one of the deepest and most mysterious conceptions of biblical thought underlies the name of God. Of course this thought has nowhere been submerged or even lost in the ultimate depths of 'naming', but has plainly set up the name of God like a rainbow of reconciliation and consummation over all that is earthly and historical, over all the world and all nations. The name is ultimate and permanent like God: 'On the last day the Lord will be one and his name one' (*Zech.* 14.9). In one respect it is the first, primordial word of God, with which he named himself before he revealed himself by word or by name in or to the world; in one respect it is also the Spirit of God, because it is the power through which God guides the world and brings it to its destiny. So on the one hand the name of God sums up his manifest presence by which he is at the same time joined to and separated from all creation, and on the other hand it embraces the multiplicity and totality of beings and things, all of which are grounded on and directed by the name of God. The name is before their beginning and after their end. Precisely because of that it is most deeply associated with the idea of the holiness of God, as it is the very act that manifests God's hidden holiness. So too it comes before everything else that can be named and is named in this petition, before God's kingdom and his will. Both these speak, each in their own way, of things in and about God, but only the name loses any individual reference, to look towards that personal unity and totality which, though ruling over it, still lives from all creation.

4. The words of the first petition are so brief and general, so little supported by kindred expressions in the Gospels, that they seem

open to a number of interpretations. It has often been supposed that they are an introductory formula, beginning with the praise of God's name like an ancient doxology, or that they are to put the suppliant in a right state of mind for prayer. Bengel, however, already raised an impressive objection to such views: *modus in 'sanctificetur' eandem vim habet quam in 'veniat' et 'fiat,' adeoque est rogatio, non doxologia expressa.* This objection is rightly made. The Lord's Prayer is too brief and deliberate to have room for the flourishes and formulas of a doxology; nor is it for prayer itself to prepare the person who makes it for praying. It was a Jewish custom for a man to prepare himself for an hour before he prayed.

Of course these explanations conceal a difficulty which emerges if they are rejected: if the message of the coming of the kingdom of God is the very core of Jesus' preaching in the Synoptic Gospels, why does this prayer for the coming of the kingdom stand only in second place? Because of this, people have sometimes resorted to taking the content of the first two or even first three petitions so closely together that either the second and third enlarge on what is said in the first or the first prepares for the content of those to come. This does not, however, do justice either to the internal and external parallelism of these three petitions or to the impressive brevity of each single one. They stand side by side in asyndeton, each with a different subject and predicate and interrelated only by their common reference to God, whereas the following petitions are connected inwardly by the 'we' which they share and formally by a series of conjunctions. Consequently each of these first three unconnected petitions has a content of its own and demands an interpretation of its own, however closely God's name may belong with his kingdom and his will.

A first pointer is given by the affinity which can be traced between the petitions and the beginning of the Decalogue. The address, 'Our Father, who art in heaven,' corresponds with the so-called first commandment, 'I am the Lord your God. . . .' and this petition, 'Hallowed be thy name', corresponds with the second commandment, 'You shall not take the name of the Lord your God in vain.' This similarity suggested the explanation which Augustine, in the steps of a number of predecessors, summed up in the simple sentence: *cum ergo dicimus: sanctificetur nomen tuum, nos admonemus desiderare, ut nomen eius quod semper sanctum est, etiam apud homines sanctum habeatur, hoc est non contemnatur*. One explanation has been given of the way in which the name of God is kept holy; through holy teaching and holy life. This explanation has continued down to the present day. Luther took it over almost word for word in the *Kleiner Katechismus*; only once did he make a characteristic alteration, saying that the name is hallowed not 'in men' but 'in us'. He explains this in the *Grosser Katechismus*: it means to praise, laud and honour God's name in our way, in word and in deed. Thus the sentence becomes a petition which is concerned with the form and the content of human life; it is about men's affairs.

Now this is indeed a profound idea of the Old and New Testaments and corresponds with the ancient promise: 'I will sanctify myself in you' (*Isa.* 29.23). But is this idea expressed in the petition? The sentence clearly avoids referring to men; it speaks rather of what concerns God and his name. In what follows, too, it does not speak of human desires or human affairs; its mention of God's kingdom and his will are equally devoid of any human reference. These considerations are supported by a further point. Augustine's and Luther's explanation speaks of a petition and a task which confronts men again and again; it is concerned with a hallowing of the name which is to be done daily and hourly, and regards it as the pedagogic goal towards which men will and should aim with the help of God. But the first petition does not speak of such a constant, never-finished task of human and historical life; the tense of the predicate suggests a single event which may happen sooner or later. This once-for-allness is further stressed by the constant use of the aorist not only in the two subsequent petitions but throughout the whole prayer. Moreover, this single event is an act of God—otherwise it would not be prayed for—even if it

79

is not yet decided whether the person who prays will not also share in it. Primarily, therefore, it refers to the eschatological act by which God hallows his name before and in and over all the world, the act which is both the beginning and the end of all eschatological happenings. For the world can only be hallowed by God if his name is hallowed (that is why this hallowing is the beginning of all such happening) and the name can only be hallowed if the world is hallowed (that is why this hallowing is also its end). Only the once-for-all character of the aorist corresponds with this act of God; for whatever men can do does not have the strict character of once-for-all decisiveness that is demanded.

It might perhaps be objected that the corresponding Aramaic verb-form, a *yitqaddaš*, does not have the same temporal character but leaves more room for variation. But while this is correct in itself, it would be an error of method to argue from a reconstructed text against a text which is quite plain; at least, the Greek shows how the disciples who first translated the prayer understood their master's petition. This understanding of the once-for-allness is unmistakably confirmed by the 'come' of the second petition, which speaks of a sole eschatological event not only in form but also in content. Within this eschatological event of sanctification with which the petition is concerned, the idea that God's name should be kept holy 'in us' or 'in men' fits well. For it also contains the other idea that the individual or the people will repent in the last time and 'give glory to the Father in heaven' (*Matt.* 5.16), and in the view of all the New Testament this *metanoia* is as much an act of God as an act of men. The Revelation of St. John thus speaks of an 'eternal gospel', which runs (14.7):

> Fear God and praise him . . .
> and worship him who made heaven and earth,
> the sea and the fountains of water.

Fear and praise and worship: these three actions describe from a human standpoint what is called from God's standpoint the hallowing of his name. But precisely for this reason this hallowing is also only one element in the larger course of events implied in this petition, just as the vision of St. John the Divine is only one vision among others which depict the eschatological drama from its beginning to its end. For even the petition does not speak of men. It is put in the passive, after the reverent custom in Jewish prayers. But while the words conceal the bearer of this holiness, the sense speaks all the more clearly of him, and because it is God to whom the prayer is made, the hallowing is to be greater and more comprehensive than anything that men can achieve. Once again, the Revelation of St. John can give us at least an idea of the greater character of this hallowing; its first vision depicts how the new, pure, 'Holy, holy, holy' (4.8) rings out from the mouths of the four creatures and in the worship of the four and twenty elders, and its last vision speaks of the holy city, Jerusalem (21.11,22f.; 22.3,4):

> *Having the glory of God. . . .*
> *God the Lord Almighty*
> *He is its temple, and the Lamb . . .*
> *The glory of God is its light . . .*
> *and his servants shall worship him;*
> *they shall see his face,*
> *and his name shall be on their foreheads.*

The petition in the Lord's Prayer is more restrained and at the same time greater than this vision; it speaks only of the hallowing of the name, thereby presupposing the earthly reality of an unhallowed world and the eschatological possibility of its hallowing: at the same time, however, it ignores all that is meant by world over and above the one factor of this name. The petition speaks of an eternal act of God in which the holy God hallows his name above all the world, and the emphatic once-for-allness is the one fleeting sign that here it is also concerned with the hallowing of the world created by God and consummated by this hallowing. Only in this way is the passive rightly understood; for in concealing the action of God and its effect in an eschatologically perfect world, it leaves everything in the inexpressible wonder of the eternal divine activity, losing all sight of men's own work and nature and praying for the open hallowing of God. This comes first and last, before all worlds and after all worlds, the ground from which and the end towards which the once-for-all eschatological hallowing of his name in all the world also leads.

To interpret the petition in this way does, of course, seem to introduce the unbiblical tone of abstract speculation which may be characteristic of a late gnosis or theology, but not of the original preaching of Jesus and the directness of this one prayer. All that has been said, however, only expresses the biblical idea that God's thoughts are as infinitely higher than all man's thoughts as the heaven is higher than the earth, and the theme of the petition is that these holy thoughts of God may become an eternal, once-for-all act of God. But even to put it in this way is still too abstract for the concreteness of this petition. This is not a hidden or unspeakable name for God to hallow; it is the most familiar, the richest name on which the life of each individual and the existence of the world depends: 'Our Father'. So the perceived presence of God in human life is bound up with that inconceivable transcendence: God's unapproachable holiness *is* his fatherly presence, and what seemed to be no more than an instant in the great event 'now rests'—to use Goethe's familiar words—'in inmost depths on God's eternal breast'; the hallowing of God's name 'Father' also means the hallowing of all those to whom he is Father. Consequently the ancient explanations are justified afresh in a larger setting: 'We pray in this prayer that he may also become holy among us.' The paradox of separation and nearness, of holiness and fatherliness is neither capable of, nor in need of, resolution; it is the foundation of New Testament preaching.

5. If this is the right way to understand the petition, some important historical and factual consequences follow. First, it is no longer remarkable, but necessary, that the petition for the hallowing of the name should precede that for the coming of

the kingdom; for only God's name can form the basis for God's kingdom, only holiness can form the basis of his kingship and rule. The same thing happens in Jesus' thanksgiving: first comes 'Father', and then 'Lord of heaven and earth'; in the same way the whole of Primitive Christianity prayed, 'Abba, Father', and in so doing and by so doing confessed its 'Lord'. There is already an analogous principle in the Old Testament too: because God is the holy One of Israel, he is the king of Israel. This relationship can also be found expressed in Jewish institutions: 'The holy God dwells in his temple, the Lord and king rules by the Law.'

So the petition for the hallowing of God's name rightly precedes that for the coming of the kingdom. Now as this second petition embodies the substance of the synoptic preaching of Jesus, the hallowing of God's name must have formed an equally large and important part of his message. Just as the proclamation of the kingdom is eschatological, in other words, is the fulfilment of all God's previous kingly action towards his people, and is therefore a completely new and hitherto unseen rule, so too this proclamation of the holy name must be eschatological, i.e. must fulfil all the revelations which God has given to his people and the sentence which stands written over their history: 'You must be holy, for I am holy', thereby announcing and achieving a completely new and hitherto unheard of hallowing of God's name.

There are some features even in the Synoptic Gospels which seem to support this conclusion. The first healing miracle in St. Mark's Gospel gives Jesus the name 'the holy one of God', and the paradigmatic character of the title is shown by the formulation of Peter's confession in the Fourth Gospel: 'We have believed, and have come to know, that you are the holy One of God' (6.69). The narrative of the entry into the temple at Jerusalem, the eschatological character of which is unmistakable, comes to a climax in the joyful shout of the people: 'Blessed be he that comes in the name of the Lord.' The first two Gospels are permeated, though perhaps only incidentally, with the fight against the sanctification which is expected from cult and sacrifice. As a rule, however, there are only a few allusions here, for in the centre of the Synoptic message stands the sentence, 'The kingdom of God is at hand.'

The presence of the substance of the first petition in the Fourth Gospel is all the more important in the light of this, as we have already seen: 'I made known to them thy name, and I will make it known' (17.26). These words sum up the whole of Jesus' activity during his earthly life and even beyond it, and not just at this one point. We may not call this formula 'peculiarly Johannine', as apart from Old Testament instances it also occurs in the eucharistic prayers of the Didache (10.2), which are at least contemporaneous with, if not earlier than, the Fourth Gospel: 'We give thanks to thee, O holy Father, for thy holy name which thou didst make to tabernacle in our hearts'. The evangelist's own words run (1.18): 'The only Son, who is in the bosom of the Father, he has made him known.' So we may term 'Abba, Father', an original heritage of the Gospel tradition.

No wonder, too, that St. John's Gospel alone records the short prayer of Jesus which was described as the Johannine form of the first petition of the Lord's Prayer: 'Father, glorify thy name.' It is spoken in an hour when 'his soul is troubled', and is contrasted with another petition, 'Father, save me from this hour', so much more understandable and yet rejected. The answer comes from heaven, saying, 'I have glorified it, and I will glorify it again.' The objective content of these words is clear from the context, for they are spoken when the Greeks come to Jesus, and the world of the Gentiles presses on him, when the hour of the world's judgment dawns and the prince of this world is cast out, when the earthly day of Jesus' life comes to an end and the earthly night of his suffering and death, which is also the heavenly day of his glorification, begins. From this context it becomes quite clear that this petition and the promise which goes with it represents, according to St. John, the centre of that eschatological revelation of which the Gospel is the record. It is summed up in the words 'Father', 'name' and 'glorify', which is, as we know, a synonym for 'sanctify'. The Johannine approach thus has its origin and character in the content of the first petition whereas the Synoptic Gospels take the theme of the message from the second petition. Or, in other words, the first two petitions of the Lord's Prayer include the germ and nucleus of the preaching of the Fourth Gospel as well as that of the first three, though details of both groups may have been interpreted in some respects from tradition or in the light of a special approach.

This clear parallelism, however, also prepares us for the fine distinctions which nevertheless exist between this first petition and the Johannine prayer. Where glorification is spoken of, attention is drawn to the glory and majesty of the eschatological revelation in which all that is unholy and sinful is blotted out from hearts and minds and men and peoples and lands, and the victory is won over every enemy. But this manifest holiness is so to speak hemmed in by two shadows: before it on earth there stands the dark hour of passion and death, and behind it in heaven there stands the hidden holiness of God. The Fourth Gospel has done all that it can to remove these two shadows; it has made the hour of the darkness of death into the hour of glory and has in addition suppressed the concept of holiness (which appears only in the address 'holy Father' and in the prayer to God to sanctify the disciples), including its content in the fullness of the glory which is now manifest in the Father and in the Son. So there is a clearer mention of something which still remains unsaid in the more familiar and more restrained language of the first petition. Consequently, we have the open active 'glorify' here instead of the concealment of the passive, 'be hallowed', and instead of being a petition of the disciples it has become a prayer of Jesus, from the Son to the Father. So the way and the means, but not the end, the word, but not the reality, has changed; both petitions, the Johannine and the Synoptic, deal with the same eschatological revelation.

There is one last theme here. The idea of the hallowing of God's name points to an eschatological act before which all historical differences of peoples and languages vanish and in which at the same time the world is presupposed as a well ordered and 'sanctified' entity. So it is understandable that this first petition has become so to speak the petition for the mission to the Gentiles. Just as *Ps.* 86.9 already says:

> *All the nations thou hast made shall come*
> *and bow down before thee, O Lord,*
> *and shall glorify thy name,*

so *I Clement* gives thanks that: 'He has called us from darkness to light, from ignorance to the full knowledge of the glory of his name' (59.2), and warns: 'Let us then be obedient to his most holy and glorious name, that we may tabernacle in confidence on the most sacred name of his majesty' (58.1).

But comprehensive as the petition for sanctification is, its origin and content point far more to the life and historical career of the people of God: 'You must be holy, for I am holy', thereby associating it closely with the documents of the revelation which are preserved by this people of God. So this eschatological petition completes the history and the community of the people of God in the world. It also, however, begins it, as it reaches back to before the creation of the world. And then it reaches forward to after the consummation, to an eschatologically new community, of those who pray and worship in this way, sanctified and glorified, sanctifying and glorifying children of God, 'in my Father's house'. It therefore points in two directions, to the universality of the whole creation and to the exclusiveness of the eschatologically perfect community, and thus in both preserves only the fact that this is a hallowing of God's name, before which even creation and consummation are only parts of the whole.

It has now become clear why the petition 'Hallowed be thy name' is important enough to have first place among the petitions of the Lord's Prayer. It is also understandable why people have always wanted to see it as a doxology like those which so often characterize the openings of Old Testament and Jewish prayers. The expression 'doxology' is not inappropriate if it is understood in the broad sense which the Bible gives to it: here it is a matter of God's *doxa*, i.e. the praise of his name, for which 'Thou, Lord almighty, didst create all things' (*Did.* 10.3), and therefore of his manifest glory, which is the revelation of his holiness; it is a matter of that ultimate theme which resounds and will continue to resound in and almost after the abiding world to come, as it has done in and before this transitory world, in the coming people of God as in those who have been before. Here is a petition which joins both worlds and both communities in a unity, through the very name of God, which stands over them both, and through the act of hallowing which is made to his name.

IV Thy Kingdom Come

1. The wording of the second petition raises only a few minor questions. Some manuscripts read the predicate in the imperative form of the Greek aorist I ἐλθάτω, others in that of the aorist II ἐλθέτω. The change has only linguistic significance; it points to the increasing confusion of the two forms in the *koine*, which has led to the complete abolition of the difference in modern Greek. In Church use, the form, 'Thy kingdom come to us' also occurs; Matthias Claudius comments on it in his commentary and Grillparzer used it in his unfinished poem on the Lord's Prayer. The sole support for it is a reading of Codex D (*Cantabrigiensis*) at *Luke* 11.2. It is certainly not original, as the parallels of the first and third petitions show; the very lack of any point of reference for the 'come', attested by all manuscripts of the Matthaean text, is one of the peculiar characteristics of these first three petitions. The origin and character of the variation can only be decided on when we have discussed the Lucan deviations. The Old Latin versions also show that it was felt necessary to define the purpose of this coming rather more closely, because of the immediate practical use of the prayer and a number of New Testament parallels. Some Old Latin manuscripts translate the phrase *veniat regnum tuum*, others, which the Vulgate follows, *adveniat regnum tuum*. This 'coming to' has subsequently found its way from the Vulgate into the French and Swedish versions of the Lord's Prayer. The simple 'come' corresponds more closely to the Greek text. In Aramaic, the petition would probably run *tētē malkūtāk*, and this is in the

88

Peshitto and in the Curetonian Syriac. In both Syriac versions an 'and' comes before the second petition; it is a reference to an ancient interpretation rather than the trace of an ancient tradition. For this text, the first and second petitions belong closely together, and are in this way separated from the third, which is added in asyndeton.

One external feature seems at first sight to separate the second petition from the first; the sentence 'Hallowed be thy name' stood by itself in the Gospel tradition, but was deeply rooted in Old Testament passages; 'Thy kingdom come', on the other hand, while quite common throughout the Synoptic tradition, has no corresponding phrase or object in the Old Testament. But we must investigate the position rather more closely. The Synoptic Gospels speak in many places of the kingdom of God, and the occurrences of the word '*basileia*' spread over the whole of the New Testament show that it is a basic concept in Primitive Christian preaching. But the word 'come' is associated with the concept of the kingdom of God only here in Matthew. Mark has the connection twice: in 9.1 he reproduces the Lord's saying, 'before they see the kingdom of God come with power' (in 16.28, Matthew writes, 'before they see the Son of Man coming in his kingdom'), and in 11.10 he is the only one to have the jubilant cry of the people, 'Blessed be the kingdom of our father David that is coming!' at Jesus' entry into the temple. Luke combines the two words of this petition three times (twice in 17.20 and once in 22.18).

But it would be wrong to draw any major conclusions from these minor differences. For the small number of instances can easily be increased if we include the kindred words 'draw near' (ἐγγίζειν) and 'reach' (φθάνειν); the first occurs in *Matt.* 3.2; 4.7=*Mark* 1.15; *Matt.* 10.17; *Luke* 10.9,11, the second in *Matt.* 12.28=*Luke* 11.20. But in that case we can see some differences, for ἔρχεσθαι and ἐγγίζειν are distinct from φθάνειν in that both are used both in a temporal and a spatial sense, whereas the former is used only in a temporal sense; ἔρχεσθαι then differs from the other two in that they already imply a 'being on the way', whereas to 'come' says nothing about that. In the first case the 'coming' has already begun, and the person is near his destination; in the other not only is the end of the journey undefined, but even its beginning; the only assurance is that the journey will at some time be completed. Nowhere outside the first three Gospels does the New Testament speak of the 'coming of the kingdom of God'.

Nor is there any explicit mention of it in the Old Testament or in earlier or later Jewish writings. The rabbis speak not of 'coming', but of 'being made manifest', or even of 'taking upon oneself the kingdom of God'. There are only a few expressions which come any nearer to this petition. *Daniel* 7.22 runs, 'and the time came when the saints received the kingdom'; and Josephus says once of the Herodian kingdom, 'so that even if the kingdom came to him he would still not be able to enjoy it' (*Ant.* 17.66). But phrases like this at most show the common currency of the idea and say little about the concept in question. We must take the two words separately.

2. To ask at the beginning or the end of a prayer for the god (or goddess) to come to hear its words is a well-known Greek custom. Even in Homer, Odysseus prays to Athene (*Iliad* 23, 770):

κλῦθι θεά, ἀγαθή μοι ἐπίρροθος ἐλθὲ ποδοῖιν

('Hear, goddess, graciously come to my aid')

The phrase later becomes a stereotyped formula in the Homeric and Orphic hymns, so that Plato can say (*Leg.* iv 712b): 'Let us invoke the presence of God; and may he hearken, and hearkening may he come, propitious and kindly to us-ward.' And if this is often only an introductory formula, to begin the inter-course with the god or goddess, it still retains its concrete significance. 'Women, weep, for the goddess to come', runs a fragment of Euripides (Nauck, fr. 353). But this 'coming' is not that of the person of the deity: in a wider sense, it refers to all that the gods give or sustain. A prayer by the Chorus in

Aeschylus' *Supplices* (804) has words which match the form of this petition exactly: ἐλθέτω μόρος (let fate come); in prayers of the magical papyri, which are also full of appeals for the coming of the god, we find: 'Let the throne of God come' (v 32, cf. 35, Preisendanz). Josephus, too, knows this Hellenistic prayer-formula, 'O come, Lord of the universe, to judge my cause and to attest as witness incorruptible' (*Ant.* iv 46, xx 90). And later, in the Acts of Thomas, we not only have, 'Jesus: let his victorious might come' (157), or, 'Let the powers of blessing come' (133), but also, on the ancient Greek pattern: 'Come, thou holy name of Christ. . . . Come, thou power of the Most High . . . Come, gift of the Most High . . . Come, compassionate mother, come, communion . . . Come, revealer' etc. (27, also 50).

Although this language is widespread in non-Jewish prayers, it is rarely used in the Old Testament or in Judaism. True, the Psalter has a petition like the one in Aeschylus, 'Let death come upon them' (55.15), and others of a similar kind: 'Let thy mercy come to me' (119.77), or, 'Let thy steadfast love come to me' (119.41). There is even a direct address, 'And come to save us' (96.13). But such a 'come' does not invite God to hear a petition, nor does it ask for him to appear in some kind of epiphany. It is not even specifically a phrase used in prayer— it became that only partially and in a completely new sense through the primitive Christian cry, '*Maranatha*=Come, Lord Jesus' (*Rev.* 22.20). This 'coming' describes the beginning of an action or an event and on the lips of the faithful signifies that the intervening hand of God has become perceptible in some happening. In this general, but also very definite sense, it is deeply bound up with the fundamentals of Old Testament and New Testament thought.

In the New Testament, the word 'come', in a transferred sense, primarily denotes a certain point of time at which something will happen: 'The days will come', 'the hour has come', 'the time had fully come' (*Matt.* 9.15; *Mark* 14.41; *Gal.* 4.4); this also corresponds to a well-known Old Testament usage:

'The day of the Lord comes' (*Joel* 2.31; *Isa.* 63.4; *Mal.* 4.1,5) or, 'The days are coming' (*Amos* 4.2; 8.11; 9.3; *Isa.* 39.6; *Jer.* 7.32; 9.25; 16.14; 19.6 etc.). One can recognize the different application of the phrases by comparing the familiar verse in Homer: ἔσσεται ἦμαρ ὅτ'ἄν ποτ'ὀλώλη ''Ἴλιος ἱρή (*Iliad* vi 448) (The day will come when holy Ilium shall fall).

In Homer, the day which 'will be' is one of a series of days; this is a constant and equal flow which runs according to its own laws from an unknown origin to an unknown goal. In the Bible, the days 'come' irregularly, like the visits of friends or the attacks of enemies; no fixed rule governs their sequence; chance or purpose arranges for it to be so. Other events or states come, like time, whether they are processes in nature or happenings in human or historical life; good and evil (*Rom.* 3.8), faith or apostasy (*Gal.* 3.23-25), the law (*Rom.* 5.20), temptations (*Matt.* 18.7), perfection and the kingdom of God all come (*I Cor.* 13.10; *Luke* 22.18).

This matches Old Testament usage; there too good and evil (*Jer.* 17.6), heat and cold, sunshine and hail, 'the word of God' (*Jer.* 17.5), death and corruption, grace and mercy (*Ps.* 55.15; *Prov.* 1.26; *Ps.* 119.41,77), come, and *Isa.* 5.19, very similar in form and content to the petition in the Lord's Prayer, runs: 'Let the purpose of the holy One of Israel draw near, and let it come, that we may know it!' So firmly is the concept of coming bound up with that of time that the Septuagint renders the almost mythological statement in *Isa.* 30.27, 'The name of the Lord comes from far', with one that is almost speculative: 'The name of the Lord comes through much time.' Often, of course, the word 'come' seems to be simply a synonym for 'happen, take place' (a word which, of course, echoes a similar thought with its derivation of 'to eye', 'perceive with the eyes'), but the expression reaches still deeper; for it is well known that the world itself is called 'time' ('ōlām= αἰών), and whatever exists and takes place in it, whatever it is itself, in short, all its being, is a 'coming into time or through time'. This 'coming', then, is not an ultimate concept which in principle cannot be transcended, like the Greek 'being'; it is merely the expression of a happening and a becoming which itself originates in a principle, or, in biblical terms, in a will, which stands outside the time that is the world, and by means of this time brings it into being. Being, then, means being enacted, 'activity', and 'to come' is a periphrastic expression for an action of God which so to speak creates the world and all reality from outside. Being is only possible as 'being there', as 'existing', i.e. as an *ex-sistere* in the literal sense, a breaking out from the realm of divine being into the framework of time; and if 'the time comes', then that too is a product of this work. This coming is distinguished from the idea of a 'being enacted' only by the fact that it belongs not with the action of the will but with the being that is there enacted, thus severing at the root any substantial connection between 'being in the world' and 'being in God', not to mention the being of God. At the same time, however, it rejoins the two by the ideas of action and being enacted, or the idea of creation.

So biblical thought recognizes a distinction, but not an opposition, between time and eternity; for both 'come' from God's hand, and just as the world is time, so too God's eternity (though with a degree of clarity only since Deutero-Isaiah) is 'time' or even 'the age of ages'. God's time does not reach from eternity to eternity, but 'from age to age' or 'from ages to ages'. Therefore here, too, time is not a constant and uninterrupted flow, without beginning and end, but it stands at the beginning, divides itself into 'ages' and reaches an end which is the transition into the 'ages of ages', i.e. into eternity. It therefore does not obey a special law or a special nature, but is always achieved anew; the predominant idea everywhere is not that of an empty, merely fleeting, time, but of an experienced time, or, more exactly, a historically filled time which is in fact expressed in this 'coming'. Rabbinic evidence still attests this in replacing the notion of the continuity of being by another one, that of renewal. 'Every morning God creates the world anew,' runs a well-known rabbinic saying. It is further part of such a view that attention is focused particularly on the future, on what is 'to come', for if all reality 'comes' from the will of God, it has its existence precisely in the fact that it is created new every morning. So what 'has come' and in this sense 'is', exists only because it prepares or waits for what is to come.

If, then, both Old and New Testaments often speak of the 'coming' of divine things and events, it is clear that this is the context in which the word is given its full and true sense, and that the 'coming' of earthly things and events is only a derivative expression. For here it quite literally happens that 'with mighty acts the All breaks into reality'. And if not only the world 'comes', but even God himself is in an exclusive sense 'He who is to come' (*Rev.* 1.4), this phrase too confirms with considerable accuracy the great pattern of thought: Because God is the fullness of all that is to come and the power of all that is to come, he is, as the God who acts, himself the final destiny of his action, and therefore quite simply '*the* Coming One'. So too the world which belongs to him in such an eschatological sense as the pure and permanent place and the pure and permanent manner of his action is precisely the age to come ('*ōlām hab-bā*= ὁ αἰὼν ὁ μέλλων). While this age to come is comparable and yet dissimilar to the present age, it is not exclusively opposed to it, as even the present age is God's creation; we see it, rather, as a perfect example of what this 'coming' means: all being and happening is, because it is made *through* God, also made *for* God; its being in time and through time is a steady transition from being made by God to being fulfilled by God. Each step and each pause in this transition, each existence from day to day is, seen in the light of God, a being made or a being renewed, and, seen from the point of view of men, a new 'coming' from the hand and will of God. So being itself has the almost dormant possibility of the eschatological, and everything eschatological has the true reality of all being.

So this coming appears in a twofold aspect. Whatever comes is only what has already been for a long time, for both are God's work, yet at the same time it is something completely new and

94

other, created by God, because it 'comes'. Therefore the process of becoming and changing is God's language to men and God's work among them. There is no infinite flow of becoming which streams incessantly onwards, but only a coming and a becoming, new like the sun every morning, until through God's counsel this becoming reaches its true destiny and arrives at the end of all coming. Then will be the reality which is appropriate to God: the holy God in his holy world. But before this end, desired by God, hoped for or feared, longed for or despised by men, the whole life and existence of men and things is a coming and a passing away, and this passing away leads in various stages from the same, which was always there, to something completely new which can be contrasted with all existence. So even the Old Testament 'day of the Lord' is a day like past or present days and therefore the completely different day which ends all days, and the age to come is an age just like the present and at the same time completely different, which ends all days—and both are and come only because God, who created both, is the same; He was and is and is to come.

3. The concept of the kingdom of God, the 'coming' of which is prayed for here, has been discussed so frequently that a brief survey of its structure must suffice. It has become a unity of many aspects and of many meanings from three patterns of thought and three different origins. The three can be recognized from the verbs connected with the kingdom of God.

A first pattern is indicated by words like 'sit at table' (*Matt.* 8.11), 'eat and drink' (*Luke* 22.30), 'enter the kingdom' (*Matt.* 5.20; 7.21; 18.3, also 8*f.*; 19.17,23*f.*; also 25.21,23), 'be thrown out of the kingdom' (*Matt.* 8. 12). Here the phrase 'the kingdom of God' evokes the picture of a house or a city of God. There are 'keys' to this kingdom (*Matt.* 16.19), and men can 'close' it (*Matt.* 23.14). There is also a counterpart, 'the kingdom of Satan', which is itself compared with a house or a city (*Matt.* 12.25*f.*); one can go on from there to talk about a householder,

Beelzebul, and his household (*Matt.* 10.25). So the kingdom of God is first of all a place or a locality and the picture also takes in the community of those who belong to this house, like its Lord and founder. So in numerous parables we find the king, who invites guests (e.g. *Matt.* 22.1-14) or makes a reckoning with his servants (*Matt.* 18.21-35), the householder who hires labourers for his vineyard (*Matt.* 21.28-31; *Luke* 15.11-32), and entrusts them with his goods before he goes away (*Matt.* 25.14-30). All these pictures and parables have their clear inner limits, revolving round the father and the king to whom this house and kingdom belong, and round the community of inhabitants who are called 'sons of the kingdom' (*Matt.* 8.12) or 'guests' or 'invited' (e.g. 22.3,8f.). This eschatological 'Father's house' (*John* 14.2) has its clear historical counterpart in the house of God which is now God's dwelling-place in Jerusalem and the unassailable and holy centre of the community of all pious Jews.

In some places, however, the inner concentration of this picture is suddenly opened up so that it becomes capable of embracing the vast immensity of all nations (*Matt.* 8.11f.):

> *Many will come from east and west*
> *and sit at table with Abraham, Isaac, and Jacob*
> *in the kingdom of heaven,*
> *while the sons of the kingdom will be thrown*
> *into the outer darkness.*

These words disclose a different pattern of thought from the earlier one; whereas the last words still suggest a brightly lit house, whose comforting light makes a happy contrast with the surrounding gloom of night, the first words presuppose the great apocalyptic ideas of the 'world to come', which transcend all boundaries; for these 'many from east and west' represent the idea of 'this world' from which the 'sons of the kingdom' are separated. It has primarily spatial and temporal connotations and is associated with well-known Jewish apocalyptic ideas: 'For they shall behold the world which is now invisible to them, and they shall behold the time which is now hidden from them, for in the heights of that world shall they dwell' (II *Baruch*

51.8). This world is the 'kingdom' (*Matt.* 13.24). So this kingdom of God also 'comes'; it will be 'seen' (*Mark* 9.1; *John* 3.5), 'inherited' (*I Cor.* 6.9f; 15.50; *Gal.* 5.21; cf. also *Matt.* 5.5; 19.29; 25.34), men 'eat and drink' in it (*Luke* 22.30), there are 'many mansions' in it (*John* 14.2), and the 'righteous will shine like the sun in the kingdom of their Father' (*Matt.* 13.43). In the language of later Christian expressions it is 'the new Jerusalem, the heavenly city', a world 'of eternal life and blessing', of peace and glory. With such a character of divine openness, this idea of the kingdom of God is combined with the earlier ideas of the house or city of God to form a unity full of deep tensions and even deeper resolutions. It is enclosed like a father's house, yet unbounded like God's world, it embraces the 'sons of the Father in heaven' (*Matt.* 5.45) and the 'many from east and west'; it is familiar and yet hidden, known yet unimaginably new and different. It is like a treasure that a man finds (*Matt.* 13.44), that he seeks and discovers (*Matt.* 13.45), and at the same time a power which permeates everything (*Matt.* 13.33), a grain of mustard seed which grows and becomes a tree (*Matt.* 13.31) 'so that the birds of the air come and make nests in its branches.'

The shape and derivation of these two ideas of God's house and God's world, in which the immensity of the world is contracted to the safety of the home and the home is opened out to become the boundless heaven, while the heaven of this kingdom is at the same time God and the father's house, are clearly recognizable. They are, however, only rarely mentioned by name and are far more frequently combined in the unifying word *basileia*. Here a third pattern of ideas emerges. The expression 'kingdom of God', or, as Matthew usually puts it, 'kingdom of heaven', is almost unknown in the Old Testament. It occurs only in a few passages in the later Psalms (22.29; 45.7; 103.19; 145.11f., also *I Chron.* 29.11f.) and the book of Daniel (2.44; 4.28; 7.28), and finds its way from there into Jewish apocalyptic (*I Enoch* 84.2; 90.30; 92.4; 103.1; *II Enoch* 24.3; *Ass. Mos.* 10.1ff., etc.).

The idea that 'The Lord is king for ever and ever' (*Ex.* 15.18), reaching back to ancient times, is far more vivid and has much deeper roots. This kingdom exists in the world which God guides in accordance with his will, and in the people which he has chosen and directs. His kingly rule is exercised through creating and sustaining, guiding and ordering, beginning and ending: God holds the reins. As it was in the beginning, and is now, so one day it will be in perfection, untouched by the enmity of men and peoples. This eschatological kingdom differs from all earlier acts of the Lord, not in character, but only in degree and extent. It is an act of God in the history of his people and consequently of all other peoples, and yet at the same time it is God's kingly rule over his own people, chosen from of old, whom he still guides and will continue to guide to their destiny. This idea is expressed with all clarity, at least at the time of the later prophets, in the idea of the covenant that God concluded with the patriarchs of the people, which regulates their whole life. It is a covenant of the past and the present and therefore also of the eschatological future; although in the here and now of this age it is involved in deep tensions, so that the people again and again disobey or transgress the royal will of God, the eschatological covenant will establish and strengthen a union with God in their hearts and lives which will never be broken.

So God's kingdom, too, is eternally established. No one can say of such a kingdom, as Jesus does, that a man can enter into it, and outside the earliest Christian Gospels there is no instance of an expectation of its 'coming'. The old hope is preserved right into the rabbinic period: because 'God's kingdom is established' (*Targ. Onk. Ex.* 15.18), 'it will be made manifest' (*Targ. Onk. Isa.* 24.23). There is only one new feature in rabbinic evidence: we often find the phrase 'take up the yoke of the kingdom of heaven' (passages in Billerbeck I, 173*ff. passim*). But here the Old Testament idea merely lives on in a rabbinic way: God has laid 'the yoke' on his people because he was and is and will be king, and both the individual and the people take it up to honour and obey him as their king and lord. It is no new and unknown yoke, but the old law which assures an abiding kingdom to the people of God.

A wide gulf separates this idea of the kingdom from the two earlier ones. In Judaism, the kingdom is a royal function of God, while here in the Gospels it is an entity defined in space and time, established and given by the one God and Father; in Judaism, God's kingdom comes to pass in the eschatological future because it has been coming to pass through all the past and the present though concealed by the veil of history, while in the Gospels a kingdom 'comes' in an imminent 'tomorrow' which was not there before; in Judaism it is royal and familiar, while in the Gospels it is fatherly and royal, strange and unknown. Nevertheless, in the concept of the kingdom the idea of God's kingly rule has been fused with that of God's house and God's world to form an almost paradoxical unity. This amalgamation, attested only in the Gospels, has stripped the idea of the 'coming world' of the characteristics of apocalyptic fantasy and mystical indeterminacy and has given it the imminent reality of an historical event; it has removed the kingdom of God from its previously historical context and enlarged it so that it becomes the 'coming world' of God, to which 'many come from the east and from the west'; it has taken the 'house of God' out of its narrow restriction to the cult and banished 'kingdom' and world into the intimate secrecy of a father's house in which 'there are many mansions', or the joy of a family meal where children and beggars, the sick and the needy, Gentiles and tax-collectors and sinners, recline at the table. Like that world to come, this kingdom too gives life and righteousness to the individual (*Matt.* 7.14; 6.33), and like that Old Testament kingdom it is a realm in which the community of the elect is realized, or a home in which the children cluster round their father. Like that world, the 'kingdom' is an entity defined in space and time, in which all life and existence is fulfilled; like the house of God it is a place where God's name dwells and is hallowed, where those who may be called his children pray to him, the embodiment of God's presence; and like that kingdom it is finally a permanent, historical and eschatological function, it is God's future activity. That is the significance of this unity, that God's apocalyptically unique and eternal reality and his historically unique activity are regarded as an event which happens here and now and in the future. The idea of 'coming' points the way to such an inexhaustible and almost paradoxical unity, since it is clearly connected with the contrast between the two worlds and at the same time understands this opposition as a transition 'from age to age'.

4. The connection between the first and second petitions is a straightforward one. For 'to hallow God's name' also means to recognize and praise him as the sole Lord of creation: where his name is praised, there is his kingdom. Jewish prayers are also familiar with the same transition; the Kaddish has, 'Magnified and sanctified be his great name in the world which he hath created according to his will'; this is followed by the words, 'May he establish his kingdom during your life and during your days.' Similarly, the Revelation of St. John puts the hallowing of God at the beginning of its apocalyptic visions (4.8):

> Holy, holy, holy, is the Lord God, Almighty,
> who was and is and is to come!

And this is followed in the next vision by the enthronement of the king with the hymn (5.9):

> Worthy art thou
> to take the scroll and to open its seals,
> for thou wast slain
> and by thy blood didst ransom men for God
> from every tribe and tongue and people and nation,
> and hast made them a kingdom and priests to our God,
> and they shall reign on earth.

Because of this it has often been said that the second petition repeats the contents of the first, or that the first petition prepares for the expressions of the second. In view of the terseness of the prayer, however, we must ask whether the petition does not have a content of its own, although—or even, because—it is closely related in form and matter to the one which precedes it.

Ever since the first commentaries on the Lord's Prayer there have been two contrasting interpretations of this petition. One envisages a gradual coming of the kingdom and an increasingly deep and extensive penetration of it into the hearts of men, like the great Old Testament image of the Word of God, the rain and snow, which 'come down from heaven, and return not thither but water the earth, making it bring forth and sprout, giving seed to the sower and bread to the eater' (*Isa.* 55.10). Or, to use the New Testament picture, the kingdom develops in men, in nations, in the whole world, through a steady growth like the grain of mustard seed. Although this growth is quite clearly in pursuance of the will of God and is brought about by him, men are still his co-workers, or, in other words: the fact or the task of missions at home and abroad underlies this petition; men take the kingdom of God to men and nations, men preach as God's message that human life is to be directed in thought and deed in accordance with his holy moral will so that the conduct of the individual and the ordering of society is founded afresh upon it. So the idea of the kingdom of God becomes the ordering of moral or social or religious life in accordance with the demands of the Gospel of Jesus. God brings it about among men, and through a constantly repeated *ora et labora* men are his instruments, until it is fulfilled in very truth through the action of God at the end of the world and of history. The beginnings of such an interpretation are already present in Origen; many commentators of the Greek Church developed it, and it was finally established firmly by Zwingli and Calvin.

The other interpretation envisages the perfect kingdom of God at the end of time and history, the *regnum gloriae*. It has not yet appeared on earth, but it will 'come' one day, and that means that it will manifest itself in great glory, will put an end to all dispute and injustice, all evil and godless powers, and exist eternally in peace and holiness. Tertullian understood the petition in this way, and many fathers of the Latin Church followed him; Bengel took the interpretation up in more recent times. Unmistakably it has an intimate connection with the Old Latin translation, *adveniat regnum tuum*, which is characteristically different from the simpler 'Thy kingdom come' of the Greek text. But it does not in any way exclude the first one, as that too speaks of such an eschatological coming, just as the second one itself also already sees the coming of the kingdom in the *regnum gratiae*, as it calls it, and finds that mentioned not in the second, but in the third petition. So from Chrysostom right up to Luther and Calvin, commentators have found both points of view here; as Luther put it, 'God's kingdom comes here once in time through God's word and faith, and a second time in eternity through his revelation.'

Now one thing is clear from the start. The second petition does not speak of a twofold coming of the kingdom. The tense of the verb clearly precludes this and allows only the idea of a single coming; similarly, the subject itself resists being split in Old Latin fashion into a *regnum gratiae* and a *regnum gloriae* or, in a more modern way, into an age of gradual progress and extension which will lead into one of consummation. The first and most obvious meaning of the sentence is that this kingdom comes once for all and that it is therefore final and eschatological. In other words, this kingdom is the kingdom *of God*, and that in turn means that it is his final and eschatological kingdom; the petition is only concerned that the eschatological character of this kingdom should no longer surrender it up to apocalyptic dreams and obscure hopes, and that the eschatological character of its coming should become a unity created by God. Nevertheless, the difficulty of understanding it lies just at this point; for are we not justified in asking what this coming means if it does not mean to come 'to us'? Must we not then supply this 'to us', as has sometimes been done in manuscripts, and as it is clearly and simply expressed in Jewish prayers: 'May his kingdom reign in your days and in your lifetime'? And is there not a further justification for such an addition in the fact that the Master is here instructing his disciples to pray 'like this'?

The question may seem obvious, and it may seem reasonable to pray, 'Thy kingdom come to us', but it is still important to note that this petition, like the first, gives no promise of such an end to the person who prays. One reason for not expanding the petition is that there is a clear stress on this reference to 'our' life and hearts only from the fourth petition onwards; in the first three petitions, the reference is purely and simply to what God is and what God does. True, there is a hint of a human reference occasionally elsewhere in the Gospels, but they also suggest that it is impossible to add one here as a matter of course. 'The kingdom of God is in the midst of you' (*Luke* 17.20); this saying is addressed not to Jesus' disciples, but to the Pharisees. 'But if it is by the finger of God that I cast out demons, then the kingdom of God has come upon you' (*Luke* 11.20). This sentence is directed sharply against the charge that Jesus drives out demons through Beelzebul.

The one positive human consequence of the coming kingdom is unmistakably shown by Jesus' cry: 'Repent, for the kingdom of heaven is at hand.' But one who 'repents' because of the nearness of the kingdom is not yet one who prays for the coming of the kingdom. Elsewhere it is not that the kingdom comes to men, but that certain men will enter it, when it comes, the sick and the poor, the persecuted and the oppressed. So the coming of the kingdom has its own meaning and its own end; it is so to speak the unexpected and unimaginable grace of God that men whom he calls—and they are those who 'sit in the region and shadow of death' (*Matt.* 4.16=*Isa.* 8.23*f*)—may also enter his kingdom. Just as by God's will the sun rises in the morning and gives light and life to good and evil alike, so too God's kingdom comes on the eschatological 'morning' regardless of men's prayers and longings, hopes and fears; once again, 'there was light'. If men are nevertheless to pray for this coming, it is not only because the greatest proof of the love of the Father which is the coming of this kingdom is given in this divine objectivity to those who pray, but also because through their prayers they may count themselves among those who may enter this kingdom because they are the children of their Father in heaven, or even because they will 'reign on earth', as the Revelation of St. John puts it (5.10; 20.6; 22.5). They pray, like the angels who sit in the council of God, they implore what is God's counsel and God's work alone, they concern themselves about the creation and the consummation of the world, and because of this concern, not only for their own fate, but for the eschatological things between heaven and earth, their prayer goes up: 'Thy kingdom come.'

For this kingdom is first of all the 'coming age', and its day corresponds to the day which first beheld this 'world-age'. All the contrasts and all the similarities there are between this world and the world to come therefore also define the content of this petition. The world to come is God's world, the present world is that of demons and the devil; God's world is holy and righteous, this world is sinful and guilty. God's world is one of life and glory—that is why even the Synoptic Gospels speak of 'inheriting eternal life' (*Matt.* 19.29 *par.*) instead of 'the kingdom', or of 'entering into life' (*Matt.* 7.13*f.*) instead of 'into the kingdom' —this world is one of death and corruption. So in this petition those who pray ask that the powers of this world, whether they are called 'sin, death and the devil' in familiar Pauline words, or 'debt, temptation and the evil one' as in the last three petitions, will be overcome by the powers of the world to come, righteousness, life, God. So too there is no reference to men, because the coming of the kingdom first of all affects the powers who restrict their life and action.

This kingdom is also the coming house of God, or the coming city of God, and is thus in contrast to the present, historical house of God. The consequences of this conflicting relationship can be expressed in the old prophetic saying which St. Matthew's Gospel twice puts into the mouth of Jesus (9.13; 12.7): 'I desire mercy, and not sacrifice.' Its content is described in many ways: not holiness of service but purity of heart (*Matt.* 5.8) and action

(*Matt.* 13.11, 19*f.*), not segregation but love (*Mark* 12.29*f.*), not sacrifice but prayer and worship, not Temple feasts but feasting in 'My Father's kingdom' (*Matt.* 26. 29). All this is not a gift and a task in an earthly life but the sole reality through which the father is united with his children in his house.

This kingdom is finally the consummation of the people of God who have hitherto supported the kingship of God as a gift and a task in their history and in their life. Here, too, the opposition and the agreement is clear. Not a political and national kingdom and people, but a community which, under God's care and protection, lives its life in love and worship, in righteousness and purity. This is the link which leads from the heavenly entity of the world of God and the house of God to the historical reality of those men who pray for the coming of the kingdom, and as they pray can know themselves to be invited guests. But there is only a faint echo in this petition of this human reality as a possibility asked from God; the one who prays knows that all the significance of this kingdom for men is reserved for the will and the action of God.

So this petition still retains its peculiar ambivalence. It speaks of an order which is to come about through God's eschatological action. This order is a revelation of God, as was the hallowing of his name. It exists of its own power and in its own self, unaffected by worldly orders, yet at the same time it fulfils in 'this world' and among this people whatever lies in the province of the powers and objects of a divine ordering. Because of the first element, this 'kingdom' is a substantial entity defined in space, which God will reveal in his own time—and it is now clear that this spatial, substantial character, deviating from Old Testament ideas, merely gives it final and definitive form—because of the second, it is the act of an eschatological revelation through which God fulfils in his people his kingdom which has existed from the beginning. As both these elements, however, are included in the one word *basileia* and in the one petition, there is room for a completely new order in which it is left to

God's overwhelming grace whether he fulfils men and things according to his will, or whether he eschatologically creates something unimaginably new and yet still primeval. This utter abandonment of everything to God forms the basis of the freedom and the trust as a result of which children may pray to their Father, 'Thy kingdom come'. If hitherto they seemed to pray as though from the counsel of God, they are now those who are put under other rulers—whether men or demons—and are in their grasp. This twofold aspect, which almost tacitly points to the divinely ordained fact of a community of God, is alone sufficient to define the picture of those who pray like this, but through it the eschatological character of this kingdom emerges into that rich and pure light which is no longer disturbed by the obscurity of apocalyptic or the confusion of history.

A petition which is so exclusively directed at the coming of the kingdom seems, however, to expose itself to one grave suspicion: should it not know that this kingdom is already 'at hand' in the very work and preaching of Jesus? Here the old explanation, which in various ways talks about a twofold coming, seems to be justified, and it is not easy to refute it. Some much-discussed sayings speak of the kingdom of God as having come and being present. It 'has come upon you' in the driving out of demons (*Matt.* 12.28), 'Behold, the kingdom of God is in the midst of you.' Many parables of Jesus about the kingdom of God would be incomprehensible if we tried to exclude this idea of the nearness and presence of the kingdom. The two sides do not, however, contradict each other; these very sentences which speak about the tangible nearness of the kingdom of God make it clear that the coming of this kingdom is still utterly in God's counsel and in God's hands. The words of Jesus can proclaim it, his signs may prepare for it in many ways, they may even bear witness to its existence—the kingdom nevertheless remains something which comes from heaven, as it is the final eschatologically fulfilled kingdom. So the prayer can and always must be, 'Thy kingdom come'. The suspicion mentioned above, then, is not directed at the eschatological character of this kingdom, nor does this eschatological character exclude its nearness and presence; it merely gives clearer testimony and definition to the position of those who pray for its coming. They stand in what is almost the projection of the light of this kingdom, as they can ask for things which rest purely in the eschatological counsel of God, and at the same time stand in prayer in the darkness of this world, in this people and this land, given over to its powers and afflictions. To put it in Johannine words, which exactly describe the twofold character of the situation: they are still *in* the world, but they are no longer *of* the world. They have in common the fact that they can pray 'like this', underneath which there lies another, never expressed and yet always secretly presupposed, namely that they are the disciples. They are not a *regnum gratiae*, much less a *regnum gloriae*, but the community of those who pray and from their grace and need ask for the glory of the kingdom of God.

This suggests a number of further consequences. First, the petition tacitly rejects the idea that the kingdom of God could ever be built by men or even by those who make this prayer. God alone can achieve it: man, no matter who, can at most prepare to 'enter this kingdom', if God calls him. So no one is, as Origen thought, following a well-known saying of St. Paul's (*I Cor.* 3.9 etc.), a 'fellow workman' for God. Whatever even Jesus may achieve in the present power of his words and his works is, in the light of this petition, only an occasion for fervent prayer for the coming of this kingdom. So, secondly: even if Jesus' works prepare for the kingdom of God and testify to it as something present, which is growing and being achieved in the here and now, there stands above everything the hidden will of God, which means the coming of his kingdom. Even the signs of his presence are never infallible guarantees of God's coming in the sense that they bind his will and make a prayer for his coming unnecessary. God alone is the guarantor, because he is the father of those who pray, and all signs and words therefore only strengthen the one petition, 'Thy kingdom come', even if this kingdom seems to come nearer, indeed to stand 'before the door' (*Matt.* 24.32f. *par.*)

One can understand from this why the petition does not speak of 'being near' or 'being in the midst of you', but simply of 'coming'. The very colourlessness of this word conceals the depth of the surrender in which the suppliants look for the kingdom, and the magnitude and grace of the divine will, which its coming implies. This simple surrender to grace of the divine will, which alone determines the day and the hour, leads to one last thing: the Jewish hope painted some pictures of how all salvation and all blessedness would be found in this future kingdom, how the righteous would be gathered in and all the ancient prophecies be fulfilled. There is nothing of all this in this petition; there is no reference, not even a slight allusion, to any promise; it conjures up no reminiscence of the past and no hope for the future, but is solely given over to what is to come, which will appear like the sun each morning to righteous and unrighteous alike, and which is in this very way as inconceivable as God's eschatological world and house and kingdom.

5. We have now discovered that the second petition has a content all of its own, but this very discovery once again raises the question of its relationship with the first petition. With his terse profundity, Bengel notes: *Sanctificatio nominis divini ex Vetere Testamento quasi derivatur in Novum, continuanda et augenda apud nos: sed adventus regni Dei est Novi Testamenti quodammodo proprius* (*Gnomon*, on *Matt.* 6.10). If the eschatological coming of the kingdom of God is 'peculiar to the New Testament', this is no less true of the eschatological sanctification of God's name, though the idea is prepared for and expressed in the Old Testament in many ways. Numerous other attempts have been made to distinguish between the content of the two petitions, e.g.: the first describes the beginning of the divine work, 'in us', which means the observance of God's holiness, the second describes the means, and the third the end, the complete unity

of heaven and earth, of creator and creation; the ancient *Glossa ordinaria* refers the first to the *humilis adventus regni*, the second to the *adventus regni gloriae*, and the third to the *perfectio nostrae beatitudinis*. As all such distinctions relate more or less to 'us' men, whether dogmatically or psychologically, whereas the three petitions give no hint of such references, they can hardly be right.

If we pay strict attention to the wording, however, the difference in the petitions is not hard to recognize. The first begins with the hallowing of God's name which is the same today and tomorrow as it was yesterday, and which remains the same from age to age. The second speaks of the coming of the one age which is the 'age' of God; and if this coming at the end of time corresponds with God's creation at the beginning of time, the difference becomes still clearer: 'Holy is the Father' has resounded over all ages since before this world was created, and will continue to resound after it has been completed, in other words, even after the kingdom has come. In the creation, God's holiness broke into the realities of this world; with the coming of the kingdom, this world is so to speak restored to the holiness of God. The 'holy' of the first petition also implies the idea of one world, this second petition now speaks expressly of the 'coming' of this world and of this kingdom. The former names the innermost being of the Father with his supreme name, while the latter names the sphere and the order which belong to him, as a father's house belongs to the father and the place of consecration to the act of consecration. To put it in words used by the Greek Bible: the first petition prays to the one who is in the deepest and the holiest sense called God, the second to the one who is the Lord and in this role rules the world and orders the coming of his kingdom. In this duality, the two petitions at the same time fulfil a rule of prayer which is, of course, only expressed in later formulations: any benediction in which (God's) kingship is not mentioned is no benediction (*Berak.* 40b, in Billerbeck I, 419, where there are further instances).

Over and above this duality of the names 'God' and 'Lord', which are only hinted at, there is here the one name which *is* expressed: 'Father'. The elements of holiness and kingly rule are taken up into it. So once again the basic significance of the name emerges: the one name 'Father' so to speak includes the two others, 'God' and 'Lord', and the fatherly love which draws those who pray like children to their father is shown forth itself in holiness and glory, before which they bow the knee and worship.

V Thy Will be Done

1. A number of minor details of the text of the third petition, which has been transmitted only by Matthew, are not completely certain. Codex D and some Old Latin manuscripts omit the 'as': this simplifies the text and abruptly resolves a rather knotty problem. The Vulgate is therefore right in restoring a *sicut*. There is no agreement on whether there should be an article before both οὐρανῷ (heaven) and γῆς (earth): the reason for this is probably that an attempt has been made to approximate the formula to the language of the Old Testament, from which it derives.

The wording, too, calls for some brief remarks. Although the verb γίνεσθαι and even the aorist ἐγενόμην are quite frequent in the New Testament, the passive aorist ἐγενήθην is relatively rare in the Gospels. The first three have it in common only in the Septuagint quotation from *Ps.* 118.22: οὗτος ἐγενήθη εἰς κεφαλὴν γωνίας (*Matt.* 21.42 = *Mark* 12.10 = *Luke* 20.18); otherwise neither Mark nor Luke knows it. It does not occur in the Fourth Gospel, but does so seven times in Matthew, five of them in the imperative form γενηθήτω, so that it seems to be a Matthaean peculiarity, perhaps with a biblical foundation. There is, however, considerable interplay between the passive and middle aorist forms in the rest of the New Testament, as there is in the Septuagint and in Hellenistic papyri, just as later Greek language virtually prefers the passive forms in the deponents. The usage peculiar to Matthew occurs only in his special material; in every case the ἐγενήθησαν (11.23; 28.4) or the γενηθήτω (further 8.13; 9.29; 15.28; 26.42) stands by itself and supports the weight of the expression; the subject is either 'thy will' (as here and at 26.42) or a paraphrase: as you will, according to your faith, as you have believed (8.13; 9.29; 15.28). Thus all the passages reflect the active forms 'do the will of', etc. which are common in the Greek Old Testament.

The word 'will' seems to be so common and widespread an abstract that it might be expected everywhere in the Greek Bible as the designation of the divine will. But neither the New Testament nor the Greek Old Testament uses it particularly often. It occurs in relatively few places in the Septuagint (about twenty times), and in the Gospels only once each in Mark and Luke; it does, however, occur seven times in John and six in Matthew, and it is far more frequent in the rest of the New Testament. In accordance with its form the word does not so much describe the act of willing as the content of what is willed. The corresponding word in Hebrew, rāṣōn, often translated by the Septuagint, is more frequent; in Aramaic it is rē'ūtā; both characteristically express desire or longing and, indeed, joy and delight. So the word does not describe a decision made in rational thought, but the will that is born of physical desire. The extent to which this colouring is still perceptible in the New Testament and has been transferred to the will of God is, of course, questionable.

In rabbinic language the phrase, 'Do the will of the Father in heaven', etc., is a stereotyped formula (examples in TWNT III 54). It is therefore probable that 'Thy will be done' here is a passive and impersonal form of the active; in Aramaic it would be yit'abēd re'ūtāk (Dalman). Alongside it there is often the expression yᵉhī rāṣōn or yᵉhī rāṣōn lᵉpānekā, but here 'the will' is used adjectivally and is not therefore comparable with this petition. Lucan usage corresponds more with such a formula, which occurs in Luke 22.42 and Acts 21.41, 'The Lord's will be done' (γινέσθω).

For the first time, the brief petition is given an addition: 'in earth as it is in heaven'. The connection ὡς — καί need hardly be explained; it is usual in the *koine* as well as in the New Testament, and also in an abbreviated form, in which a οὕτως is easily supplied as a second member (cf. *Luke* 6.31D; *John* 20.21; Plut., *Mor.*, 460a, already Herod. vii 128; viii 64). The word καί, which stresses one of the two members, can come either in the first one or in the second, indeed sometimes in both; New Testament examples are: *Acts* 7.51; *II Cor.* 7.14; *Gal.* 1.9; 4.12; *Phil.* 1.20; *I John* 2.27, further *Matt.* 18.33; 20.14 (cf. Blass-Debrunner, *Grammatik des neutestamentlichen Griechisch*[10] §453,1). The function of this connection is not only to compare two entities, but to refer them generally to one another or even to substantiate one through the other or, for that matter, simply to put them in series one after the other, as with the Latin *tam . . . quam*. The καί is an impossible addition in Aramaic; it is purely Greek. More important, however, are the two things which are associated through this copula.

'Heaven and earth' is a common expression throughout the Ancient East and in the Old Testament, and is used to paraphrase the spatial concept 'world', which, as is well known, does not occur in the Bible and is partly replaced by the temporal concept 'ōlām. The twofold division, which matches the immediate viewpoint of the landsman, is supplemented by a threefold division into heaven, earth and sea or even heaven, earth and underworld. Both heaven and earth are the creation of God, and he is therefore called 'Lord of heaven and earth' (*Matt.* 11.25). But in comparison with earth, heaven is nearer to the Creator; as the Sermon on the Mount has it in the well-known words of a psalm, heaven is God's throne (*Matt.* 5.34f.) and the earth is his footstool. So the earth is subordinate to heaven. But this relationship can become one of complete equality or complete contrast. Both are equally parts of the world, because both have been created by the one God and are therefore subject to him, but also because both are transitory; for 'heaven and earth will pass away' (*Matt.* 5.18; 24.35). Again, they are contrasted, because everything on earth will be devoured by moth and rust, whereas in heaven all is incorruptible. Between these two extremes there is a wide range of connections by which heaven and earth are related: what is on earth has powers and rights in heaven, like 'binding and loosing' (*Matt.* 16.19; 18.18), or prayer; what happens in heaven guides and determines what happens on earth (*Heb.* 8.1,4f.). The kind of relationship which is intended on any one occasion is thus indicated by the sense of the expression in question and is not simply determined by the word-association.

Heaven and earth are only the twofold, yet complementary, realms in which 'thy will is to be done'. Only in the first member is the reference ambivalent: earth is imagined as a plane 'on which' all life, action and will takes place; heaven as an enclosed realm, the interior of which is inaccessible to man, so that he can see it only from outside. The preposition $\dot{\epsilon}\nu$ can therefore mean 'on the heavens' (seen from outside), as at *Rev.* 12.1, 'And a great portent appeared on the heavens' ($\dot{\epsilon}\nu$ $\tau\tilde{\omega}$ $o\dot{\upsilon}\rho\alpha\nu\tilde{\omega}$) or 'in heaven' (happening unseen within), as *Matt.* 18.18; 19.21; 28.18; 'All authority in heaven and on earth has been given to me.' Whichever possibility is chosen depends on the sense of the sentence as a whole. The lack of an article is hardly significant; in the Septuagint, too, the article is sometimes present (e.g. *Gen.* 1.21; 2.1), sometimes omitted (e.g. *Gen.* 2.4; *Ps.* 148.13). It is rather more striking that 'heaven' here is put in the singular, whereas in the address of the prayer the Semitic plural is used. But again, it is the almost invariable Septuagint usage, which is followed by the New Testament, that the word 'heaven' is always put in the singular where it is associated expressly, or by implication, with 'the earth'. The reason may be one of form, so that the two entities which together make up the one concept 'world' are made parallel and connected even in number. But perhaps we may also infer an objective reason, namely that the plural is always put where heaven is spoken of in its separation from all earthly things and in its relationship with and validity for God, as, say, in the expression, 'Our Father who art in heaven'. In short, the singular is used wherever heaven and earth are combined in the unity of creation, the plural where 'heaven' means God's world away from all the bustle and distraction of earth.

2. Although the third petition has been handed down to us by Matthew alone, its content is nevertheless expressed in some other passages of the New Testament. We need only recall Jesus' prayer in Gethsemane; in Matthew even the wording corresponds with this petition (26.42). Luke deviates only slightly, Mark varies rather more. A second instance, Paul's farewell in Ephesus, ends with the words, 'The Lord's will be done' (*Acts* 21.14), and Polycarp, prepared for his martyrdom, prays and exhorts in almost the same words (*Mart. Pol.* 7.1). So the third petition belongs among the few whose words and content are also attested outside the Lord's Prayer.

Of course, this evidence does not seem to say a great deal: for if religion is reverence and submission to the will of God or the gods, should it not be possible to find similar echoes in all religions? There is, for example, in Greek and Roman religion the kindred formula 'If God wills', or 'According to the will of the gods'; it puts all human action and will under the one will of God which alone should be effective both in the life of the individual and in that of the nations. Nor is it rare in the New Testament (*I Cor.* 4.19; 16.7,12; *Heb.* 3.6; *Acts* 18.21; *James* 4.15; cf. also Ign., *Ad Eph.* 20.1), but there is hardly any evidence of it in the Old Testament. Its ancient significance is described in the anecdote which is told of the Pythagorean Thymaridas: when he was parting from friends to go on a sea journey, one of them called to him, 'May the gods grant you what you will.' He retorted, 'God forbid, I would wish to be granted what the gods will.' So the formula asks not only that the gods should make man's own will their own, but also that the will of the gods should be that of men.

This connection is perhaps still more clearly recognizable in the kindred formula, 'with God', for which parallels are equally vainly sought in Judaism. It already begins in Homer and goes through almost the whole of the Greek and the Roman world until it reaches Christianity. From the context which the formula suggests, there emerge in the first century A.D. the well-known ideas with which the culture of the Graeco-Roman world is filled; Epictetus teaches, 'I account God's will better than my own,' or Seneca says, '*placeat homini quicquid Deo placuit*' (Epict., iv 7,20; Sen., *Ep.* 74,20). The content of this will of God, which the individual must resolve to follow, can be put in a few words: 'Do not seek to have everything that happens happen as you wish, but wish for everything to happen as it actually does happen, and your life will be serene' (Epict., *Enchir.* 8, cf. *Diss.* ii 14.7, also i 12,15). This Stoic wisdom is simply expanded to a general rule which Socrates acknowledges to Crito in prison, 'Well, if so it is pleasing to the gods, so let it be' (Plato, *Crito* 43D). Here is the idea of the harmony of the divine and the human will which has man finding the adventure of his life in the obscure realms of history.

We can understand why this religious idea, obvious though it seems, has not struck deeper roots either in Judaism or in the New Testament. For there the will of God is not to be discerned gradually in the events of human life; it is revealed in the Law as the norm of all life and conduct; it is therefore not so much a matter of *willing* what God wills, but of *doing* what God wills and man should will. The goal set for man is not harmony, but obedience. Consequently the will of God is not to be recognized in the pattern of events; there it is obscured, to be manifested in the words of his revelation. History, whether of men or of nations, can indeed be the scene on which the will of God is worked out, but above it, like the heavens, is spread the holy and moral will of God, which never enters wholly into history, although it is partially recognizable there. We may add a second point: in Judaism, too, it is recognized that God guides the life of the people and of mankind; 'Whatever the Lord pleases he does, in heaven and on earth, in the seas and all deeps' (*Ps.* 135.6). It does not, however, follow from that that whatever happens is his will, but in the dark complexities of life the revealed will of God guides the individual on a sure and certain path. So it does not really matter whether what happens is man's will; the only important thing is that he does what he ought.

Nothing shows this more clearly than the late rabbinic rule which bids the priest pray for himself at the close of the blessing: 'Lord of the Universe, we have done what thou hast decreed upon us; fulfil with us what thou hast promised us' (*Sotah* 39a). That does not mean that the pious Jew could not also pray to God for help in danger and necessity. We have a prayer of Rabbi Eliezer (about 90 A.D.) in mortal danger: 'Do thy will in heaven above and give quietness of spirit to them that fear thee in the earth, and do that which is good in thine eyes' (*Tract. Berak.* 3.7). But such a prayer also gives way to the firm assurance that looks beyond life and death: 'But as his will in heaven may be, so he will do,' says Judas Maccabaeus before the battle (*I Macc.* 3.60) and in so doing only repeats Samuel's prayer, 'Let the Lord do what seems good to him' (*I Sam.* 3.18=*I Chron.* 19.13). But such confidence rests on the foundation that as the Lord who has chosen his people for himself, God can order and dispose what he wills, and that his people, as his servant, is obliged to obey in will and in conduct; both the life of the individual and the history of the people have their significance in this covenant. Hence a rabbinic saying runs, 'Make God's will as thy will that he may make thy will as his will; Efface thy will before his will that he may efface the wills of others before thy will' (*Pirke Aboth* 2.4).

In this context we can understand why we find the formula 'if God wills' in the New Testament and classical antiquity but not in the Old Testament and in Jewish writings. We can also appreciate the distance separating the Greek idea of the will of the gods from the Israelite idea of the one revealed will of God. Instead, another formula seems to appear. Prayers often begin with the phrase 'May it please thee', 'May it be thy will'. Thus, for example, R. Johanan ben Zakkai prayed on his sick bed for his pupils, 'May it be (God's) will that the fear of heaven shall be upon you like the fear of flesh and blood' (*Berak.* 28b).

But this formula does not conceal its origin from the court language of the Near East; it is the expression of reverence with which a servant puts his request to his king and lord, to all intents and purposes an 'I beseech you'.

So the third petition seems to be strangely isolated and yet at the same time to have some strange affinities. It shares with Old Testament ideas the Psalmist's assurance, 'Whatever the Lord pleases, he does,' but why then the petition, 'Thy will be done'? It shares with Greek thought the attitude, 'Not my will but thine be done', but why then the addition, 'In earth as it is in heaven'? We must enquire more closely into what is meant by the will of God.

3. Following the example of the Old Testament, the New Testament speaks of the will of God in a number of ways; sometimes, of course, there is no mention of what was earlier considered important, and at others mere hints are now clearly brought out. The Old Testament has many ways of describing the manifestation of the divine will, which created heaven and earth. We might expect the same also to be true for the New Testament, but there creation is only once associated with the concept of the will of God, in the Revelation of St. John, whose theme leads from the creation to the consummation (4.11):

> For thou didst create all things,
> and by thy will they existed
> and were created.

Instead, however, the will and the work of God can be seen all the more often in the things of daily life and the phenomena of nature. 'Look at the birds of the air', 'Consider the lilies of the field' (*Matt.* 6. 26ff.), 'But even the hairs of your head are all numbered' (*Matt.* 10.30). So there is nothing that is not done by the will of God; whatever is real proclaims this will, whatever happens happens as a result of this will. But in such a context the phrase or the idea of 'the will of God' hardly ever appears.

THE WILL OF GOD

Nor do we often find that the history of people or even of nations is the setting in which God's will is worked out, leaving a pattern and a model for others to consider. The events of the past are more a dark confusion of human errors and sins than the clear mirror of the divine will. History is the time of 'God's forbearance' (*Rom.* 3.25); its course is pointed here and there by the proclaimers of his will, but they themselves reveal that this course runs through darkness and sin. They are the prophets and patriarchs of the Old Testament; his will is only expressed where they speak by their words and acts, and their message is not so much an interpretation of past and future events as an indication of present action. God's will is the holy moral commandment and the aim of human life and action.

The New Testament often speaks of the will of God from this point of view, particularly in the phrase which already occurs in the Old Testament and is often attested later in rabbinic writings, 'to do the will of God'. The disciples of Jesus are, like any pious Jew, obliged to do this will; only the one who does it, and not the one who says, 'Lord, Lord', will enter into the kingdom of heaven (*Matt.* 7.21); only he 'is my brother and sister and mother' (12.50). What this will involves is simple and evident: there are the admonitions of the Sermon on the Mount, in which law and prophets are fulfilled, there is the double commandment of love which even for Paul is 'the fulfilling of the law'; the will of God is the way indicated in the words of the Law and the prophets and in the words of the Master, which leads to eternal life.

In this phrase we must also remember that the Greek language uses more abstract and colourless expressions for what would sound colourful and concrete in Aramaic. For 'to do the will of God' means literally 'to do what is well pleasing to God', or even, 'to do his pleasure'. Here the old idea is preserved that what is involved is not the fulfilling of a particular commandment which can be reckoned up afterwards, but a relationship between God the Father and his child and servant in all moral actions; his work is merely the reflection of the will and thought of his

119

lord and master. For the action of men who fulfil God's will is
in truth an action of God in and to men. Paul's saying, 'God is
at work in you, both to will and to work for his good pleasure'
(*Phil.* 2.12) applies generally; it can also be heard in the prayer
of the Psalmist (90.17), 'Establish thou the work of our hands
upon us' (cf. also *Psalm Sol.* 16.9), and is further echoed in the
words of the Epistle to the Hebrews (13.21), 'God equip you
with everything good that you may do his will, working in you
that which is pleasing in his sight, through Jesus Christ.' Here
a new and yet ancient significance is attached to the concept
of the will of God: it is signified not only in the words of Holy
Scripture, by which men are to act, but also in the work through
which men fulfil his words; God not only commands what he
wills, but he also does what he commands. To put it in the
well-known words of Augustine: he not only says *fac quod
jubeo*, but also *do quod jubeo*. And this twofold activity, however
much it may already be anticipated in the Old Testament, is
now also rooted in the situation which already bears signs of the
end and of the consummation.

Here the concept of the will of God takes on a new definition;
it is not only an eschatological word but also an eschatological
work; not only a holy, moral norm but also an eschatological
event: 'So it is not the will of your Father who is in heaven that
one of these little ones should perish.' The same thing is said
in a common Jewish phrase which recurs in Jesus' thanksgiving:
'I thank thee, Father, Lord of heaven and earth, that thou hast
hidden these things from the wise and understanding and revealed
them to babes; yea, Father, for such was thy gracious will'
(*Matt.* 11.25). In the Fourth Gospel, the will of God is simply the
work of eschatological consummation (14.31) and the aim of this
will is 'that I should lose nothing of all that he has given me'
(6.39), or that 'all that the Father gives me will come to me; and
him who comes to me I will not cast out' (6.37). If these words
already sound like the Matthaean saying about the 'little ones',
the other element associated with the concept of God's will that
is attested in Matthew is also present: 'I seek not my own will

but the will of him who sent me' (5.30). The prayer in Geth-semane has a connection with this, and not only in language. Similarly, the Acts of the Apostles speaks of the divine will when Paul there describes his conversion (22.14): 'The God of our fathers appointed you to know his will, to see the Just One . . . for you will be a witness for him to all men.' Ephesians 1.9 says the same thing in grander and fuller language:

> For he has made known to us in all wisdom and insight
> the mystery of his will,
> according to his purpose which he set forth in Christ
> as a plan for the fullness of time,
> to unite all things in him,
> things in heaven and things on earth.

Hebrews 10.1-9 puts it in Old Testament words, 'Lo, I have come to do thy will' (=*Ps.* 40, 8*f.*), and this will runs, 'By that will we have been sanctified.' In all these expressions the concept of this will is directed to the idea of an eschatological community in which the work of eschatological consummation is being completed.

From this standpoint we can understand the numerous remarks, particularly in St. Paul's letters, which refer to the divine will and use it to vindicate external earthly matters. For even outward things like journeys and visits which Paul or his fellow workers plan or undertake serve the primitive Christian mission, serve the primitive Christian community, and so further the work of eschatological consummation. So attention is turned as in a new light to the days which are still passing, for their course leads to a day of consummation; they are themselves merely the transition from this age to the age to come. So these remarks have an apparent affinity with Greek and Roman ideas, even down to the formulas, 'As God wills', or, 'Not as I will, but as the gods will'. For in the events of the last days on earth the apostles, like the disciples of Jesus, find traces and actions of the eschato-logical will of God everywhere; they see from their eschato-logical standpoints what was visible to the Greeks from looking at human life and natural events, the hidden will of God, which guides the destinies of this world and of mankind to their eschatological conclusion by the way that has been revealed. Therefore Paul has become an apostle of Jesus Christ 'by the will of God' (*I Cor.* 1.1; *II Cor.* 1.1; *Col.* 1.1; *II Tim.* 1.1), the communities have given 'themselves to the Lord and to us by the will of God' (*II Cor.* 8.5), and the goal set for each community for whom the Apostle and his helpers pray is 'that you may stand mature and fully assured in all the will of God' (*Col.* 4.12). In this passage the concept of the will of God combines the traditional moral—so to speak Old Testament—motive with the newly-made eschatological—so to speak New Testament—motive; the former furthers the performance of the eschatological will, the latter makes possible and achieves the doing of the holy, moral will. Matthew has already given a profound and exact description of the mutual involvement of these two sides in always saying only 'the will of your Father in heaven' even where, say, Mark uses the expression 'the will of God' (*Mark* 3.35= *Matt.* 12.50).

Now if the concept of the divine will draws attention to happenings in the present, in which, seen only by faith but also unmistakable to it, there are traces of his eschatological power, then we can understand why the old maxim 'Regard God's will as better than your own' and the primitive Christian prayer, 'Not my will but thine be done' should be so similar outwardly and yet so different inwardly. Both times the history of the life of the individual or even of the universe is the field in which God manifests his will; in the one case, however, the outward event and the divine will are an inseparable and indissoluble unity, whereas in the other, history is something transitory and passing away, which is nevertheless shaped by abiding indications of God's eschatological will. In the one case the will of God is like the course of events; in the other it runs against this course, but is at the same time the eternal goal of all things, which is also its end. In the one case, the maxim is based on the correlation between the divine will and natural events, in the other, the petition is based on the discrepancy which marks the suffering and corruption of this world and at the same time the miracle of eschatological consummation.

4. The third petition has continually been interpreted as though it were recommending and praising the renunciation of all personal human will and the acceptance of God's will in all things.[10] As a result, it goes together with Socrates' vow, 'If so it is pleasing to the gods, so let it be.' And is this sense not confirmed by Jesus' prayer in Gethsemane? Did not Paul go into prison and Polycarp to martyrdom with the words of this petition on their lips, and was not Tertullian correct in his terse remark; *in hoc dicto ad sufferentiam nos admonemus?*

Impressive though such an explanation may be, it does not, however, fit the sense of this petition, nor does it correspond to the prayer of Jesus in Gethsemane. For too little notice is taken of the fact that the words, 'Not what I will, but what thou wilt' (*Mark* 14.36), occur only in this one place in the Bible, that they are spoken at a time and in a situation in which not only Jesus' own personal fate is at stake but also the eschatological event between heaven and earth in which God is now beginning to achieve his eschatological will. So the speaker there is not a trembling man, extended to the limits of his being, but the Son of Man who knows the magnitude of his work and his task; his prayer is a conversation between the Father and the Son before his work begins, while there still seem to be two choices open, that 'this cup should pass' or that it should be drunk. And when it becomes clear in this conversation that the Father has decided that the Son is to be 'betrayed into the hands of sinners', his attitude is not one of quietness and patience, as the words of the prayer suggest, but a clear decision, 'Arise, let us be going.' Nor does the decision mean surrender, but the beginning of the eschatological work in the way which God has fore-ordained; it leads, not to the capture of Jesus, but to the self-surrender of the Son of Man. And even if a suggestion of surrender could be detected in the words of his prayer, it should be remembered that neither the Old Testament nor the New knows any thought of an opposition of the human and the divine wills.

Man can have his own will and persist in it, in which case he is godless and hostile to God, or he can trust in God's will and obey him, in which case his existence in faith is a constant renunciation of his own will and a constantly renewed surrender to that of God. At all events, the question of a man's outward fate, of life and death, becomes meaningless and insignificant: 'Whom have I in heaven but thee? And there is nothing upon earth that I desire besides thee' (Ps. 73.25). All comfort and all hope that God guides the suppliant even in all difficulties lies rather in the fact that God 'is the strength of my heart and my portion for ever' (Ps. 73.26). So this petition, too, does not speak of surrender and does not even counsel patience—for in that case what would the words 'in earth as it is in heaven' mean? Such an interpretation derives from ancient religious ideas, just as 'surrender' too is virtually a pre-Christian term. We have to begin with an explanation of the New Testament concept of the will of God.

As this concept extends on two sides, towards the idea of the holy, moral norm and that of the eschatological consummation, as it—to use the traditional dogmatic terms—develops both as *voluntas praecipiens* and as *voluntas decernens*, two explanations are possible and both have frequently been put forward. If the holy, moral will of God is meant, the petition asks that God should prepare men to live for all time in word and deed according to his holy will, as happens eternally in heaven. We can also see how such a meaning fits in well with the content of the second petition; for if that spoke of the eschatological event of this kingdom, the third petition speaks of the significance of this event for the heart and will of each individual; it therefore asks that this kingdom shall be embedded in the heart and soul of the person who prays and that from such a seed, the fruit of a life according to God's holy will should grow and ripen. This interpretation was advocated particularly by the Fathers of the Latin Church, Tertullian and Augustine. But the explanation is not without suspicious features, because here it introduces man in a way which has not happened before. It speaks of man, and not of God, and a paraphrase of its prayer would run, 'Let me do thy will with heart and hand!' And in this version, would it not be a paraphrase of what the second petition had said and meant for the individual? Now if repetition is *a priori* doubtful in these brief clauses, this repetition is particularly so, for it speaks not of the heart of the individual, but of what surpasses all human things in heaven and on earth.

In the light of this we can understand the attempt to translate the phrase ἐν οὐρανῷ as '(written) on the heavens' and to interpret it of the firmament and the course of the stars, so that there would be here almost a prefigurement of the two Kantian sources of all worship: the starry heaven above me and the moral law within me. Now it is not at all strange even for the Old Testament to point to heaven as the place where 'the morning stars sang together, and all the sons of God shouted for joy' (*Job* 38.7). It can also speak of the immutability of the ordinances under the stars (*Jer.* 31.35*ff.*) and it has even seen in them the mirror of the infinite wisdom of God. But it has not found there this expression of a holy, moral will:

> *How then can man be righteous before God?*
> *How can he who is born of woman be clean?*
> *Behold, even the moon is not bright*
> *and the stars are not clean in his sight* (*Job* 25.4f.)

So the addition to the third petition points away from an ethical interpretation to an eschatological one. For 'heaven and earth' are God's creation; so fixed is this expression after the first words of the Bible that we hardly ever have 'Lord or Creator of angels and men', or, like rabbinic usage, 'Lord of the world', but 'Lord of heaven and earth' (*Matt.* 11.25 etc.); for heaven and earth are greater than the beings who live in them. But if the work of creation is visible 'in heaven and earth', so too will be the work of consummation. At the end of St. Matthew's Gospel we have just the same thought, 'All authority in heaven and on earth has been given to me' (28.18); on the last day everything in heaven and on earth will be made one in Christ (*Eph.* 1.10, similarly *Col.* 1.16-20), every knee in heaven and on earth and under the earth will bow, and every tongue confess that Jesus Christ is Lord, to the glory of God the Father (*Phil.* 2.10*f.*). And when the Lamb of the Revelation has taken the book with the seven seals which contains the final destinies, the four 'creatures' and the four and twenty elders sing a new song in which the angels join, and 'every creature in heaven and on earth and under the earth and in the sea and all therein' (*Rev.* 5.13). The idea of the unity of everything in the final age is well established in the New Testament, and is occasionally also attested in Judaism, though at a late date: 'May it be thy will, O Lord our God, to establish peace among the celestial family, and among the earthly family, and among the disciples who occupy themselves with thy Torah' (*Berak.* 16b-17a). Whatever the verdict on the details of this evidence, all of it shows that the phrase 'in earth as it is in heaven' has a constant reference to the two *data* of creation and consummation. In the light of such an understanding of the eschatological will of God we can also see how we are to understand the ambiguous sentence.

The petition presupposes that heaven and earth are still separate, or at least different, whatever the basis of this difference, whether it is divine counsel, human failure or deliberate rebellion against God—and so it asks for this difference to be abolished at the end of time. It asks for a single will to be made powerful and effective against all divergent ones so that the world's original destiny may be fulfilled in one event. Then this world becomes God's world 'in earth as it is in heaven', a world which has its sole reality in the will of God, who permeates it without difference and without opposition, and is its life and its light. Not only the creative will of God is expressed in this petition, but also that governing will which commands the coming of his kingdom; the two can no longer be distinguished, as the kingdom is also the perfected world and its lord and king is also its creator and perfecter. So the earth is almost raised to heaven, or heaven descends to earth; both are now the one place where God's will is done.

One can understand here how for the earliest commentator, Clement of Alexandria, the third petition has become a petition for the Church; he explains: 'The Church guided by the Logos is a city on earth which cannot be plundered and cannot be ruled by a tyrant, the divine will on earth as it is in heaven' (*Strom.* iv 172.2, cf. also 66.1), and this interpretation is followed not only by Tertullian, who therefore boldly puts the third petition before the second, but also by Augustine, who asserts that the petition for the *regnum gratiae* follows that for the *regnum gloriae*. All these interpretations can refer to the original idea of the New Testament, in which the consummation of the world and of the kingdom is the consummation of the eschatological community, and the consummation of the community is the founding of the Church. But in view of these later interpretations it is significant that the third petition speaks neither of the way in which nor of the end to which 'God's will is to be done' 'on earth as it is in heaven'; indeed one might find its eschatological character expressed precisely in the fact that it is silent and must be silent about historical agencies of any kind; for the idea of either a way or an end would differentiate between willing and happening, between the thought of God and the reality of God. The special character of the petition seems to be that it should no longer be possible for such a distinction to exist, that in the almost external spheres of heaven and earth God's deepest will should be done— and done without any agency, even that of the Word—that in such a sense of eschatological miracle, which would be analogous to the miracle of the hallowing of his name and the coming of his kingdom, 'Thy will be done'.

In view of this apparent indeterminacy it is no wonder that attempts have been made to give the petition some definite content. This is the context of the old dispute whether there is a real comparison between heaven and earth or merely an emphatic co-ordination; in the first instance we would have to interpret it as follows: May God's will be done on earth as it is in heaven—

the person who prays sees a picture of that heavenly kingdom in which the angels are his holy servants and always 'do his will' (cf. *Ps.* 103.21, *Heb.* 1.14) and on earth a picture of another kingdom, the Church, which leads its life according to the heavenly pattern. So in a remarkable mixture of Stoic and Primitive Christian elements, Chrysostom has paraphrased the petition in this way: 'He bade us indeed long for the heavenly city, but meanwhile we are to pray not to do God's will by halves, but to perform all things as he wills.' In Primitive Christian terms this heavenly city is none other than the heavenly city, the new Jerusalem, into which the believers will enter, and which will itself descend at the end of the work of consummation so that the old promise will be realized: God in heaven, with his own on earth!

In addition, there is another possible explanation: if God's will is to be done on earth as it is in heaven, then the reality of the divine will must first of all be established in heaven. For what else is the meaning of sentences like, 'All authority in heaven and on earth has been given to me', 'that every knee should bow, in heaven and on earth and under the earth'? What is the significance of the many descriptions of the Risen One being enthroned in the heavenly council as though unknown (*Rev.* 5, I *Tim.* 3.16, etc.)? They simply say that God's will is now being done and his eschatological kingdom is being established. Of course these ideas are bound up with definite Christological ideas, and in that case the content to be given to the will of God would be, 'May the Son of Man be Lord on earth as he is in heaven!' In view of such possibilities the terseness of the petition is again significant; God's will does not refer to the Son of Man or to the community, nor to the Lord and his Church, but to the whole of heaven and earth and to every individual in them; it refers both to the 'event' which lies over men, between heaven and earth, and to that which lies in men. In this respect it is as near to all eschatological consummation as it is to all historical and human incompleteness; it can embrace the nearest thing upon earth as well as the farthest in heaven. But there is no mention even of this, but only of the will of God and the realm which he has created, in which it is to be done. This realm is the new element in comparison with the previous petitions: the world, which God has made and has not yet completed, rises on high from the timelessness and spacelessness in which his name is to be hallowed and his kingdom is to come.

There is still one final point to consider: if the third petition refers to God's will to achieve the work of eschatological consummation and prays for it to be realized, this seems to imply that this will has not hitherto been perceptible and effective in the history of the world or even in the history of one particular people. But is not this will in fact always done, is it not done every morning, when he makes the sun rise again, and will it not be done as long as the earth endures and the heaven is spread out over it? What is the relationship between this petition for the 'particular' eschatological event and the general fact that nothing exists and is done without the will of God? The question here is the same as that in the first and second petitions, and the answer runs on the same lines. For God's kingdom and rule were also everlasting, and they have 'come upon you' precisely in the presence of the Master. Yet the Lord's Prayer still asks 'Thy kingdom come'. For before the eschatological character and power of this coming whatever can already be seen and heard of God's kingdom in this world pales to nothing. So, too, God's will has always been done hitherto, because there is no reality which his will does not create and sustain, and the Johannine saying, 'For I have come down from heaven, not to do my own will, but the will of him who sent me' (6.38), applies in this very present. The will of God in both past and present goes almost in secrecy through the world; it can be traced in any and every thing, and yet it is full of obscurity; 'Silently goes God's will over the earthly struggle' (W. Raabe).

But this petition is concerned that it should be done in all its eschatological fullness 'in earth as it is in heaven'. Indeed one might almost say that the petition could not ask for such a happening in heaven and on earth if it did not know and see that the will of God had always been done in the past, and again, that it would not see this will effective there if it did not now pray, 'Thy will be done'. For this will is that by which the world was made 'in the beginning', and as an eschatological will it is also the completely different new will which 'at the end' will complete the world that has been begun. So, too, those who pray this petition occupy a twofold position. They pray 'only' for the eschatological will of God to be done as though they were familiar with it, for they stand under the sign of the imminent end which has been revealed to them as to babes. They therefore ask as though heaven and earth are for them only the scene of an event, whereas they already belong to the eschatologically fulfilled community. And yet at the same time they pray as those who are under the heavens and rooted to this earth, who long finally and once for all to see the will of God done in a world which hitherto has only followed the deviations of its own disrupted will.

Each of these aspects supports and strengthens the other. The anxious longing yearns for an imminent eschatological event, and the knowledge of the will that is so soon to be done is comforted by the signs which already proclaim it and still the former longing. And in this duality, born of revelation and longing, of strength and weakness, the petition gently slips from the Old Testament ground on which it has grown up; for what matters now is no longer the firm, earthbound security which their own elect history and their own elect people hitherto gave the faithful in addition to the work of consummation; all is surrendered without remainder to the unknown eschatological will of God, not in land and in people, but in heaven and on earth. And at this point it returns from afar with a new significance to the ancient 'pagan' piety, for just as the latter seeks and finds the pattern of a heavenly will in the fabric of earthly events, so now this knowledge of the revealed eschatological will gives those who pray the obligation and right of discovering its unmistakable sign in their own present and directing their will and their longing in accordance with it. So here we find traces of that particular Primitive Christian attitude and that particular Primitive Christian message which seems so near to and yet so far from antiquity and Judaism, and represents something unmistakably new which is nevertheless grounded in them.

5. After the first two petitions, the third seems to have a double function. First, it continues the pattern of ideas which has been followed so far; for the first petition begins with God's innermost being, the second moves on to the external kingdom or action of God, and the third ends with the existing world, heaven and earth. As a result, these petitions lie almost like concentric circles round the one point, the address, 'Our Father who art in heaven'. The event of eschatological consummation for which all petitions pray shines out over increasingly extensive areas and with ever-increasing strength; the third petition gives the final and extreme boundary. But precisely here it gives a clear summary of what has been asked for hitherto. Just as God's kingdom and God's name are in the last resort matters of his will, so too the content of the two previous petitions is included in this 'Thy will be done'. The third petition relates God's deepest nature and the thoughts of his innermost heart to what is farthest removed from him, the earth; in this way it asks that God's name may be hallowed on earth as it is in heaven, that God's kingdom may come from heaven to earth, and that if this is achieved, then God's will may be done in earth as it is in heaven. The summarizing function of the petition may be expressly underlined by the two-membered form of the sentence.

We can now discuss whether this petition originally belonged to the Lord's Prayer, as it is missing in the Lucan version, although Luke knows both its words and its content as a petition of Jesus (*Luke* 22.42, cf. also *Acts* 21.14). If this petition so to speak repeats what the first two say, ought we not to conclude that it was only inserted by the community into an originally shorter Lord's Prayer? Since the beginning of New Testament criticism, the Matthaean petition has frequently been judged to

131

be a community formation or a saying of the Lord transferred from the Gethsemane narrative, and the Lucan form has been taken to be 'original'. But the reasons advanced for this view are hardly satisfactory; for if the petition is superfluous because of its content—leaving aside the difficulty of making a ruling about what is superfluous and what is not—then it is as probable (or even improbable) that this superfluous element has been inserted into the context as that it has been deleted from it. Indeed, in Matthew's case one might think that in view of the rule (only handed down to us by him) which precedes the Lord's Prayer, not to use vain repetitions in prayers like the Gentiles, the insertion of something superfluous in a prayer which is meant to be a pattern of 'non-repetition' is almost inconceivable. But what is 'superfluous' here? The third petition does not repeat what has already been said, but sums it up, and it does not only sum it up but at the same time develops it and paves the way for the following petition, leading from the prayer for the coming of the kingdom to the prayer for daily bread; it has, as we have shown, elements of its own which are not at all clearly expressed, so that they reveal all the internal characteristics of authenticity.

With all the reasons which are advanced against the authenticity of the third petition, must we not also ask whether the same reasons which caused the community to insert the sentence might not also have influenced Jesus? Why should it not have been possible for the prayer for the eschatological consummation, the sole concern of the first petition, the sole concern too of the message of Jesus and of the whole New Testament—to have been expressed a third time, once it had been expressed twice? The threefold emphasis simply expresses still more strongly than a twofold emphasis the intensity of eschatological expectation which is purely concerned with God's cause, removed from all human points of reference, for which this cause is so infinitely great that heaven and earth alone can be the stage on which it is enacted. But the fact that for the third time something new is spoken of here is betrayed by external characteristics: while the petition is indeed related to Jewish ideas, they are by no means commonplace in Judaism; and it bears so unmistakably an eschatological stamp, both in the Lord's Prayer and in the Gethsemane narrative, that it is clearly distinct from Jewish or Hellenistic commonplaces. So it need only be a 'community formation' in the sense that the rest of the tradition of the story of Jesus is 'community formation'.

There remains only the question why the third petition does not appear in the Lucan version of the Lord's Prayer; the answer will be found when we investigate the numerous peculiarities of this Lucan version. But one thing is already plain: to conclude that anything in Matthew which does not appear in the Lucan Lord's Prayer must have been inserted later by Matthew is a dubious procedure; the primitive community clearly used different forms of the Lord's Prayer, and perhaps the first disciples of Jesus already prayed their Master's prayer in different forms. For such developments as have taken place in the Lord's Prayer have a complex beginning as often as a simple one; in fact it is more likely to be complex. For we now possess only a varied echo, while the one voice which rang out has been stilled.

VI Our Daily Bread

1. The tradition of the text of the fourth petition in Matthew is secure and there are no variants. The fact that the Curetonian alone among the Syriac versions writes, 'And give us . . .'—introducing the conjunction 'and' and putting the imperative in first place—is hardly to be regarded as a variant, but simply as an attempt at interpretation. The divergence between the Matthaean and Lucan forms therefore emerges all the more clearly. True, Luke has almost the same words and the same word-order, but instead of δός he puts the present imperative δίδου and instead of σήμερον he has τὸ καθ' ἡμέραν. There seems to be an inner connection between the two deviations; the Aramaic form *hab* which presumably underlies the Greek, has no mark of tense. The difference in the verbs is therefore simply a matter of Greek translation. As the other difference, between 'this day' and 'each day', is connected with this difference of tense, it is probable that one is not a correction of the other, but that both reproduce independent versions, each the tradition of his own community. Matthew's aorist is confirmed by the fact that all his other petitions have the verb in the aorist; Luke has made free with this rule in other places as well as in the fourth petition.

The form of the petition differs characteristically from those which precede it and follow it. Here alone the verb is not put first, but is preceded by an object in the accusative, which is clearly emphasized. This object is further defined by an attributive adjective, the only one in the whole prayer. It differs from the previous clauses in the absence of the passive predicate and the disappearance of the word 'thine'; it is connected with those that follow by the appearance of the predicate in the active and the presence of the word 'us' or 'ours'. This is probably also the reason why the petition stands in asyndeton alongside the first three, whereas it is connected with the last three by the 'and' of the next petition. So this petition remains in isolation and yet is connected with the later ones.

The petition itself seems to be clear and comprehensible— leaving aside the riddle of the word ἐπιούσιος—but in spite of (or even because of) this clarity it is not unimportant to make clear the exact meaning of the individual words and phrases. First we have the phrase 'give bread'. It is strange that it occurs only in the Gospels; wherever it is said later that bread is distributed to the hungry or that the Lord's Supper is held in the community, this particular expression from the Gospels is no longer used. The apostles 'serve tables' in the primitive community when they give food to the poor and the widows (*Acts* 6.2), and the celebration of the Lord's Supper is called 'the breaking of the bread' (e.g. *Acts* 2.42). The phrase 'give bread to someone' does not occur anywhere at all in the Apostolic Fathers and in the Apologists. Its use is even rarer in the Gospels. The prayer 'Give us our bread' is made to God only here; otherwise it is said three times of Jesus that 'he took bread, gave thanks, broke it and gave it to them' (*Matt.* 14.19; 15.36; 26.26). It happens in the unforgettable and yet familiar gesture which accompanies the miraculous meal by the sea of Gennesaret, as it does in the last meal in Jerusalem. But outside this narrow and holy circle the phrase occurs nowhere else in the first three Gospels, so that it seems to have been usual only in religious language. Perhaps a clear sign of this is the fact that it is not the simple verb διδόναι but the compound ἐπιδιδόναι (*Matt.* 7.9) which is used in a parable-saying of Jesus, 'Or what man of you, if his son asks him for a loaf, will give him a stone?' Finally, in the Fourth Gospel, 'give bread' has become a purely religious phrase; even Jesus' distribution of bread and fish is sometimes called διαδιδόναι here (6.11; 21.13 differs). But God 'gives bread' from heaven and Jesus himself gives 'the bread of life' (6.31*ff.*); in this context we also have the only passage in the New Testament which corresponds to this petition in more than a formal way, for the Jews ask Jesus, 'Lord, give us this bread always' (6.34).

Of course the Old Testament offers a different picture; here the phrase is more frequent, and by no means limited to God. In the narrative writings, 'to give bread to someone' merely means to give him something to eat, to look after him, to feed him; in the poetic and prophetic books, on the other hand, only two contexts are usual; first God is praised for giving bread to everyone, and especially to the hungry, and secondly, men are commanded to give their bread to the hungry. It is clear that the commandment merely reflects the praise of God. As the phrase will not be found in the later narrative books of the Old Testament, from Chronicles to Maccabees, a purely religious application of the phrase seems to be developing even here. It can also be traced in the great picture which *Isa.* 55.10 paints of the Word of God, 'As the rain . . . comes down from heaven, giving seed to the sower and bread to the eater.' But here the word 'give' no longer seems to be associated with the situation of the meal; it is used in a quite general sense which may be particularly suitable and appropriate in a prayer, 'to give, to grant as a portion or a possession'. We could therefore render the petition, 'Give us something to eat', just as the Old Testament often says, 'He gave them bread to eat', or even, in short, 'He gave them to eat'.[11] Such a sense seems more suitable in a prayer which longs to receive from God what it asks. The word-order, however, tells against understanding the sentence in such a general way; special stress is laid on the word 'bread' and it is put first, emphasized further by two qualifications. Only then does the verb follow, so that we might use Luther's words to translate the petition, 'Our bread, our daily bread, give us to-day'. Even if we regard this 'give us' merely as an expression of prayer and not also as referring to the actual situation of eating, the whole phrase is out of the ordinary.

Old Testament faith above all others regards man's possessions and his heritage as a gift and a loan from God: 'The Lord gave, and the Lord has taken away' (*Job* 1.21). Even the bread which feeds a man every day is no more than a gift from God to mankind, new every morning. Countless words and prayers of thanks have come down to us which testify to this view, and this thanksgiving is continually expressed in the daily grace at meals, so that anyone who omits it is to be accounted pagan and godless. Thus the first benediction of the grace at mealtime (*Berak.* vii 11a.35) runs: 'Blessed art thou, O Lord our God, king of the universe, who feedest the whole world with thy goodness, with grace, with loving kindness and tender mercy: thou givest food to all flesh, for thy loving kindness endureth for ever. Through thy great goodness food hath never failed us: O may it not fail us for ever and ever for thy great name's sake, since thou nourishest and sustainest all beings and doest good unto all, and providest food for all thy creatures whom thou hast created. Blessed art thou, O Lord, who givest food unto all' (Billerbeck iv 631). The ninth petition of the Eighteen Benedictions is more general: 'Bless this year unto us, O Lord our God, together with every kind of the produce thereof! . . . . Give dew and rain, for a blessing upon the face of the earth. O satisfy us with thy goodness! . . . . Blessed art thou, O Lord, who blessest the years.' All such prayers either give thanks for gifts received or pray for the fruitfulness of the land, for blessing on the harvest, and so on, but no prayer has been handed down to us which puts it so directly, 'Give us bread!' If a Jacob asks God to 'give him bread' in a foreign land (*Gen.* 28.20) or if in *Ps. Sol.* 5.10 the singer acknowledges, 'For if I hunger, unto thee will I cry, O God, and *thou* wilt give to me,' the reason for such directness is evident. It is the need and the right of the hungry and the foreigner to pray to God like this for their bodily wants day by day; the only phrase in the Old Testament which is a close parallel is the rule 'share your bread with the hungry' (*Isa.* 58.7) or the praise of *Ps.* 146.6–7:

> *Who keeps faith for ever;*
> *who executes justice for the oppressed;*
> *who gives food to the hungry;*

or even that of *Ps.* 107.9:

> *For he satisfies him who is thirsty,*
> *and the hungry he fills with good things.*

From this standpoint, the special character of the fourth petition in comparison with the usual Jewish prayers is understandable; for it is now a petition of the poor and the hungry, and the affliction in which they speak is further underlined by the 'today'. For the middle course is dear to the heart of the pious Jew, as *Prov.* 30.8 shows:

> *Give me neither poverty nor riches;*
> *feed me with the food that is needful for me,*
> *lest I be full, and deny thee,*
> *and say, 'Who is the Lord?',*
> *or lest I be poor, and steal,*
> *and profane the name of my God.*

Similarly, *Ps. Sol.* 5.18 runs:

> *Happy is he whom God remembereth in (granting to him)*
> *   a due sufficiency;*
> *If a man abound overmuch, he sinneth.*
> *Sufficient are moderate means with righteousness,*
> *And hereby the blessing of the Lord (becomes) abundance*
> *   with righteousness.*

A last sign of this uniqueness lies in the expression '*our* bread'. Nowhere else in the New Testament, and rarely in the Old, is there evidence of the word 'bread' with a personal pronoun; where it does occur, it has a special meaning and emphasis. The phrase, 'Share *your* bread with the hungry', means 'Share what belongs to you with the hungry even though you need it.' In the curse with which God drives Adam out of Paradise, it is only the Septuagint which has inserted the personal pronoun (*Gen.* 3.19): 'In the sweat of your face you shall eat your bread', and once again this 'your' means 'the bread for which you labour, and which you need'. So here too 'our bread' probably has a special meaning; it is the bread that we need and for which we ask, because without this necessary bread we hunger.

The objective content of the word 'bread' also points in the same direction. It is well known that both the Hebrew *leḥem* and the Aramaic *laḥmā* describe not only what is baked from wheat flour but any food whatsoever; in particular, the phrase 'eat bread' simply means 'have a meal'.[12] The Greek word ἄρτος has taken over some of this wider meaning in the Septuagint, but it is still not used everywhere. Wherever the Massoretic text in *Lev.* 21.6,8,9,17,21 speaks of the 'bread of God', i.e. the sacrifice, the Septuagint has 'gift'; where *Prov.* 30.8 speaks of 'the bread which is needful for me', it has general terms, 'what is needful and satisfying', and the translation of *leḥem* by 'nourishment' (τροφή) points in the same direction (*Ps.* 135.25; 145.7; 146.7; *Prov.* 6.8; 24.8). For the Greek ἄρτος is only given the general meaning 'food' when and because bread is the chief nourishment of the poor and the less well-to-do. So the word keeps its proper meaning in the New Testament even in this petition, and its words are coloured by the fact that the bread of need for which the hungry pray is at the same time the bread of grace which God gives. Even where the word is used in a transferred sense, the two elements may still be traced. When the Jews make a request which is so astonishingly like this petition, 'Lord, give us this bread always' (*John* 6.34), Jesus replies:

> *I am the bread of life;*
> *he who comes to me shall not hunger,*
> *and he who believes in me shall never thirst.*

So the petition 'give us bread' is also a petition of the hungry

One last reason for thinking of the bread for the hungry and the poor lies in the word 'today', which, together with ἐπιούσιος, distinguishes this petition from all comparable ones. Wherever else in Old Testament or Jewish prayers God is asked for food and drink, either there is no suggestion of a temporal limit, or the interval is limited by a human life or even by a season. The third grace at meals asks: 'O our God, our Father, feed us,

nourish us, sustain, support and relieve us, and speedily, O Lord
our God, grant us relief from all our troubles. We beseech thee,
O Lord our God, let us not be in need either of the gifts of flesh
and blood or of their loans, but only of thy helping hand,
which is full, open, holy and ample, so that we may not be
ashamed nor confounded for ever and ever' (Billerbeck IV 631).
In the Eighteen Benedictions the corresponding petition runs:
'Bless this year unto us, O Lord our God, together with every
kind of produce.' It is the petition of the farmer who prays
for the fruit of the field which will feed him until the next seed-
time and for the 'work of his hands'. The fourth petition is
prayed, say, by a day workman who does not know in the morning whether he will find work and bread for the day, or by a
traveller who takes nothing on his journey, no bread, no purse,
no money, as Jesus bade his disciples (*Mark* 6.8 *par.*). This 'today'
probably also corresponds with the Near Eastern custom, at least
in simple circles, to bake each day only the necessary unleavened
bread for the day, so that what is baked in the morning is con-
sumed by the evening; it does not calculate on keeping food
for a meal which goes beyond today. Perhaps it does not even
know of such a practice; like a beggar or a traveller it looks for
a small gift 'for God's sake'.

The word 'today', however, is not only intended to put a
temporal limit on the petition for bread and thus to indicate a
most modest measure of human nourishment; it also limits the
prayer and the desire to the immediate present. This 'today' is
therefore usually associated with Jesus' instruction not to take
thought for the morrow (*Matt.* 6.34). Man's care for today,
however, is something different from the prayer to God for this
very today; the two are not mutually exclusive, but they are
not immediately connected. If a man is not to take thought for
the morrow, then he is to expect that he can and must pray for
this morrow and for the day after; this expectation is not raised
by thoughts of the day; in Luke the fourth petition is not
limited to 'today', but is extended without qualification to
'day by day'. We may even ask which prayer is more faithful

to Jesus' preaching, the one which knows that the whole of man's life, however long or short it may be, is dependent on God's care, or the one which limits itself to the tiny span of a day and is so to speak rooted in its unavoidable, but at the same time transitory, needs. There is, of course, no sure answer to the question, but it teaches us to recognize that perhaps tomorrow will bring something different from the dawning of a new day, especially that it need not be particularly accentuated as this fleeting today, since this is already intimated by the action of praying, where it is brought to God's attention with all its demands and all its needs. But perhaps this temporal qualification is connected with the still unexplained ἐπιούσιος, for both are attributes which give the petition its special stamp, the one as object, the other as predicate, both standing at the end of each half-line. We must therefore turn to the riddle of the adjective.

2. A small library has been written about the word ἐπιούσιος since the first remarks made by Origen, but its riddle has only partially been solved, and that with no degree of certainty.[13] Origen (De Orat. 27) explained that the word did not occur either in the language of Greek literature or in popular usage, and that it had probably been coined by the Evangelists. Now, of course, the word has been found once again. In a papyrus from Upper Egypt (Preisigke, Sammelbuch griechischer Urkunden aus Aegypten 5224, 20), which is the text of an account book, there is the item '½ obol for ἐπιουσ . . .' It is quite probable that the word is an abbreviation for ἐπιουσίων, as there are other abbreviations in the list, which consists of fodder and provisions. In that case, τὰ ἐπιούσια probably means 'what is appointed or sufficient for the day', in other words, the daily ration. This conjecture is partly supported by an inscription on a wall at Pompeii (CIL IV suppl. 4000g) which also contains in a list of expenditures an item 'five asses for diaria' alongside items for oil, straw, hay and bran. This diaria, as other evidence indicates, means a day's ration. So ἐπιούσια and the Latin diaria might

be equivalent expressions. In that case, is at least the literal meaning of the word ἐπιούσιος explained? The evidence comes from
the fifth century A.D., from distant Upper Egypt; what bearing
can it have on the same word occurring four hundred years earlier
in Palestine, in a prayer which during these four centuries has
taken the whole world by storm? The mere posing of the
question produces a negative answer, so we need not consider
further the possibility of the word ἐπιούσιος having found its
way from the daily recitation of the Lord's Prayer into everyday
language. We are left with three different possibilities, all
uncertain: etymologies, the ancient versions and the ancient
commentators.

There are two possible derivations of the word. The first
begins from the preposition ἐπ' and the participial root of ἰέναι
and makes use of the stereotyped expression ἡ ἐπιοῦσα ἡμέρα
(so e.g. *Prov.* 27.1 LXX; *Acts* 16.11; 20.15; 21.18) in its interpretation; this designates the day following, the day after the
present one, the day that is breaking. The relationship between
the word ἐπιούσιος and the participle is the same as that between,
say, the form ἑκούσιος and ἑκών, ἑκοῦσα; the meaning would
be either general, 'future, following on, coming, approaching', or particular, 'for the next day'; it is therefore related both
to *crastinum* and to *venientem*. A second etymology begins with
ἐπί and a form of εἶναι; there is of course one difficulty to
begin with, though this is not insuperable, that ἐπιούσιος has
a hiatus which is not otherwise found with ἐπεῖναι. Here,
too, there are several possible variations: either the word
derives from ἐπὶ τὴν οὖσαν *scil.* ἡμέραν, i.e. for the present day,
or from ἐπὶ τὴν οὐσίαν i.e. what pertains to existence, to life.
These interpretations arouse linguistic suspicions because there
is as yet no evidence of a stereotyped expression ἡ οὖσα
meaning 'the present day', and because while οὐσία means
existence, even the nature of things, in philosophy, its popular
meaning is simply 'possession', 'means', etc. So etymology
leads to no certain explanation; there is no consideration of the
tension which exists between derivation and usage, especially in

countries whose inhabitants speak a language originally not their own.

The versions have followed various courses. The Syriac versions, of which unfortunately *Sinaiticus* lacks *Matt.* 6.9-13, hesitate between different renderings, *continuus*=continual and *panis necessitatis*; once we even have *panis abundantiae*. The meaning 'constant' is evidently formed on the analogy between 'our bread' and the Old Testament shewbread, which is called *leḥem hattāmīd* in *Num.* 4.7; the Septuagint translates it οἱ ἄρτοι οἱ διὰ παντός, while in *Num.* 4.16 it renders the phrase *minḥat hattāmīd* by ἡ θυσία ἡ καθ' ἡμέραν. The meaning 'daily' is thus not far off. Ulfilas (*sinteina*) and the Armenian version follow the Syriac pattern. A second group puts forward the meaning *crastinus*. According to Jerome's well-known remark in his Commentary on St. Matthew, the Gospel of the Hebrews read *māḥar* in this petition, meaning: 'Tomorrow's (i.e. the future's) bread, give us today.' This rendering is followed by the Memphitic; the Sahidic has *venientem*. Here *māḥar* is simply back-translated from the Greek, as otherwise it would be incomprehensible how the familiar word 'tomorrow' could have been rendered by the quite remarkable ἐπιούσιος. The reverse, on the other hand, is quite conceivable, as it removes the obscurity of the Greek word. It is therefore equally dubious to look for the Aramaic original of this mysterious ἐπιούσιος, and the methods of retro-translation or even comparison with rabbinic evidence break down completely. In the Latin versions, finally, there are two translations: *cotidianus*, read by the Old Latin, and *supersubstantialis*, Jerome's interpretation. Both interpretations, *supersubstantialis* in St. Matthew's Gospel and *cotidianus* in St. Luke's, have come down to the Christian West through the Latin Bible. The manifold deviations clearly show that the original meaning of the word was no longer understood and was, in fact, completely lost.

If, finally, we investigate the Greek Fathers, we find great uncertainty even among them; this impression is further confirmed by the devious exegesis which they offer for the whole petition. Origen considers two possibilities, one arising from οὐσία, which produces 'bread of substance', and the other from ἐπιέναι, which, according to him, produces 'bread for the future'. But in both cases the word ἐπιούσιος indicates that 'bread' is merely a metaphor for the Logos. Cyril of Jerusalem, without dwelling on the linguistic problem, thinks of earthly bread—not the usual 'daily' bread, but that of the eucharist. Gregory of Nyssa again has a different interpretation: ἐπιούσιος simply means 'daily' (ἐφήμερος), but physical bread is meant; in this petition the suppliant is instructed to ask only for what serves the simplest needs of the body. Chrysostom interpreted the petition and the word in a similar way.

It is not unimportant to see that these different explanations go back to quite an early period and can sometimes be supported by details of the New Testament. Thus the New Testament often has the word 'daily': in the primitive community there was a 'daily distribution' by the apostles (ἡ διακονία ἡ καθημερινή Acts 6.1), and James 2.15 admonishes the Christians about the brethren who are 'ill-clad and in lack of daily food' (τῆς ἐφημέρου τροφῆς). The idea of 'daily bread' is therefore a familiar one, but that makes it all the more difficult to understand how such a rare word could be used in the daily prayers of the disciples for so frequent an idea. In James 2.16, the concept of daily food is immediately taken up by another, that of 'bodily need' (τὰ ἐπιτήδεια τοῦ σώματος), and, as we have already seen, this idea has its roots in old Jewish wisdom language: 'Feed me with the food that is needful to me' (Prov. 30.8). Rabbinic sayings explain the expression 'bread which is needful for me' by the phrase 'food that is enough for me' (Examples in Billerbeck I, 420ff.). So the fourth petition would agree with a traditional Old Testament view which desires and chooses a modest mean between riches and poverty. It was doubtless widespread in the Judaism of Jesus' time, but was it also the view of the one who said, 'Blessed are the poor, blessed are the hungry' (Luke 6.20f.)? Moreover, if our mystery word meant this, the passage would be almost tautologous; for the emphatic 'our bread' can only be explained as 'the bread that we need', and in that case, should it be necessary to add 'that is enough for us?'

The idea of 'future bread' is already an old one, as is shown by the reading of the Gospel of the Hebrews, which has preserved some early phrases and ideas elsewhere. Of course, if we follow this Gospel in understanding 'future bread' directly and literally to mean the bread for the next day, it remains obscure why the 'today' at the end has not led to the use of the far commoner 'tomorrow' ($αὔριον$). What is the significance of this periphrasis, which describes the following day in a narrative account but not in a conversation? But perhaps the 'tomorrow' of the Gospel of the Hebrews also or only means the coming day which will give 'us' eschatological food, as Origen already explained. Marcion too was probably of this opinion when he rendered the fourth petition in his Gospel: 'Thy bread, the future ($τὸν$ $ἐπιούσιον$) bread, give us today.' This is hardly a tendentious alteration, but an objective interpretation which was also current outside Marcionite Christianity; for the Syriac rendering of this phrase with the expression describing the 'bread of God' (e.g. *Lev.* 22.7), the holy shewbread, in the Old Testament, shows that it took a view not far removed from that of Marcion. The way in which in the Fourth Gospel the Jews use almost the exact words of this petition, 'Lord, give us this bread always', and Jesus' reply, 'I am the bread of life' (6.34*f.*) are also closely related. In that case, this heavenly bread can then be defined in two ways, as the proclamation and the activity of Jesus (just as in *Mark* 7.27 his work can be described as 'bread' for the children) or as the 'spiritual food' (*Didache* 10.3) which is given in the Primitive Christian feast of the Lord's Supper.

So there seem to be four explanations to choose from, all of which have more or less strong reasons to support them or to rule them out: tomorrow's (future) and daily, needful and future (heavenly). The scope for choice once again highlights the difficulties of the position: in a prayer which is intended for daily use and which deals with the simplest and deepest matters of human life and divine action, in a prayer which is as clear and brief as it is close knit and comprehensible, we find a Greek word which appears here for the first time and which for a number of centuries occurred only here. There is no Aramaic word which clearly suggests itself as the basis for this Greek word; and yet the word must have been comprehensible, and it must at the same time have given the petition a content, or at least a colouring, all of its own. In the earliest translations and commentaries this basic simplicity ('daily' bread, necessary for sustaining life) and this ultimate finality ('future' bread, heavenly, for the salvation of the soul) is reflected in a variety of colourings and forms. We will attempt to progress towards the solution of this riddle by considering briefly Jesus' view of 'food', of eating and drinking.[14]

3. It is a familiar feature of the Synoptic Gospels that they speak more often of eating and drinking, of food and nourishment, than any writing or even group of writings in the Old Testament. As a parable or an event, as a warning or a promise, as a threat or as an assurance, the mention of food and drink pervades every strand of the tradition. True, the Old Testament too speaks about daily food and speaks of it more strongly and more profoundly than any other ancient religion; the reason for this is perhaps the transition from a nomad life to a more settled one, supported by the soil, which even in ancient Israel seemed a great miracle of divine salvation and divine leadership. The significance of this food is expressed above all in two passages (leaving aside here, where we are concerned with the inner content, the great cultic festivals at the beginning of sowing and the end of the harvest): God is praised because he 'satisfies the desire of every living thing' (*Ps.* 145.16), and in particular because he 'gives food to the hungry' (*Ps.* 146.7), and he is looked to in hope of a time of fulfilment which is depicted for us under the image of a banquet. In pre-Christian times there was hardly any connection between these two ideas other than the thought that God now gives man what he now needs for his life and that

he will one day give to the faithful all that they need for eternal life with him; hence it is only natural that above all there is a duty to be thankful: 'And you shall eat and be full, and you shall bless the Lord your God for the good land he has given you' (*Deut.* 8.10), a duty which is renewed day by day and year by year, and before which the future picture of a distant hope almost fades away.

Two ideas in particular are expressed in this thanksgiving: God gives food to all things living, the birds of the air, the fishes of the sea, beasts and men on earth, kings, rulers and peoples (*Ps. Sol.* 5.11-13, cf. *Ps.* 147. 8f., *Job* 38.25-7); it is a sign of the power with which he has created the world and sustains it. Nor does he have respect for persons: as the rain and sunshine come upon righteous and unrighteous alike, so too the food ripens for righteous and unrighteous alike. Secondly, God gives food before all else to the hungry: 'For if I hunger, unto thee will I cry, O God; and *thou* wilt give to me' (*Ps. Sol.* 5.10; cf. *Ps.* 107.9); it is the sign of his merciful goodness, 'for who is good and gentle but thou?—Making glad the soul of the humble by opening thine hand in mercy' (*Ps. Sol.* 5.14). Behind such questions lies the great question of hunger among men, and this is still answered with an almost childlike trustfulness: God feeds even the hungry. But there is a duty bound up with this confident assurance: 'Share your bread with the hungry . . . then shall your light break forth like the dawn' (*Isa.* 58. 7ff., cf. *Prov.* 22.6; *Tobit* 1.16; 4.16), and Judaism especially taught and practised this duty of well-doing in exemplary fashion.

These basic ideas can still be traced in the Synoptic proclamation of Jesus too, but the emphasis is placed elsewhere. We still hear of the power with which God satisfies all things living: 'Look at the birds of the air: they neither sow nor reap nor gather into barns, and yet your heavenly Father feeds them' (*Matt.* 6.26). But the problem of hunger is realized immeasurably more sharply and it is given a far more profound solution. There is still a duty to feed the hungry and to give drink to the thirsty, but whoever does so belongs to 'the blessed of my Father', for whatever 'you did to one of the least of these my brethren, you did it to me' (*Matt.* 25.34*ff.*). The idea that it is precisely the hungry whom God feeds is hardly touched on (only *Luke* 1.53); instead, we have the greater saying, 'Blessed are you that hunger now, for you shall be satisfied' (*Luke* 6.21), and this points to the greater hope which 'fulfils' all things and almost takes the place of the idea of God's creative power, 'you shall eat and drink at my table in my kingdom' (*Luke* 22.30). The problem of hunger is solved by reference to the eschatological kingdom, where 'they shall hunger no more, neither thirst any more . . . for the Lamb . . . will be their shepherd, and he will guide them to springs of living water' (*Rev.* 7.16*f.*). This solution is twice confirmed by the opposite picture: 'Woe to you that are full now, for you shall hunger' (*Luke* 6.25); and whoever does not feed the hungry is condemned 'to eternal fire' (*Matt.* 25.41). The well-known parable of Dives and Lazarus has given unforgettable expression to the idea.

So there is a first link, more powerful than that in the Old Testament, between eschatological fulfilment and the fact of eating and drinking; it is not, or not only, bound to the ordering of creation, but also to that of the fulfilment, not to the God-givenness of this world, but to the 'divine promise' of the future world: all need and all doubt which the hungry can suffer on earth is itself the sign of the eschatological blessing which they will taste in the kingdom of God. And this thought is further underlined by the fact that while in the Old Testament there are many vivid pictures which paint the glory of the final kingdom, in the words of Jesus there is only one, which is drawn many times, the picture of the marriage feast or the king's feast, of eating and drinking or reclining at table with the patriarchs, in Abraham's bosom, and the pictures of harvest or sowing only serve to show the great context in which 'our bread' is situated. One might almost say that from this point of view to pray for the coming of the kingdom and to pray 'Give us our bread today' amounted to the same thing.

Now these ideas of food and of meals are valid not only for an eschatological future, however near it may be, but also for the earthly presence of the Master. He has come to 'invite' sinners (*Mark* 2.17 *par.*) and this 'invitation' is also the word which describes how guests are invited to a meal. In fact, a meal is spoken of precisely here. 'The Son of Man also came not to be served but to serve' (*Mark* 10.45), or, as the form of the saying runs in Luke (22.27): 'I am among you as one who serves,' and 'serve' (διακονεῖν) in the strict sense means 'to wait at table'. The first service, therefore, that the apostles practised in the primitive community, from which the 'service of the word' is derived, is the 'daily service at the tables' (*Acts* 6.1-4). The phrase has been preserved elsewhere as well as in sayings about Jesus' mission; the people to whom he was sent rejected him with the words, 'Behold, a glutton and a drunkard' (*Matt.* 11.19) which distinguish him from John the Baptist, who 'neither ate nor drank', and both verdicts are accurately reflected in the dispute over fasting: the disciples of John fast, the disciples of Jesus are 'wedding guests, and how can they fast while the bridegroom is with them?' (*Mark* 2.18 *par.*). Their daily eating and drinking with the Master is thus a wedding feast, present and yet future, because it provides a full eschatological communion despite the constraints of the day. Nor does this meal remain limited to the disciples, seeing that the Master has come to 'call sinners'.

This saying stands like a title under the picture which Jesus paints as he shares bread with publicans and sinners. For this fellowship with men who were regarded by the Jewish Law and by pious Jews as outcasts of God and the people and were therefore unclean is not meant to break such supposed prejudices in favour of a higher human freedom; it is not even exercised in unbounded love to anyone who is a member of the human race or in mercy towards all who are in need. This narrow community of eating and drinking partially realizes that eschatological kingdom to which it is the sinners who are invited, in which one day the beggars and cripples from the hedges and fences, the Gentiles, 'will sit at table with Abraham and Isaac and Jacob' (*Matt.* 8.11). So we can understand why a vulgar caricature of Jesus, 'the glutton and drunkard', should be followed by another, 'the friend of publicans and sinners' (*Matt.* 11.19). The remark to the Canaanite woman who asks for her daughter to be healed says and means the same thing in a different way (*Mark* 7.27*ff. par.*): if it is not good to take the bread from the children and throw it to the dogs, then Jesus' work in preaching and healing acts is itself a giving of bread; and this giving of bread is, like 'serving' or 'calling', the embodiment of the eschatological 'coming', while the eating of the bread at this time is the sign of the salvation which has now become present and real.

From this aspect, all Jesus' sayings about eating and drinking, being hungry and thirsty, and giving feasts, have a sense of eschatological fulfilment; it is clear too how the imagery appears in all the features of Jesus' activity from paraenetic wisdom sayings to eschatological prophecy, from the prayer of the disciples to the mysterious revelations of the Son of Man. In 'bread', we find the duty of feeding the hungry, the need to go short and the grace of being full, and finally, the fellowship of being a guest at God's table as in his kingdom. This significance of bread is at its greatest and its most profound in the two narratives of the miraculous feeding; for both these meals display, in action and in event, all the features revealed by Jesus' sayings about bread. They are simple meals, Jesus is the host, he feeds his guests, like a Jewish householder, in accordance with pious custom and with frugal fare, and the purpose of the meal, like its result, is that hunger should be satisfied and that all should be full. But this meal is also, as the miracle shows, part of the reality of the consummation, when his elect will 'eat and drink in his kingdom' (*Luke* 22.30); the bread that he gives here, today, is also the bread that he will share with them and eat with them in his kingdom. From such a conception of the meal, the custom of a meal continued day by day, a miracle once performed, there derives at the end of his life the institution of the meal for

his disciples, a legacy of yesterday, a feast for today, and a promise
for tomorrow.

4. Perhaps the mere fact that the Lord's Prayer contains a petition
for bread accords with Jewish custom; for the ninth petition
of the Eighteen Benedictions, which are prayed daily by Jews,
asks for God's blessing on bread. But the view taken over from
the Old Testament is surely expressed in the fact that the prayer
for bread is here made as the first of all prayers for human need,
for God's care is most clearly and most deeply to be seen in the
fact that he 'fills all things living according to his well-pleasing'.
Nor is it just the first petition: it is also the only petition which
is concerned with the bodily life of men, and it does not sound
the same as a Jewish prayer. For it merely asks God to give us
bread today, and does not for a moment transcend the narrow
boundaries of this one day. This limitation is all the more
important as hitherto the petitions have been about things which
concern God to all eternity, and those which follow deal with
things which constantly come between God and men. Only
here, almost between the eternity of God and the eschatological
future of man, does there appear this single 'today'. There may
be numerous reasons for it: this is the language, as we suggested
earlier, of a poor man who in the morning does not know how
he will nourish himself and his family beyond the day, or of a
traveller who begins his journey early without bread or money
or purse, or even of a day-labourer who waits in vain for work
in the market place. But the 'today' expresses not only the
external need of the poor, but also the inner freedom of those
who pray, who have cast their cares for tomorrow and the next
day trustfully on God's goodness. In this dedicated freedom,
which asks everything, even the needs of body and life, from
God's hand, our petition may indeed follow Old Testament
belief, but no saying from the Old Testament or from Judaism
envisaged this freedom as being so unlimited, so unencumbered
as almost to do away with the need for the works of a man's

own hands (e.g. Eighteen Benedictions, ninth petition). In this attitude it merely reflects the great saying of Jesus, 'Look at the birds of the air: they neither sow nor reap nor gather into barns, and yet your heavenly Father feeds them' (*Matt.* 6.26). It need hardly be said that such a petition negates not only concern for bread but also 'the right to bread', which is in any case a concept unknown in the ancient world.

The petition also introduces a second limitation, which has already been touched on: the bread which the needy seek for this today is also quite simply the bread that God assigns us, that is sufficient for us. This limit is further hinted at in the phrase 'our bread', just as in the Old Testament too the personal pronoun is used when a man is shown as it were the limitations to which he is subjected, within which he is to delight in God's goodness; 'Eat your bread with enjoyment' (*Eccl.* 9.7). If, however, 'our bread' means the bread that we need, some interpretations which find here simply a brief expression of all the needs of bodily life are almost ruled out of court. Today's bread, then, is not, as Luther thought in the *Kleiner Katechismus*, 'all that is needed to nourish the body and to remove need', from eating and drinking to 'good friends, trusty neighbours and the like'; it is only the piece of plain barley bread which stills today's hunger. 'Bread', then, does not stand for the physical ordering of a man's life—the Bible knows no other meaning for the word than human food—but at most the act of divine care which preserves human life. All else is left to God, who alone knows 'what you need before you ask him' (*Matt.* 6.8). Again, this limitation does not mean that the individual is to learn to be content with that, but that he should take delight in it and at least learn to thank God for his grace.

It is probably significant that these few words of the prayer sweep away whatever rights and duties may be and have been derived from the fact of natural life, and that they teach rather that even this fact should be regarded as a loan dependent on God's grace, which occupies only a tiny space in the whole of God's works and activity, like a drop in a bucket. But the sense of the petition is not exhausted even yet. For the question arises whether this prayer for the bread which is today's food does not presuppose the right for a man to stress his concern for his own life precisely in such a petition to God; does the sentence not veil the right of the creature to be sustained by his Creator? Whatever the objective, historical justification for such questions, they first of all direct attention to one fact. It is not an 'I' which asks for the bread it needs, but a 'we', who ask for 'our bread'; and the 'we' first of all stands for the circle of those who pray like this to their Father in heaven. It is more closely knit together through this Father than any earthly group, whether social or national, professional or family, but for this very reason it is impossible to interpret the 'us' without further ado as referring to each single one of us; this 'we' asks as a praying and living community here and now for 'our' bread.

There is one other striking point: in every thanksgiving or prayer for daily bread, in the Old Testament or in Judaism, we find either the individual or the totality, not only of the nation, but also of all peoples, involved. For the basis and assurance of being heard is that God fills the whole world with his good treasures (see Eighteen Benedictions, ninth petition), just as *Ps.* 145.1 praises God for filling 'all things living' as he pleases. Closely connected with this view is the fact that the possessive pronoun is rarely added to the word 'bread' in the Old Testament: hardly ever in prayers, and just occasionally in commands to give bread to the hungry.[15] But here the restriction to the circle of the 'we' is expressed twice over. Could or would Jesus not have taught a prayer for each and every individual to be fed, such as each pious Jew learned from the Old Testament and from his teacher? To put the question means to answer it in the negative; this twofold 'our' and 'us' makes a special link between the bread and those who pray for it. They are not only those who need bread—all men do—they are also blessed with 'their' bread; and an investigation of Jesus' views and customs of eating has shown what that means: bread is the image and the reality of the eschatological kingdom of God, described by the saying, 'Blessed is he who shall eat bread in the kingdom of God' (*Luke* 14.15). The bread therefore does not cease to be physical, indeed frugal and scanty bread, to still 'our' hunger (afterwards, as before, it is a testimony to God's creative power and protective goodness); but this very bread, with which God satisfies all living things, is also 'our bread', with which God blesses us today; it is the bread which the Father gives to his children and which no one can take from them, and consequently it is also a testimony to the eschatological grace of God. Only in such a context do we seem able to explain the emphatic and singular stress on the 'our' and the 'us'.

It may perhaps be objected that such a deep double meaning, which speaks of physical and eschatological hunger, of physical and eschatological bread, can hardly be read out of this brief sentence. But first, this petition is unique not only in the Lord's Prayer, but also in the whole of the New Testament, and secondly, the one word which otherwise makes up the riddle of the fourth petition has not yet been taken into account. And the very word ἐπιούσιος seems to correspond exactly with the two points of reference which are touched on throughout the whole sentence. It is hardly a description of 'sufficient', or 'appropriate' bread, for this meaning is already implied in the 'our', and if it were taken to revive the Old Testament phrase about the bread 'which is needful to me', we would overlook the fact that the Jewish view which underlies it is not the view of Jesus. He knows nothing of the 'moderate means' (*Ps. Sol.* 5.20, cf. also *Pirke Aboth* iv 3), of a divinely appointed existence with which the pious Jew is to content himself or to be contented; he required the surrender even of the most moderate means capable of assuring life: 'Sell what you possess' (*Matt.* 19.21); he demands the acceptance of hunger and thirst for the sake of the poor: 'Blessed are you that hunger now, for you shall be satisfied' (*Luke* 6.21). The word ἐπιούσιος is already a clear preparation for the 'today', and all the special content of the petition seems to lie in the agreement and the difference between these two words.

It therefore means the future, the coming bread, the bread of and for tomorrow, which God is to give today, and hence it is a hint of the dual character inherent in Jesus' idea of bread, which in turn fits the situation indicated by all the Gospels, that of standing on the threshold between this world and the world to come, and being in the grasp of the powers of both worlds, of both grace and need. This 'future bread', as one might then translate the phrase, is not yet the perfect bread which the guests will one day eat in the kingdom of God, nor is it today's physical bread; it is the future bread in that of today, today's bread in that which is to come, as is shown in the great picture of the miraculous feeding, the bread which is shared by the disciples with their master during his lifetime. This dual character does not in any way rob the bread of its earthly reality, but at the same time it has become the vessel of eschatological communion and consummation. This 'coming' bread also stills present, earthly hunger, while this 'present' bread also gives all the eschatological grace to come.

Because of these complex relationships we can understand why the common word 'tomorrow' ($\alpha\check{v}\rho\iota o\nu =$ *māḥār*), which was chosen later by the Gospel of the Hebrews, was not put there. The Aramaic word which Jesus used is irrevocably lost; one might suppose that it would have spoken even more simply and plainly of the eschatological grace of the present and future bread, and that it was the Greek translation which chose an unusual word to express the underlying meaning of a common one. But in that case, the whole fullness of eschatological mystery and eschatological revelation is contained in the very rareness and ambiguity of this one word, which elevates the frugal eating and drinking in the here and now to be the sign and the reality of the coming of the kingdom of God, thereby making the 'today', which is still here but already passing away, the temporary vessel of his eschatological fullness.

5. For a long time it has been thought remarkable, or even highly

significant, that Jesus has a petition made for physical bread as the first of all human concerns, as he forbids all such thought elsewhere. Origen therefore saw in the bread the heavenly food of the Word, and Gregory of Nyssa read it as an urgent warning to be content with what was absolutely necessary, while Luther saw in it the idea of the ordering of the world. It is easy to see how such interpretations reveal the speculative theologian or the monastic preacher or the practical reformer of his people rather than the original meaning of what Jesus said in this fourth petition, however clearly each has stressed one aspect of what was meant. But what is the original sense which embraces all these different aspects?

Bread is prayed for here first because it is holy. In many Jewish prayers, we can find, scattered among much else, that God 'gives bread' to men; this is one of the many signs of his grace, with which he preserves and guides the outward life of man. Here it is the sole and all-embracing sign, and the following petitions which ask for preservation from powers and things that are hostile to God will make this one-sidedness even clearer. The bread is holy, first because it satisfies the hungry, and then because God's all-victorious and tender care can be seen wherever the pangs of hunger are stilled. But it is holier still, because for those who receive it and taste of it as God's children it is the image and reality in this transitory age of the eschatological banquet and therefore of the kingdom of God. Of course, within the wider context of the conception of the feast this petition also has a particular significance of its own; for wherever else we encounter the eschatological grace of this feast in word or deed it is bound up with the person of the host: he is the bridegroom, he gives a wedding banquet for those he has chosen, the 'future bread' today. But here it is not associated with the person of the Master in any way. The petition does, however, share this impersonal character with the whole of Jesus' preaching in the first three Gospels; for the call, 'The kingdom of God is at hand', rings out without any thought of the one through whom it is to come. It is the fact of the meal which makes those who partake of it certain of the presence and the reality of this kingdom.

We can now also understand the position which the petition occupies in the Lord's Prayer as a whole. It stands between the first three petitions, which are concerned with God, and the last three, which are concerned with man; it asks particularly for bread, which is given in a special way by God to man. So it is the threshold leading from the kingdom of the longed-for eschatological consummation to the kingdom of present human need, and therefore belongs to both kingdoms. At the same time it also speaks of the historical and eschatological justification for 'our' praying for God's name, kingdom and will, for 'our' trusting him in debt, temptation and evil, and for 'our' being the children of 'Our Father who art in heaven'. On the other hand, the petition for this present and future bread is also an expression of the communion from which we pray to God. We must guard against defining the two sides of this reference too exactly and too firmly along the lines of later Church concepts. This bread is not the bread of the Church's sacrament, nor is it even the bread of the Primitive Christian Lord's supper, nor is this communion as yet the later Church or even the Primitive Christian *ecclesia*. Both sides are still loose and undefined, like seeds which incomprehensibly develop into the forms which are predetermined for them and grow out of them. The bread, then, is earthly bread, the bread of the poor and needy, and at the same time, because of the eschatological hour in which it is prayed for and eaten, it is the future bread in this today, the bread of the elect and the blessed. This communion is the loose circle of those who pray here and there to God, 'Give us our future bread today', and it is at the same time the eschatological communion of the children of God who today eat 'our bread', their Father's gift, as they will soon eat it in their Father's house. One might almost suppose that this petition, and with it the Lord's Prayer, was imagined as a grace before the beginning of the common meal of the disciples, or even as the morning prayer of those who, poor and hungry and homeless, look

for the place and the bread which will unite and feed them
'today'.

This petition also explains the plan of the whole prayer.
The children of God, together, so to speak, sharing a meal at
their Father's table, are those who in the first half of the Lord's
Prayer pray for what belongs solely to their God and Father in
heaven; they can and may do this, because like the angels of
God they are in his service. And they are the sons of men
hungering after food, who pray for freedom from hunger and
debt, from temptation and enmity; they must and should do
this, because they are needy and debtors upon earth. In this
twofold character they belong to both realms, to the former, in
which God's name and kingdom and will prevail, and to the
latter, in which guilt and temptation and suffering are all around.
They are the link between God and the world, between tomorrow
and today.

Finally, we can understand from this the many interpretations
and explanations which have been given to the word ἐπιούσιος.
If the explanation we have given is correct, the strange word
holds the key to this petition, in adding the expression of
eschatological fullness and tension to its familiar Old Testament
and everyday character. It is therefore permissible to take this
word at first sight in the sense of 'daily' as the Lucan version
suggests, and to understand it to mean 'sufficient', 'appropriate'.
Such an interpretation reflects the Old Testament, and, at the
same time, the natural basis of this petition, with which it is
inalienably associated. It is equally clear, however, that the two
other interpretations, 'tomorrow's' and 'supersubstantial', are
equally justified, because they speak of the eschatological element
which characterizes not only the message of Jesus, but also the
situation of his disciples. The word ἐπιούσιος with a meaning
of 'future' similarly contains two elements, as does the call 'The
kingdom of God is at hand': it, too, speaks of being present as
well as of being near, of 'now' and the future. The idea of the
eschatological coming is also stamped on the first three petitions
and is concentrated in the one word ἐπιούσιος, because this

petition for bread shows that we must speak not only of an eschatological future but also of an eschatological present which makes today, the place of all need, at the same time the place of all blessing. The three following petitions can therefore turn exclusively to what oppresses and tempts the praying community in this 'today'. So the content confirms what has already been suggested by the discovery of a rhythmic form in the prayer: the fourth petition is the heart and centre of the Lord's Prayer.

VII   Forgive us our Debts

1. In the fifth petition, the manuscript tradition offers more textual variants than it has done hitherto; they are connected with the differences between the Matthaean and Lucan versions, which are also more considerable than they have been. Matthew uses ὀφειλήματα, Luke ἁμαρτίας, and the Didache ὀφειλήν; the religious use of Matthew's word, like that of the Didache, is found only at this point. Luke has replaced the rare word by a common one with the same meaning and has betrayed his action by keeping the metaphor of the debtor in the apodosis. It is more difficult to decide between Matthew's word and that of the Didache; both have the same literal and metaphorical sense and both often occur in the *koine* (the second particularly in papyri and ostraca, the first also in Hellenistic literature); Matthew also has the word ὀφειλή in the parable of the unmerciful servant (18.32). His deviation here probably means that ὀφειλήματα is original; the plural seems to give a more concrete colour to the expression than the commoner and unobtrusive singular ὀφειλήν. If this is so, it is easy to decide between a second pair of variants: Matthew writes τοῖς ὀφειλέταις ἡμῶν; the words match the end of the previous sentence 'our debts' almost like a rhyme, and at the same time reproduce the assonance of the original Aramaic words. Luke has παντὶ ὀφείλοντι ἡμῖν, which is better Greek, but is no longer the language of prayer; it has become a command or a regulation. Its form is like, say, *Matt.* 5.28, 'Everyone who looks at a woman', and its content like the rule which can also be found in *Matt.* 6.14f.; 18.35; *Mark* 11.25. Here, the rhyme, which was there in the Aramaic, and could still be detected in Matthew, has completely disappeared.

The other differences all seem to be of the same kind and to have the same origin: Matthew makes a close connection between protasis and apodosis with ὡς καί, Luke's καὶ γάρ is looser; similarly, Matthew has introduced the saying about the Son of Man coming to serve with ὥσπερ, Mark with καὶ γάρ (*Matt.* 20.28=*Mark* 10.45). Both go back to the Aramaic *kᵉdi*, which is similarly used both in explanations and in comparisons. Then the form and tense of Matthew's predicate vary in the manuscripts; we find ἀφήκαμεν, ἀφίεμεν, ἀφίωμεν and ἀφίομεν. Luke simply has ἀφίομεν, the Didache ἀφίεμεν. It is impossible to choose between the two present forms; ἀφίεμεν is the classical and more 'cultured' form, ἀφίομεν a popular neologism. The subjunctive weakens the expression on dogmatic grounds which are to be discussed later. So we have to decide between the present and the aorist, both of which tenses point back to the Aramaic form *šᵉbaqnan*, which is of indeterminate tense and can therefore be rendered by either present or aorist. As Matthew has used the aorist throughout the Lord's Prayer, the form ἀφήκαμεν will also be original here; but we should beware of drawing theological conclusions from this past tense, which means no more than that the earliest community regarded the forgiveness as a single event, and not something extending over a long period. One last difference concerns the subject of the apodosis; Matthew emphasises it with a ἡμεῖς, Luke with αὐτοί. It is impossible to suggest a reason for the difference here, but it shows all the more clearly that in the two versions of Matthew and Luke an original Aramaic wording has been 'translated' in different ways. We must consider the significance of this 'translating' in a bilingual country, where almost everyone uses now Aramaic, now Greek, according to needs and circumstances. This consideration will then hold not only for the fifth petition, but also for the text of the whole prayer.

In both versions, the strict parallelism between the protasis and the apodosis is worth noting. Each of the two clauses is constructed in exactly the same way: each has the same verb as predicate, has forms of ἡμεῖς twice in the same place, and has an object from the same root with the same sound. In Aramaic this similarity was perhaps even more striking (see above p. 28); it prevents us from taking the apodosis as a parenthesis within the sequence of the fifth and sixth petitions, as the great philologist Lachmann once wished to do, and indicates that the two petitions should correspond in content, as well as in form.

2. The content of the fifth petition is determined by two concepts, those of debt and forgiveness. We must first establish their exact range and meaning.

The word ὀφείλημα (debt) occurs in a religious sense in the Greek Bible only in Matthew, and this sense is unmistakably established by the rule following *Matt.* 6.14, which puts 'trespasses' (παραπτώματα) in place of 'debts'; the Lucan difference, 'our sins', which has already been mentioned, adopts another course. The religious use of the root ὀφειλ and its derivatives is not unknown elsewhere in St. Luke's Gospel. The apodosis itself speaks of 'one who is our debtor', meaning, 'who wrongs us''; *Luke* 13.4 says of those on whom the tower of Siloam fell, 'Do you think that they were worse offenders (ὀφειλέται) than all the others who dwelt in Jerusalem?' Matthew himself, or his tradition, seems so completely familiar with the word that he also tells the parable of the unmerciful servant, which is built up round the concept of debt—in both the financial and the religious sense. The LXX, of course, uses the word ὀφείλημα three times (*Deut.* 24.10; *I Esdras* 3.20; *I Macc.* 15.8), but only to mean 'offering, tax'. Naturally the Aramaic word ḥōbā has the same double meaning as its Greek equivalent; it is also the commonest expression for sins in the Targums; in Hebrew the word seems to be an Aramaism (*Ezek.* 18.7; cf. *Dan.* 1.10; *Ecclus.* 8.6; 11.18). It is in itself instructive that Aramaic, as against Hebrew, which is already over-rich in words for 'sin', has produced a new, perhaps comprehensive, perhaps alternative expression, which is, moreover, taken from commercial life. It is still more instructive that St. Matthew's Gospel is the most important evidence of this usage, in the first and fifth petitions of the Lord's Prayer. While we do not know how far it was already current in the time of Jesus, it increasingly dies out in Primitive Christian literature (it does not occur again either in the apostolic writings of the New Testament or in the Apostolic Fathers) but it grows and flourishes in rabbinic literature. We may conclude from Luke's replacement of the word and from the avoidance of it in favour of other words in the rule which has derived from this petition (*Matt.* 6.14*f.*) that the use of the word was a limited idiom. It is therefore probably a 'Galilean' expression, just as so much of Matthew's special material is of Galilean origin, and it shows how religious thought is not only dominated by traditional concepts, but also affected by new words and therefore new ideas.

The association of this word 'debt' with the verb ἀφιέναι (='remit, loose') is a common feature of Greek linguistic usage. The verb is often used in a juristic context, where it means to free from various legal ties and obligations. There is evidence of this sense not only in Greek literature and the language of comedy and the papyri, but also in the Septuagint, where it is almost a stereotyped term for the Old Testament Sabbath year for which the regulation runs (*Deut.* 15.2): 'Every creditor shall release what his neighbour owes (ὀφείλει) to him.' In Greek, then, the legal sense of the word is predominant, and a religious sense has not developed anywhere; the Septuagint usage varies between two different meanings. But these changes have also altered the colour and meaning of the word: in the Old Testament, ἀφιέναι chiefly renders the Hebrew *nāsā* and *sālaḥ*, once even *kāpar*, that is, words which mean the sin of cultic impurity: as the Holy One, God blots out the unholy, he wipes it away like a stain. But wherever ἀφιέναι appears, the cultic sphere disappears; there is a legal relationship between God and the sinner. God's ἀφιέναι is therefore a voluntary renunciation of his claims; instead of asserting them and carrying them through, he lets his grace prevail. So this rendering follows Isaiah's great saying, 'the holy God is made holy through righteousness' (5.16); the purely moral element has developed from the cultic and legal elements.

The change has progressed further in the New Testament; the legal sense remains only in the context of divorce; elsewhere the word has its Old Testament content. Here too, then, ἀφιέναι means that a claim arising from the breach of an existing relationship is not pursued, but the original relationship is restored 'through grace'. Here too, then, legal or moral religious views predominate over cultic ones; in the profound literal sense mercy has taken the place of sacrifice. And this whole development is true, not only for the Greek verb but also for the Aramaic šᵉbaq, the meanings of which are roughly the same as those of its Greek equivalent. So perhaps in Aramaic, too, a line of thought has already begun or been developed which transfers the idea of the forgiveness of sins from the cultic sphere to that of law, morals or religion. So the first and literal sense of this petition is that God shall release those who pray from the debts which they owe to him. The objective content underlying this imagery is to be considered later.

The fifth petition may seem remarkable both in language and in the imagery which it employs, but the idea of the forgiveness of sins, with which these uncommon images and concepts are associated, nevertheless seems so widespread in the Old and the New Testament as to make this strangeness no more than a terminological peculiarity. However, the reason for it lies deeper. First, the idea of the forgiveness of sins is by no means as widespread and as central in the Gospels as is sometimes claimed. The Synoptic tradition has Jesus' great saying to the scribes (*Mark* 2.10 *par.*): 'But that you may know that the Son of Man has authority on earth to forgive sins', which is preceded by the greater saying to the paralytic, 'Your sins are forgiven'. There is also the strict saying that blasphemy against the Spirit will not be forgiven (*Matt.* 12.31f.). Only the First Evangelist

164

transmits the question and the teaching on the problem of forgiving one's brother's sins (18.21-35) or, in the childhood narratives, the sentence which sketches out the task of the final eschatological figure: 'He will save his people from their sins' (1.21).

This exhausts the Matthaean passages, but there seem to be more sayings about the forgiveness of sins in Luke. Here we have the saying about the 'woman who was a sinner', 'Much is forgiven her, for she loved much', and the parables of the prodigal son, the lost sheep and the lost coin, and finally, in some manuscripts, the prayer of Jesus on the cross, 'Father, forgive them'. Again the Fourth Gospel knows nothing of this tradition, but it has the saying of Jesus to the twelve, which in *Matt.* 16.19 is addressed only to Peter: 'If you forgive the sins of any they are forgiven' (20.23).

This group of witnesses can be expanded if we include kindred expressions. The noun-phrase 'forgiveness of sins' is connected in Mark and Luke with the baptism of John, in Matthew with the Last Supper and thus with the blood of Jesus. Luke again also uses this expression more frequently (ten times in the Gospels and Acts); it stands like a pointer over the beginning of Jesus' ministry (4.18) and stands equally over the works of the apostles (*Luke* 24.47; *Acts* 2.38; 5.31; 10.43), especially Paul (*Acts* 13.38; 26.18). It is thus a basic idea of the preaching of Jesus which is merely stressed to a different extent in different strata of the tradition. The petition for the forgiveness of sins is also mentioned in the conversation between Peter and Simon Magus (*Acts* 8.22), so to speak as the human beginning of turning to God and Christ.

But this New Testament concept is also a basic idea of the Old Testament; in either case it is associated with the prophetic and evangelical call to 'repentance'. In the theophany in *Ex.* 34. 6*f.*, God is already called the one who 'forgives iniquity and transgression and sin'; in the Psalter, the 'forgiveness of sins' belongs so much to God's nature and will that the whole fear of God is based firmly upon it (130.4,7*f.*). To speak of the goodness of God and of the forgiving God is one and the same thing

(25.18); so here too the petition runs: 'Consider my affliction and my trouble, and forgive (LXX ἄφες) all my sins.' It goes through the whole of the Old Testament and is echoed right up to Primitive Christianity. Moses already prays to God on Sinai, 'If thou wilt forgive their sin, forgive!' (*Ex.* 32.32) and later, in the Eighteen Benedictions, we have (sixth petition): 'Forgive us, O our Father, for we have sinned; pardon us, O our king, for we have transgressed; for thou dost pardon and forgive!', or in the New Year Prayer: 'Our Father, our King! forgive and pardon all our iniquities, blot out our transgressions, and make them pass away from before thine eyes. Our Father, our King! erase in thine abundant mercies all the records of our debts!' Such constantly repeated petitions are made not only for open misdeeds, but also for unknown sins, not only for what is known publicly, but also for what is kept unwittingly, in a man's own heart (*Ps.* 19.12; 90.8). Nor is it just a matter of theological ideas or pious confessions; all these Old Testament and Jewish ideas about the forgiveness of sins were the basis of the daily cultus at Jerusalem, just as they were supported by it. The sacrifice, the odour of which goes up to heaven, is so to speak a perpetual prayer of the faithful (*Rev.* 8.4) for the forgiveness of sins; the Day of Atonement which blots out the people's sins so that they are pure and holy like an angel of God is therefore one of the great festivals in the life of both the people and the individual. The attacks of the prophets on the cultus and the confessions of the Psalms have strengthened the inner and outer trend towards the forgiveness of sins; if God desires steadfast love rather than sacrifice (*Hos.* 6.6), if a broken and contrite heart is the sacrifice with which he is well pleased (*Ps.* 51.19), then in either case there is the same concern, 'Forgive us our sins'.

Like the prayer for forgiveness, the reference to a man's own forgiveness of debtors has some parallels in Jewish writings. Jesus Sirach exhorts (28.2): 'Forgive your neighbour the wrong he has done, and then your sins will be pardoned when you pray,' and this admonition is explained with various illustrations which seem to anticipate the parable of the unmerciful servant. Rabbinic evidence continues in the same direction: Rabbi Judah said in the name of Rabbi Gamaliel (about 90 A.D.): 'Behold, it is said, "He shows you mercy (towards others) so that he can have mercy upon you" (*Deut.* 13.18). Let that be a sign in your hand: as often as you are merciful, the All-Merciful will have mercy upon you' (*Tos. Baba Kamma* ix, 30, in Billerbeck i 425, similarly *Sifre Deut.* 13,18 §96). Or, 'He who is merciful to others, mercy is shown to him by heaven, while he who is not merciful to others, mercy is not shown to him by heaven' (*Shab.* 151b).

So the idea of the forgiveness of sins is firmly associated with the Old Testament and Jewish foundations of the Gospel. But it is also well known that scarcely any religion can survive without the contrast between the holy, powerful God and the sinful, helpless man. So the idea of the forgiveness of sins is not limited to the biblical sphere. It is widespread in a number of ancient religions. A prayer to Ishtar runs: 'I have paid heed to thee, my lady; my attention has been turned to thee. To thee have I prayed; forgive my debt. Forgive my sin, my iniquity, my shameful deeds, and my offence. Overlook my shameful deeds, accept my prayer . . . accept the abasement of my countenance; hear my prayers . . . let thy great mercy be upon me.' We find the same thing in a lament to Nergal, the God of pestilence, or in a psalm of repentance 'To Every God': 'O my God, (my) transgressions are seven times seven; remove my transgressions . . . Remove my transgressions (and) sing thy praise.'[16] The affinity of such examples to the acknowledgment of sins in the Old Testament is obvious. There are also already Egyptian psalms of penitence and Greek examples which do not have these acknowledgments or at least only have them where the influence of middle Eastern piety can be traced in Asia Minor. Some penitential inscriptions have been preserved for us from Phrygia: the sinner openly and penitently acknowledges his guilt, and this confession wins him the favour of the god or goddess. The act of confession is the act of expiation, the expressing of it frees from sin or prepares for this liberation.[17] In classical and in Hellenistic times, this confession is already a humiliating punishment which is associated with Hades (Plutarch, *Ser. num. vind.* 566f.); one can see how far this view is from our petition. True, after the Orphic movement in Greece there is a new feeling of sin and guilt, and we even hear the cry of longing for freedom, but this is freedom from the *heimarmene*, from suffering and anguish around us, and not freedom from sin and guilt in us. Wherever the feeling of sin is expressed, there is also the feeling of a doom, which embraces men: 'You make the poor guilty and then abandon them to their pain.' Conscious of such guilt, man then confesses: 'Let me pay the penalty, for I am godless, accursed, hated by all Gods and demons' (Plutarch, *Superst.* 168c). Chance has preserved for us the prayer of Apollonius of Tyana: 'O ye Gods, δοίητέ μοι τὰ ὀφειλόμενα ('grant me my due') (Philostrat., *Vit. Apoll.*, i 11). The words sound the same, but the content is exactly the opposite; here is a perfect example of the difference between the Greek petition and that of the Lord's Prayer.

3. If the forgiveness of sins is one of the central concepts of the Gospel message, the question of the meaning of the concept and the particular colouring or significance given to it in this petition now arises. Wherever the various words for sin occur in the New Testament, they imply a deviation from the way which God has prescribed for men. A human will is here opposed to the one divine will, setting itself up as a special, independent, selfseeking will against what is general and binding; the divine will is imperative and normative, the human will is disobedient and hostile in act and word and intention. In this context, *I John* 3.4 has the definition 'Sin is lawlessness' (ἀνομία). There is also another context, however, where there is mention of man's guilt before God. Here man's action and thought is not primarily understood from the objective grounds of a general law and the subjective grounds of a particular human will (or

a human situation), but from a particular relationship of God with the individual man or even an individual community. To put it in the terms of Roman Law, man's debts to God can only be *debita ex contracto* and not *debita ex delicto*, as otherwise our petition would be for the remission of *debita* and not for the forgiveness of *delicta*. But where there is already a particular relationship between God and man, God and people, there is still no general law which everything must follow; the normative factor in the relationship with the chosen partner is a personal will of God, which is particularized according to time and place, means and end. In the one case the relationship is mediated through the notion of a valid and objective norm, in the other there is a special, almost subjective, norm, i.e. one relating to the partner, mediated through the fact of a relationship concluded earlier, which is itself immediate, like that between master and servant or between father and child.

This immediacy is further defined by the picture of the debts in which the subordinate party is involved, in other words, through the idea of the loan which has been made by the master; this does not imply what this loan consists of, whether it is the handing over of a sum of money as in the parable of the talents (*Matt.* 25.14-30 *par.*), or in the appointment of someone as administrator or servant, or in another situation of responsibility as, say, with the parable of the unmerciful servant (*Matt.* 18. 21-25) or the unjust steward (*Luke* 16.1-8). There is a first difference from the concept of *sin* in the almost unlimited breadth of this imagery. Sin is clearly defined by the idea of the general norm: 'You have been told, O man, what is good'; here the servant knows 'what his master demands of him, what is to be done and what is not to be done', and the simple rule is, 'Keep the commandments'. Where the term used is 'debts', a greater breadth has taken the place of this clarity; 'debts' are determined by the loan that God has made to man, and the number of parables in which debts are spoken of emphasizes this breadth further. But what has God given to man to form the basis of man's debt to him?

169

The fact that one cannot and may not ask so definitely in the case of the relationship between God and man is the first element in which the concept of debt is distinguished from that of sin. For there is nothing which God has not given to man; he feeds and clothes him, he counts the hairs on his head, he even demands the life, 'the soul', which he has given him (*Luke* 12.20). So with all that he is and has, man is indebted to God, and there is no act and no thought, no glance and no word that is not owed to him.[18] This all-embracing idea of debt is not contradicted by Matthew's use of the plural, as it is characteristic of Hebrew and, less markedly, of Aramaic, both of which possess no great number of abstract nouns, to put the simple plural in many places where they intend a comprehensive abstract concept. Thus St. John the Divine (*Rev.* 2.2,9 etc.) says, 'I know your works', meaning by his words the embodiment of the life of the believer, as it is manifested by the community in activity and intention. So here, too, there is no objective difference between the 'debts' of Matthew and the 'debt' of the Didache. 'Debts' are no individual details of man's life, but man in his totality before God.

Parables with similar imagery teach the same thing; they allow the debtor the freedom and possibility of carrying out the consequence of his debtor's relationship to God. There are servants to whom the Lord can say, 'Well done, thou good and faithful servant' (*Matt.* 25.21, cf. also 24.45*ff*.), and there are also others who hear the verdict: 'You faithless and deceitful servant.' Over and above these specific judgments, the parables show that the relationship of the debtor never ceases. Even the most faithful servant is never free, but is 'set over many' (*Matt.* 25.21) and is thus in a new relationship of service and debt. Such examples show how this idea of debt, arising from the relationship once entered into, imperceptibly changes into another idea, that of duty, which derives from a permanent and indissoluble relationship. The word ὀφείλημα has both connotations. The religious significance intended here transcends the bounds of the picture that has been drawn. It would not be noticeable, were it not that in this petition we have 'Forgive us our debts!' without any further reason given. Here a rather different picture is drawn. In the parables, 'not being able to pay' is presupposed from the start, as though there were no other possibility than this bankruptcy, and therefore the 'forgiveness' is the subject of a petition which has emerged from the twofold feeling of trust in God and the failure of the individual.

So a second element in the concept of these debts now emerges. The idea that man owes debts to God is one according to which the relationship of man to God is either confirmed or disrupted by payment or non-payment. But here the picture transcends its legal presuppositions and indicates a deeper and greater relationship. For *this* relationship is not dissolved if a man pays his debts, still less is it dissolved if God remits his debts; in either case he is only bound the more deeply to God; similarly the legal concept of a relationship of debt does not contain the idea of forgiveness or remission, and precludes any more comprehensive grounds than those which connect creditors with debtors. But if man can never end this relationship, even if he 'pays his debts', and God alone is free to bind or loose, then here too the religious significance far exceeds the limits of the legal picture. The creator and the creature, the master and the servant, even the father and the child, are bound together like this, and the servant who has done all that he was commanded still acknowledges himself to be an unprofitable servant, because he has only done what it was his duty to do (*Luke* 17.10). So the idea of debts develops out of a more profound view, namely that the relationship between God and man is a personal one, not bound by a rigid necessity. God once gave man his earthly existence in free kingly or fatherly trust, to receive it back from him again and to confirm him in riches or poverty, the blessing or the curse of his deeds. Whatever man is or says or does, he is and says and does as a loan from God, and life and action mean the repayment of this debt of existence to God or the payment of interest on it. 'Man remains what he is—nothing else, responsible by himself to God'; man is free to pay off this debt and to increase the pound that has been entrusted to him, or he is free to increase the debt and squander the pound. So even this 'forgiveness' of sins is not an act which God can repeat for men every day; it is something unique and eschatological.

Such ideas are not far removed from the foundations of Old Testament belief. For in the Old Testament too there is a twofold foundation to the relationship which exists between God and his people; one basis is given in the law and the cult, in short, in the revelation which God entrusts to the Jewish people as their bearer, and in so doing obliges the people to follow them; the other is given in the covenant which God concluded in free grace with Abraham, by which he chose the people to be his elect. In the one place sin is transgression against the law, in the other it is rebellion against the God who has chosen his people; in one place it is lawlessness, in the other it is unfaithfulness. Because of the second idea, which lays the foundation for a personal relationship, for which all previous revelations are merely manifestations of this relationship, all the dialogues which the Pentateuch reports between God and Abraham, God and Moses, are conversations about the problem of the forgiveness of sins. It is not the law that determines the problem, but this very idea of mercy. In the former instance, the idea of righteousness prevails, in the latter, that of grace; there the speaker is God who judges, here it is God who forgives. In such contexts we can recognize the affinity of the presuppositions on which the idea of 'our debts' rests, but at the same time there is a clear difference: the Old Testament idea of the covenant is bound up with an historical act which lays the foundation for the relationship between God and people; here the 'covenant' between God and those who pray—if we may put it that way—is involved in an eschatological act. For the individual who prays is not obliged to do what God demands because God once was gracious to Abraham and Moses; because God has given him his life and existence as a loan, he must repay his debt at the end of his life, or the end of time. There is another point connected with this: whereas in the Old Testament the forgiveness of sins is bound up with special divine institutions in history, with law and sacrifice, here such institutions become superfluous. It is the free and immediate will of the king that frees the servant from his tremendous debt with a word; it is the father who restores his lost son with a kiss on the cheek.

This produces a number of consequences which result in a particular view of the whole of a man's life. If all man's life and action is the repayment of a loan made to him by God, this means that there is no end to the loan before man ends, and even when he does end there is a certain sense in which 'our debts' have not been paid, for life does not exhaust itself in the natural course from the cradle to the grave; it points to the divine ground from which it begins and the divine yield to which it leads; it represents—in another New Testament picture—the bearing of fruit for God's barns. Even the richest and most humble, the most fruitful and the most sorrowful life and action therefore falls short of the debt in which God has involved it. But far more often man does not repay by his action the debts that he owes to God; he embezzles them or repays them to strange masters; he disposes of what does not belong to him as though it did belong to him and he were powerful and free: 'Soul, take your ease, eat, drink and be merry' (*Luke* 12.19). Wherever anyone talks like the rich farmer whose words these are, he misunderstands the basic position, that all life is not contentment in this existence but an obligation and a debt towards God. Man does not have his own independent centre and significance, he is not self-sufficient, but rests in someone else, who transcends this life. Man's existence is rooted in this other, and whatever he achieves, failure or success, is simply the experience of this permanent bond with God. Throughout his life there is no deviation and doubt, no wondering what he is to do; what he does decides his fate, whether it is to be caught out, like the servant who cannot pay his debts, or to be found a good servant who has been faithful because he has done what it was his duty to do. So his life and his actions have an eschatological bearing; only on the Last Day, when the Lord comes to reckon with his servants, does it become clear what a man owes. It is not a question of which of his deeds are good and which evil; his life has already given a clear verdict and the debts need only be exacted or 'remitted'.

The imagery of this word 'debts' opens up one last theme. There is no exact dogmatic content to the concept; it is not limited in any way and has no special mark of differentiation; it embraces the smallest thing and the greatest, the crudest action and the subtlest desire. Where sin is spoken of, man is charged with utter revolt against God's holiness; he is so involved in his actions that 'all the earthborn are full of sins' (*IV Ezra* 7.68). Where men's actions against God are regarded in the light of the concept of 'debt', however, these debts are easily distinguished from the men themselves; a man may *have* debts, but he *is* not his debt. However profound, however broad this concept may be made, however great the concern to connect its content with the nature of man, there nevertheless remains a subtle boundary which distinguishes the burden a man bears as a burden from its bearer. Where there are debts, the whole man is not condemned as sinful down to the ultimate ground of his being; the debts are external to him. The decisive thing is the original relationship in which a man stands to God. True, this relationship is marred by debts, but it is not broken; it is disturbed, but not destroyed. We can recognize here the profundity of the imagery which addresses the individual merely as a person in law and yet in so doing refers to his 'soul' before the eternal God.

So it is not unimportant for the sense of the fifth petition whether it speaks of our 'debts' or our 'sins'. The idea underlying the word 'debt' is not that associated with the concept of sin. We can hardly object that a single word cannot be made the basis of a considerable construction; it all depends on the word in question, and the context in which it stands (and in the terseness of the Lord's Prayer each word is of double importance)— this particular word is supported and substantiated by a number of parables and by frequent allusions in them. We are therefore justified in using the term as the basis for a special view of sin, all the more so as it also gives a closer definition of the concept of 'forgiving' or 'remitting'. The verb almost always occurs elsewhere with a noun like 'sin' (ἁμαρτία and ἁμάρτημα) 'transgression' (παράπτωμα) or 'blasphemy' (βλασφημία); in other words, ἀφιέναι in these phrases contains the moral, religious idea of forgiving, pardoning; only here the legal significance 'remit' is also possible, without altering the objective sense. There is a strange relationship between the two concepts: the significance of the word 'debts' goes all the way from the external fact of a money debt to the most profound sense of 'guilt', the significance of the word 'forgive' begins in the heart of the 'believer' and ends with the almost commercial cancellation of the debts because of the inability of the debtor to pay. Now 'forgiving' presupposes the idea of a moral community between the person who forgives and the one who is forgiven: one has disrupted it by his action, the other has restored it by his 'forgiveness'. Just as the offending party goes against the norm on which this community rests, so the one who forgives acts in the name of this community and in the power of that norm. The norm is simply willing the good, or, in religious terms, 'love'. 'Forgiveness' is possible because of a loving concern to realize the good within the community which is based upon it; it thus means the removal of whatever is in the way, so that the good is realized and the community is founded on the good. Or, in other words which come nearer to this petition: where the communion between God and the suppliant is involved, 'forgiveness' means that God removes the hindrance, created by man, which stands in the way of the truth and reality of communion with him.

But would it not be as good, or even better, if the debtor restored the communion he had broken by 'making good again'? The question suggests two things: first, even this 'making good again' would not be possible for the debtor by himself, but would have to be 'guaranteed' by the creditor so that communion could be established again. Secondly, where the prayer is for the forgiveness of debts, the idea of a one-sided 'making good again' has already been given up. True, although 'he could not pay' the servant in the parable can still ask: 'Have patience with me, and I will pay you everything', but his master releases him and forgives him his debts (*Matt.* 18.27). So where the prayer is, 'Forgive us our debts', it has already been realized that we cannot pay our debts; the prayer is made in confidence that the Father will pay them. But if its ultimate meaning is the restoration of the communion which has been disrupted by the debts, it is clear that the word ἀφιέναι here means 'to forgive' rather than 'to remit'. For if it remained in the legal sphere, which has in any case already been transcended by the meta-phorical use of the word 'debts', the legal sense 'remit' would not establish the communion as intended, but destroy it. For it is necessary to regard the freedom from debt obtained through 'forgiveness' as an even deeper association in communion with the God who forgives. So ἀφιέναι can only be rendered appropriately in the moral-religious sense of 'forgive', as is elsewhere the case in the New Testament. In Latin, the petition runs '*dimitte nobis*', not '*remitte nobis*'.

In the fifth petition, then, ideas and conceptions from two different spheres are combined in a peculiar way. The word 'forgive' appeals to God's innermost being, the word 'debt' to an outward burden; the former to what God *is*, the latter to what man *has*. So divine action and human failure, God's word and man's disobedience, are fused into a new union, which 'takes away' (so the term runs in the Hebrew) man's freedom from him and grounds it in God; it restores him as the free child of God to what he was made by God, and relieves him of all the burdens with which his earthly life and action oppresses him. The word of forgiveness thus makes God's claim and promise in man the true reality of his existence, accepted in the goodness of God. But is it not impossible to imagine this relief from the burden of debts? These debts are man's life and actions in particular and in general, and they are as much a part of his life as the breath which enables him to live. Can he be relieved of any action or thought so that it is not and does not remain his own any more?

The answer to this question is certainly 'no', in so far as man is an earthly, historical being; for each slight emotion and each deliberate deed is so inalienably part of its subject and involved in the sequence of his days and deeds that not even the slightest link in it can be removed. A man's life is his own responsibility, unforgettable and inalienable, in failure and success, in growth and decay. But the question does make two things clear: first, that the man whose sins God forgives is no longer an earthly historical being who is caught up so to speak in the close-woven web of his thoughts and actions; with his cry for forgiveness he turns towards God and asks to become what he has always been before God and through God, the free, assured child of God who lives from God's goodness. And secondly, this 'forgiveness' is a pure eschatological act of the goodness of God who 'teaches a man his way' (Ps. 85.11). It alone can relieve a man of his human and historical inheritance and draw him out of the net of his deeds and the dark sea of this earthly life (Matt. 13.47f.); it alone can free him through the miracle of forgiveness to live as a child of God. Wherever there is forgiveness, there is God's eschatological act among men. This is simply confirmation and explanation of an Old Testament principle which R. Akiba once formulated: 'Happy are you, Israel! Who is it before whom you become clean? And who is it that makes you clean? Your Father which is in heaven!' (Yoma viii 9). The point is quite clear because the present petition says nothing about the possibility of men being able to purify themselves, or about any institution of purification, like the sacrifice; it is quite content, transcending all human historical existence, in the fact that God the Father 'forgives us our debts'.

So there are two things about this petition, which give it its special character: anyone who prays like this knows that he is called afresh by God to be his child and at the same time asks to become afresh such a child of God. He overlooks what he is made by his thoughts and actions, and even what he makes of himself, and prays for God to make him as he was intended, and so to free him from the debts which hold him like fetters, so that he can become what he is before God.

A number of further consequences arise in this context. The petition is linked with the fourth one, for bread, by a simple 'and'. The same poverty and need which there oppress a man's body here plague his heart. Just as his body cannot live without the bread that God gives him today, so too his heart cannot live without the forgiveness that God alone can give. The same grace that restores his body raises his heart; just as a man experiences the eschatological grace of God in eating and drinking, so too in forgiveness he experiences the same eschatological grace which makes him a child in his Father's house and frees him from debt and failure. The suppliant therefore needs no special reason for such a petition; just as a child will ask his father for bread to feed him, so too he will ask him for the forgiveness which 'blots out our sins'. Perhaps we ought to put it even more strongly; just as it is natural to a child to incur 'debts' and to ask for forgiveness, so it is natural to a father to grant such forgiveness. Here is a revival of the basic Old Testament thought which is celebrated in numerous psalms (103.13; 145.8,9 etc.). God's utterly forgiving grace is accessible at all times and in all places; no obstacle bars the way to it, so surely is it itself a 'property of God'. The story of the Prodigal Son (*Luke* 15.11-32) is the finest and most profound example of such forgiving grace. But even here there is a clear difference from Old Testament thought: for the Psalmist (51.17), it is the 'broken and contrite heart' that is pleasing to God and the ground and occasion for the prayer for forgiveness, and he prays for a 'willing spirit'. Here, fear is overcome by trust, brokenness by a firm promise, and it is not a new spirit which leads the suppliant to God, but the knowledge of being a child of the Father—a knowledge which can be hidden, but never lost, which has been confirmed in body and soul by the experience of present and future bread from God. Nor is this knowledge merited or inherited by the suppliant; it is the grace of God asked from God and experienced in the 'today' of the bread. Only after this 'today', when God feeds him, can the suppliant turn to what reaches from the past right down to 'today', 'Forgive us our debts', as he later turns in the sixth petition to what presses on this today from the future, 'Lead us not into temptation!' This idea, too, is an Old Testament heritage which is occasionally also reflected in rabbinic writings (Examples in Strack-Billerbeck, *Kommentar zum N.T. aus Talmud und Midarasch*, I 113f.).

One last observation should be made on the tense of the verb 'forgive'. In Greek we have the aorist; that does not mean 'some time', or even 'daily', but 'today, now'; the petition is robbed of its urgency if it is not given this present significance. This petition too, then, stands under the influence of the 'today' of which the fourth petition spoke. It is no more permissible to keep this bare 'today' by itself than tacitly to extend it to a 'daily'. The aorist, as hitherto, demands not only a single action, but an action that is once and for all: it asks for God to give us bread today because it is eschatological bread, and to forgive our sins today because they are eschatologically blotted out. In other words, although the petition refers to a forgiveness of sins now, on earth, it also refers to a final forgiveness on the one day of God, which makes the person who prays free for God's kingdom and his glory.

The same thing follows from the concept of debts which is expounded by the New Testament instances: the king's coming to make a reckoning with his servants is as unexpected as it is final; their permanent fate is then decided, and it is also the time for the forgiveness of all their debts (*Matt.* 18.27). It also follows from the objective content of the concept of 'debts', for unlike the concept of sin, this suggests the limited period which is always involved: in the Lord's reckoning with his servants, either the debts are to be extracted from the servant or—to be remitted by the Lord. So the petition 'forgive us our debts', too, can only be made when this moment, expected or unexpected, has come; then man's earthly actions and ways are at an end, he has to answer for what 'he has prepared' (*Luke* 12.20). Under the influence of this idea man's life has become a single preparation for the day when 'his life will be demanded of him'; then, too, the prayer 'forgive us our debts' is also directed towards this day and is thus an eschatological petition, just as the action for which it asks God is an eschatological action. So the 'today' and 'here' in which the prayer leaves the lips of the person who prays fuses with the eschatological 'tomorrow' and 'there' to form an indissoluble unity: in the 'today' the eschatological freedom from all debts is realized as the sole miracle of existence in faith, and in this freedom the 'today' becomes the eschatological hour when the word of forgiveness is now fact and reality. In other words, this 'today' and 'here' is the place where God acts eschatologically. We need only note here that such a fusion touches on well-known themes of the Johannine theology.

4. The simple sentence 'Forgive us our debts' is not, however, the end; at this one place in the Lord's Prayer the petition is in extended form and a subordinate clause 'As we forgive our debtors' is added.

The relationship between the protasis and the apodosis is an old question: does the apodosis speak of something which must necessarily come before God's forgiveness, i.e. in the sense of a *do ut des*, or does it speak of a consequence, that we too shall be forgiven, i.e. in the sense of a *da ut dem*, or is it merely a remote comparison, which is attached loosely and with no fully defined connection? The word ὡς, which joins the two clauses together, probably corresponds with an Aramaic k^e and permits all these possibilities. This is why the two approaches mentioned above have been put forward over and over again since ancient times. The tense of the predicate does not offer any definite information. Matthew has the aorist in both protasis and apodosis, which at least suggests that both clauses are intended to be taken simultaneously. The present, which occurs in Luke and the Didache, and in some uncials of Matthew, once again turns the single action into a repeated one and thus gives the apodosis the character of a promise which is also to hold for the time to come. But as soon as we remember that both the Matthaean aorist and the Lucan present point to an Aramaic *peal*, all conclusions from the Greek tenses become impermissible and at most are based on the understanding of the Greek translation, which is by no means clear. So only the content of the clauses can decide on their internal connection, and the question arises how the divine act of forgiveness is related to the corresponding human one. This petition, which speaks of 'our forgiving' in the apodosis, seems, like the rule added in *Matt.* 6.14f.*, to presuppose that our act precedes that of God; the parable (*Matt.* 18.21-35) teaches equally clearly that the forgiving of the servant has to follow that of the master. This variation suggests that the problem of the sentence is not which forgiveness is prior but what correlation there is between divine and human forgiveness. How could a temporal element decide the meaning, where forgiveness of debts is asked of God to whom all the past and future decisions of the heart are open? So the word ὡς seems to indicate a purely logical relationship between the two clauses.

But this raises a far larger question: is there then such a logical relationship in which divine forgiveness can correspond to human forgiveness? It is God's nature to 'forgive the debts' of sinful, utterly dependent, man; here he reveals himself as the merciful, gracious one who bears our 'iniquity, transgression and sin' (*Ex.* 34.7). But are our 'debtors' equally dependent on us for our forgiveness? Are we equally merciful and gracious to them? And finally, does 'our forgiveness' determine their lives and demonstrate our graciousness as much as God's forgiveness does in 'our' case? The question is its own answer: 'our forgiveness' is one thing—at most it is exercised at a distance among children as opposed to their father; God's forgiveness is something else—in 'all our debts' he is still near to us and is the Father. Nevertheless, our action towards our debtors is equated to God's action towards us; the apodosis emphatically uses just the same words as the protasis, and in the same place; so the equality on the one hand and the difference on the other force us to the conclusion that our 'human forgiveness' can and must be understood simply as a reflection of the divine forgiveness.

The same consequences follow from the concept 'our debtors'. If we take the metaphor strictly, as suggested by the parable of the unmerciful servant, 'we' become the creditors who have made a loan to these debtors. But in what can this loan consist? How is it possible that they are dependent on us, who are at the same time debtors, and are in turn dependent on our creditors? Because of the difficulties of answering these questions, the word is usually taken in the sense of 'sinners' (it is used once in Luke 13.4 interchangeably with $\dot{\alpha}\mu\alpha\rho\tau\omega\lambda\dot{\delta}\varsigma$), but in that case, no notice is taken of the special colouring of the word here which even Luke has preserved, though in the protasis he has used the usual word 'sins' instead of the rare 'debts'. Nor is it realized that 'sin' in the New Testament describes a departure from the course of the divine will, i.e., 'trespass', but not at the same time a deviation from the course of human justice and human morals. Of course there are some significant passages in which there is mention of trespass against a man's neighbour. The prodigal son acknowledges, 'Father, I have sinned against heaven and before you' (*Luke* 15.21). Matthew hands down as a saying of the Lord a rule which begins, 'If your brother sins', and the *koine* manuscripts add 'against you'; he makes Peter ask, 'Lord, how often shall my brother sin against me?' (*Matt.* 18.15-21) and has Jesus answering with the parable of the unmerciful servant, in which the picture of the debt and the debtor dominate the course of the narrative. So even trespass 'against one's brother' is both a sin and a trespass against God.

But what is the element that makes a comparison with a money debt possible? The term 'against your brother' gives the answer. In a community of brothers (and in the sight of God what man is not another's brother?) each lives through offering and receiving brotherly love. In so far as one man meets the love of his brother with his own love, he wipes off with his love the debt which the other owes to him and lives free from debts in the ever-repeatable act of love. But by transgressing against his brother through his action he owes him the love which sustains him and so becomes a 'debtor' to his brother. Anyone, then, who has separated himself from the community of brotherly love may be called a debtor, just as anyone who through his action separates himself from the love of the 'Father' must be called 'God's debtor'. Now there is this mutual love of the 'brethren' only because it is grounded in the love of the Father for his children; as a result, the one who separates himself from the love of the brethren is cut off from the love of God. So he is not only a debtor of God but equally 'our debtor', and we too can forgive the debts of 'our debtors' because we have experienced the forgiving love of God and support our life and action with it. So there is a deeper and more fundamental meaning in the confession of the prodigal son: 'Father, I have sinned against heaven and before you.' It is, however, also clear that all forgiveness which we can give our debtors is only the effect of the forgiveness which we have experienced from God.

If the concept of 'our debtors' is only defined and can only be defined in such contexts, we immediately note a peculiarity of our petition. It does not run, say, 'As we too forgive each other our debts', although such phraseology would come still closer to that of the protasis, but 'As we too forgive our debtors'. It therefore speaks only of our act of forgiveness, just as the protasis speaks only of God's act of forgiveness; it says nothing of the possibility of our being debtors to others and needing their forgiveness. Here is one more sign that 'our forgiving' is not contrasted with God's as though it were something separate, but that this very forgiveness for which we ask and which we grant to our debtors comes from God himself, so that our action towards our debtors is light of his light, spirit of his spirit, love of his love.

So the question of the connection between the protasis and the apodosis is easily answered; the apodosis is not meant as a boast of our own meritorious actions or as a promise of such action; both emerge so to speak from a deeper conjunction, from the relationship in which the person who prays stands to

183

his God and therefore to his debtors. We can see once again how this petition, too, has as its support and introduction the address 'Our Father, who art in heaven': only because 'we' are his children may we pray, 'Forgive us our debts', and for the same reason also confess before him, 'As we too forgive our debtors'. We could not venture to pray for forgiveness if we refused this assurance, just as we could not give the assurance itself if we might not and could not ask the Father for forgiveness. We cannot ask for reasons and conditions here any more than we can for God's fatherly love. The petition for God's forgiveness and the assurance of our own forgiveness is the double fruit on the tree which is nourished and ripened by God's fatherly love.

At the same time, however, we can then see how right and important it is that the expression 'we forgive' stands here. Behind the simple fact of forgiving or wanting to forgive there stands the eschatological gift of being able to forgive, and the moral task of having to forgive. Just as the gift does not ask for reasons and motive, but has its own sufficient justification, so too this task does not look for, but carries within itself the duty of forgiving, not only seven times, but seventy times seven; and where we fulfil this task it is simply the eschatological gift that is granted us. The task associates the present petition with numerous Old Testament and Jewish expressions; the gift distinguishes it from any possible parallels and gives it so to speak its New Testament peculiarity. As a result, the right of 'our forgiving' is also clear; it is not exhausted in the patient tolerance of the weaknesses and failings of our neighbours, but is itself an eschatological action, like the act of God with which it is compared and to which it is referred; in our 'forgiving our debtors', a part of the eschatological consummation is achieved.

5. One last question is raised precisely because of this equilibrium between protasis and apodosis: who is it who is praying to the Father for the forgiveness of debts, an individual or a com-

munity? The words 'we' or 'our', which occur four times in this petition alone, leave room for either possibility; in the matter of the forgiveness of sins, however, must one not think of the individual? It has sometimes been said in the history of Old Testament prophecy that Ezekiel discovered the concept of religious individuality when he developed a new concept of sin; and is this association of individuality and sinfulness not justified when the sin is as inalienable a part of the individual as his life and thought? No one here can take away the sins of his fellow man; because they are so much part of a man, only God can forgive them. So the present petition seems justified in relating the idea of the forgiveness of sins to the individual; the individual asks God for what he gives his debtor. So, the words of a psalm would be a good parallel:

> *According to thy abundant mercy*
> *blot out my transgressions.*
> *Wash me thoroughly from my iniquity,*
> *and cleanse me from my sin!* (Ps. 51.1f.)

Such an interpretation is nevertheless at least one-sided; for debts, and not sins, are spoken of here, and while both involve an individual, the idea of sin presupposes its inalienability, whereas the idea of debt carries with it the possibility of its repayment. From the human point of view it is characteristic of the very concept of debt that it cannot be internalized, to fuse with heart and sense, but that it quite properly remains within the sphere of external transactions and rights, however much it may refer to the innermost depths of human will and thought. In other words, anyone who terms sins against God and one's neighbour 'debts' sees through God's eyes and judges with God's judgment; a man can only appropriate this judgment if he knows that he belongs so closely to God that what basically determines his life and nature has become an element which can be removed and discarded, which is already almost overcome. Only a child of God can see and speak in this way, a child of God who no longer recognizes an indissoluble involvement of the individual in his sins, but sees them elevated in God's forgiving goodness into an equality and a community which involves everyone. Beside this objective theme there appears the word 'we', stressed four times, which still puts another obstacle in the way of an individual approach. For the psalter has given too clear and too profound examples of the power and intensity, the ardour and the broken-ness, of the human heart (even when this heart is only an expres-sion of the totality of the people), and it has stamped this language too permanently on Jewish faith for an anxious or comforted 'I' to have to hide so to speak behind the community of the 'we' in this prayer. At the same time, similar petitions, whose subject is a 'we', are also quite common in Jewish prayers, and here no one thinks of referring the 'we' simply to an individual. Thus the sixth petition of the Eighteen Benedictions runs: 'Forgive us, O our Father for we have sinned; pardon us, O our King, for we have transgressed; for thou dost pardon and forgive.'

So the present petition too is to be understood primarily as a petition in which a community of suppliants turns to its Father. We might even say that the themes suggested in the apodosis are possible only in the context of such a community, and at the same time are also necessary there. For the debts which 'our debtors' owe us are merely debts to a community (otherwise the reciprocal phrase, that 'we', each one of us, are debtors to others and ask them for the forgiveness of our sins, could not have been omitted), and in that case it would not be an individual forgiving someone else his debts, but brothers forgiving those who are separating or have separated themselves from the community of brothers—the only idea which matches the concept of forgiveness which we have discussed earlier. Then, in fact, we, and only we, can forgive our debtors; an individual would only have the authority to say 'Your sins are forgiven you' in God's name and in 'ours'. And in the face of the closer knit unity in which the 'we' are bound up before God in the community of the children of God, from which they receive the power to 'forgive sinners', 'our debtors' too are forced into a closer-knit crowd which consequently loses all traces of individuality and is still only a greater or lesser group of debtors, the more the individual in it seeks to assert himself as an individual. But this indirectly raises the question of the status of this 'we' in itself, and in relation to 'our' debtors.

Those who pray are those who ask God for the forgiveness of their debts. They know of their debts and are oppressed by them, but at the same time they know that they have the power, like God, to forgive their debtors. Because of the first element they are God's adversaries, but because of the second they are God's children; the one thing makes them like their own debtors, the other makes them free instead of captive, children instead of servants, holy instead of sinners. Because 'we' who pray are related to both God and 'our' debtors in the same way, asking forgiveness from one and granting forgiveness to the others, 'we' hand on what we ourselves receive. 'We' are thus the close and indissolubly linked circle of those who despite all their faults can cling to God like children to their father; over against 'us' there stand the debtors, as the wider and more distant circle of those who settle all their debts among themselves and are therefore also farther from God, but who precisely because of this are commended to 'our' forgiveness. Similarly, in the parable of the debtor (*Matt.* 18.21*ff.*), the unmerciful servant seems to be immediately responsible to the master, whereas his fellow-servant depends upon him and is responsible to him. To put it in the later terms of Primitive Christianity: 'we' are the *ecclesia* of God, the community of the saints in the midst of a world of debt. It is true of such an eschatological community that the debts of the individual are also the debts of all, and that the forgiveness of all is also the forgiveness of the individual. Here the original freedom granted by God to man is at the same time preserved and abolished, as it is simply association with this community, in debt and forgiving at the same time. Only as 'children' of God are 'we' these perfect individuals, and only as these individuals are we the children of God. And this indissoluble and mutual obligation and freedom in the community express themselves precisely in the fact that before God we are at the same time both sinful and sanctified, praying for his gift of forgiveness yet at the same time granting it, as it is also ours, to 'our debtors'.

Perhaps the idea of 'our' community can be explained more closely by two historical examples. One of them is prior to this conception, the other comes after it. Just as the 'we' stand here between God and their debtors, so, in a familiar Jewish view, the people of the Jews stands between its God and the nations. It knows itself not only as the children of the patriarchs, but also as the children of God; it remains in this filial relationship although, or even because, every day the fire of the sacrifices smokes in the holy place as a constantly expressed prayer of the people: 'Forgive us our debts.' We also find in late evidence the idea that not only the Jewish people, but all nations, are purified through such priestly service (cf. *Pesiqta R.45, f.185b*). Here, then, in the cult and ceremony of the whole people (in intention and, on the high feast days, in reality) we have a parallel to our petition: here sins, both of the individual and of the people, are forgiven, but it is a long way from this holy service to the assurance 'as we too have forgiven our debtors'. Here we see a first difference between this 'we' and the Old Testament people of God; a second consists in the fact that the 'we' are not a people, and do not need to be one. The foundation of 'us' and our community is simply prayer; this is an *ecclesia orans*, not in any outward form, but precisely when and in the fact that it prays. But what it has lost in historical definition and earthly power it has infinitely gained in a more profound sense: the Jewish people has no 'debtors' among the nations who might be obliged to it, and if, according to *Isa. 49.6*, its status and task is 'to be a light for the nations', this is true only for the distant time of the consummation. The community of those who pray has power and authority in the 'today' of this world 'to forgive their debtors', as a king forgives his servants or a father his children. In the light of this, we can understand how, despite their many similarities, the Jewish parallels which have been found for this petition are still insufficient, because they do not see the community of the Jewish people in the twofold character of their historical and eschatological status as it exists in the here and now.

The nearness of this petition to the basic ideas of the Johannine view is therefore all the more striking. The 'we' here are in the same twofold situation as the disciples in the Johannine writings. They are the mean and the mediators between God and the world and between the Master and the people; they have received everything from God and yet are in the world; they hand on to the world whatever they have received in word and spirit, and yet they are not of the world. Here too there is a close relationship between the forgiveness we grant to the brethren and what we ask of God or receive from him or the Lord: 'I have given you an example, that you also should do as I have done to you' (*John* 13.15). Here, too, there is the consciousness that 'if we say we have no sin, we deceive ourselves, and the truth is not in us. If we confess our sins, he is faithful and just, and will forgive our sins and cleanse us from all unrighteousness' (*I John* 1.8-9). This knowledge is based on the eschatological fact: 'See what love the Father has given us, that we should be called children of God; and so we are' (*I John* 3.1). So we may say that the nucleus of this Johannine view is already contained in the present petition.

But the differences should not be overlooked for this very reason: the present petition still does not know the sharp division between the disciples and the 'world'; here the others, whom we forgive, are the debtors, and therefore belong to the company of the same Lord and Father who also 'forgives our debts'. A second element distinguishes the two views: despite the many colours in which the Johannine view displays this mediatory work of the disciples, it hardly ever speaks in this context of the forgiveness of sin, but centres the idea all the more firmly on the person of the Master himself. The present petition knows of a work of mediation only in so far as it asks for and assures forgiveness, and says nothing about the Master and his significance.

We should not, however, overlook the identity of the basic approach because of differences of this sort. In that 'we forgive our debtors', we know that we have the power to exercise

God's eschatological work on our debtors; in that we ask for forgiveness, we know that we are helpless and in need of God's eschatological work. The common factor of the Johannine approach and this petition is thus the idea of the reality of the accomplishment of the eschatological event here and now, and this very reality is at the same time the infinite task which is posed for our thought and action in this still-present age. If for the first reason we are the elect, then for the second we are those who ask for the forgiveness of our debts. 'We' kneel as it were on the threshold of the eschatological sanctuary of God, conscious of our own debts, and nevertheless appeal for admission to the sanctuary, helpless and unworthy to enter God's presence, yet able and infinitely obliged to forgive 'our debtors' outside in the still-abiding world.

Hence we can also see the close connection between the fourth and fifth petitions. In both cases it is a matter of 'our' community, the elect of God; in the fourth petition God feeds those who hunger in both the natural and the eschatological sense; here he is asked to forgive those in debt. 'Our' community lives and rests on this twofold basis of strength and weakness, of holiness and sinfulness; it is simply the community that feeds on the bread of its God, asking for and granting forgiveness. Here is contained its whole life and action, what it can and may do, what it should will and what it can wish. In this way it stands in the 'today' which reaches from the one petition to the other and therefore from the eschatological day of God to the still historical life of those who pray, who wait for the morrow when their debts will be forgiven and they can eat and drink at God's table.

VIII   Lead us not into Temptation

1. There are no significant manuscript variants in the text of the sixth petition either in Matthew or in Luke; even the Didache has the same wording, and the Epistle of Polycarp presupposes it (7.2). This is not completely without significance, as up till now all petitions have had the imperative in the aorist, as is usually the case elsewhere in prayers, whereas here alone we find the aorist *subjunctive*. The reason for this is, of course, the negative, which also occurs only here in the Lord's Prayer; the prohibitive subjunctive often takes the place of the aorist imperative in the *koine* and particularly in the New Testament. There is no difference of meaning between the two forms; the imperative is not, say, more strict and the subjunctive more gentle; on the contrary, this particular subjunctive is used in the Gospels and outside them to express a categorical prohibition; would it otherwise be used in such well-known sayings as, 'Do not give dogs what is holy; and do not throw your pearls before swine', or, 'Do not be anxious about tomorrow' (*Matt.* 7.6; 6.34)? Luke, too, has the same subjunctive at this point; this shows that he too imagines that the event which is prayed for will happen only once—there is no room for the idea of a possibility of repetition which appears in his version of the fourth and fifth petitions.

Although there is no dispute over the wording of the petition in the earliest witnesses, there is considerable variety in the later ones, and it is not unimportant for the interpretation of the petition to know what they are. In the African Church, the petition ran *ne passus fueris induci nos in temptationem*; this is the reading of the *Codex Bobbiensis* (*k*), and other Old Latin versions have a similar reading. We should note here not only the paraphrase of the idea of 'leading', but also the frequent omission of the copula 'and'. Tertullian in the African Church seems to have pioneered the understanding suggested by this wording; he expressly declares: *Ne nos inducas in temptationem, id est, ne nos patiaris induci ab eo utique qui temptat* (*De Orat.* viii). Cyprian already recites the petition in the form *et ne patiaris nos induci in temptationem*, and this is repeated in some later Latin writers. But the wording and even the interpretation are not the creation of the African Church. Dionysius of Alexandria added this explanation to the Matthaean wording, 'That means, let us not fall into temptation' (PG 10, 1601). One hundred years earlier, Marcion knew the petition in the form καὶ μὴ ἄφες ἡμᾶς εἰσενεχθῆναι εἰς πειρασμόν. He hardly made this alteration to the wording on purpose, as in that case Tertullian would not have appropriated his interpretation. If that is so, then about the end of the first century the sixth petition was current in Church circles in Asia Minor in the form 'And let us not be brought into temptation'.

Another expansion which determined the sense of this petition later found its way into the Latin Church. *Psalm* 119.8 contains the petition *Non me derelinquas usquequaque*; on this Hilary says (PL 9,510), *quod et in dominicae orationis ordine continetur, cum dicitur: Ne derelinquas nos in tentatione, quam ferre non possumus.* Here the wording of the petition is not only changed to match that of the Psalm; in addition, a well-known saying of Paul is added, 'God is faithful, and he will not let you be tempted beyond your strength' (*I Cor.* 10.13*f.*). In his commentary on the Sermon on the Mount, Chromatius, a contemporary of Chrysostom and Bishop of Aquileia, expressly testifies that this expansion had also found its way into the Matthaean text of the Lord's Prayer: *quod ipsum in alio libro Evangelii evidenter ostensum est: sic enim scriptum est: et ne nos inferas in temptationem quam sufferre non possumus* (PL 20, 362). Similarly, Jerome mentions that 'we daily' say in the prayer: *ne inducas nos in temptationem* *quam ferre non possumus* (PL 25, 485), as do Augustine (*de serm. Dom.* ii 9, PL 34, 1283), Ps.-Augustine (*Serm.* 84, PL 39, 1909), or, in the Greek Church, the Liturgy of James in both the Greek and the Syriac versions, the Coptic Liturgy and others (Swainson, *The Greek Liturgies*, pp. 6,62,225f., 306f., 343). We can see from this evidence what questions the petition raised for the early Church. They have led to the form of the French version of the sixth petition even today: *et ne nous laissez pas succomber à la tentation.*

2. We have something similar to the request of the sixth petition only once elsewhere in the New Testament, in the Synoptic account of Gethsemane, where Jesus says to the sleeping disciples, 'Watch and pray, that you may not enter into temptation' (*Matt.* 26.41 *par.*). This rareness is all the more remarkable because the New Testament elsewhere speaks often of temptation and saw the narrative of the temptation of Jesus by the devil as the greatest and most profound example of a temptation; it is further stressed by the well-known saying which in some respects contradicts this petition, 'Let no one say when he is tempted, "I am tempted by God"; for God cannot be tempted with evil, and he himself tempts no one' (*James* 1.13). It is still more remarkable that the Old Testament has nothing analogous to this sentence, although in some ways it could be called the 'Book of Temptations'; for in the history of the people, and particularly in the figures of the men of God from Abraham to David, it displays impressive examples of those who 'were found faithful' in the most dreadful temptations (*Ecclus.* 44.21).

Some clauses of Jewish morning and evening prayers seem to stand closer to the present petition. *Berak.* 60b runs: 'Set my portion in thy law and accustom me to the performance of religious duties . . . and lead me not into sin, or into iniquity, or into temptation (*weḷō līḍē nissāyōn*) or into contempt.' We do not know when these prayers were formulated, and we cannot prove that they were used in the first century A.D., but even if they are ancient, the difference between them and the Lord's Prayer is unmistakable: in them, the pious Jew prays that if he is involved in sin or iniquity or temptation or contempt God will not give him over into their power but—as we may add from countless analogies—will give him a new spirit of assurance so that he will remain steadfast in all dangers. The petition in the Lord's Prayer is, however, that God will keep the suppliant from any temptation. Over and above such petitions there are of course warnings against a man giving himself 'into the hands of temptation' or haggadic reflections on Old Testament narratives in which God tempts the pious, or particular interpretations of the saying in Psalm 26.2, 'Prove me, O Lord, and try me'. But all such occurrences by-pass the content of this petition. It remains unique, and we must investigate its linguistic features and its contents more closely.

3. The verb εἰσφέρειν always refers to movement from one place to another in the New Testament, even where it is used in a derived sense. Just as people find a way to bring the paralysed man to Jesus in the house (*Luke* 5.18), so too people 'bring strange teaching into the Church' (Herm., *Sim.* vii 6.5) or 'bring strange things to our ears' (*Acts* 17.20). The Septuagint chiefly uses the word to render the *hiphil* form of *bō* or occasionally also of *šub* (*Ex.* 4.7) or *ᵃlal* (*Dan.* 6.19); not once is there a metaphorical use of the word. Its meaning, in Old Testament usage, is 'to effect the removal of something or someone from one place to another'. The priest brings the blood into the sanctuary, the farmer brings the grain into the barn, 'we brought nothing into the world, and we cannot take anything out of the world' (*I Tim.* 6.7). The verb is thus a causative of εἰσέρχεσθαι etc.; this is how we should understand Jesus' warning against 'entering into temptation'. The closely related meaning of this warning should not make us forget that this petition has a slightly different colouring. In the one place the disciples are to pray to God to prevent us from entering, or not to allow us to enter,

into temptation; the petition in the Lord's Prayer makes a more pointed request that God will not bring us or lead us with his own hand into temptation.

The Hebrew underlying the Greek εἰσφέρειν would be the *hiphil* form of *bō*, *hēbī*; the Aramaic *aphel* form *a'ēl* (cf. *Dan.* 6.18) corresponds to this. The Syriac versions also use the *aphel* of the same verb in their translations. This linguistic association connects the petition still more closely with Jesus' warning; both instances have the same verb, once in the *aphel* and the other time in the *p^eal*. But we may not conclude from this that the *aphel* form has a permissive sense; the causative sense remains even there. If we are still doubtful, the Greek translation itself proves that the verb was understood causatively. The Septuagint has translated the Hebrew form *hēbī* not only with εἰσφέρειν but also with ἄγειν and εἰσάγειν, thus retaining the active sense. So the Old Latin rendering *ne patiaris induci* does not draw attention to an ambiguity in the original wording, but allows dogmatic considerations to bear upon wording which seems suspicious from precisely this point of view.

This use of the verb also predetermines to some extent the concept of πειρασμός. It gives the place or the situation in which, in accordance with the etymology of the word, 'we are tested'. Just as man is led by God so to speak from outside into such a situation, so too the 'testing' comes to him from outside; we may recall the tests to which heroes and children are put in fairy tales or sagas, or the ordeals of the Middle Ages. The greatest example of such a testing in the New Testament is the narrative of the Temptation of Jesus, 'Then Jesus was led up by the Spirit into the wilderness to be tempted by the devil' (*Matt.* 4.1). The concept of 'temptation' is defined not only in space but also in time: this 'bringing' or 'leading' is not a repeatable or a recurring event, nor is it a permanent state; it is a single event. This is again made quite clear by the temptation of Jesus. Other related phrases in which the concept of temptation occurs also fit in with this picture: one can 'enter into temptation' (*Matt.* 26.41), 'fall into temptation, into a snare' (ἐμπίπτειν,

I Tim. 6.9), just as one is involved in 'ill-usage' or 'danger' (*I Clem.* 51.2, *Herod.* vi 106.2, *Thuc.* viii 27.3). All these expressions have about them an element of the danger or fear which is bound up with the temptation; the word 'lead' is free of this and also suggests the verse of the Psalm (23.3): 'He leads me in paths of righteousness for his name's sake.'

The noun πειρασμός occurs, with some significant exceptions, only in biblical writings. Matthew has it only in the Lord's Prayer and in the Gethsemane narrative, Mark only in the latter, and it is not in John; in Luke it occurs more frequently. Once the word denotes the act of temptation (*Matt.* 4.3; *I Cor.* 10.13), more often it denotes the situation in which a man is tempted, i.e. being attacked or being tempted. There is therefore an hour (*Rev.* 3.10), a moment (καιρός, *Luke* 8.13), or the day of temptation (*Heb.* 3.8 after *Ps.* 95.8), and similarly there are situations of temptation (*Luke* 22.28; *Gal.* 4.14; *I Tim.* 6.9; *James* 1.12; *I Pet.* 1.6). The faithful can fall into manifold temptations (*James* 1.2; *I Pet.* 1.6), but God knows how to rescue them from temptation (*II Pet.* 2.9). Oppression can become temptation for them, so that the word becomes synonymous with tribulation, sorrow: Paul 'served the Lord with all humility and with tears and with trials which befell me through the plots of the Jews' (*Acts* 20.19), i.e. he experienced a great deal of suffering at the hands of the Jews. In the last days there will be 'great tribulation' (θλῖψις) such as has never been upon earth (*Mark* 13.19); therefore according to *Rev.* 3.10 Christ promises those who endure that 'I will keep you from the hour of trial, which is coming on the whole world, to try those who dwell upon the earth.'

The verb πειράζειν occurs more frequently than the noun; at the same time it shows the restrictions which govern the use of the noun. In the stories about Jesus his opponents often 'tempt him' with awkward questions (*Matt.* 16.1; 19.3) so that he cries out, 'Why put me to the test, you hypocrites?' (*Matt.* 22.18 *par.*); according to the Epistle to the Hebrews his life and work was a continual 'being tempted'—and here

too 'being tempted' is the equivalent of 'suffering' (2.18)--
for he is the High Priest who 'can sympathize with our
weaknesses, who in every respect has been tempted as we are'
(4.15). This connection is once again clearest in the one
great temptation by the devil, who is 'the Tempter' *par excellence*
(*Matt.* 4.3; *I Thess.* 3.5): as Jesus was tempted, so everywhere
will the faithful be tempted (*I Cor.* 7.5; *Gal.* 6.1; *I Thess.*
3.5; *James* 1.13*f*.). But even here the one meaning runs into
the other, 'afflict with sorrow' (*I Cor.* 10.13), which is the lot
not only of the faithful (*Rev.* 3.10), but also of all men (*Rev.* 3.10).
Two questions of particular theological importance are occasionally raised. First, who brings about the temptation? James 1.13*f*.,
following a well-known Jewish train of thought, answers clearly,
'Not God, but man's own evil impulse.' To tempt here, then,
simply means to entice to sin; but precisely this enticing is,
from God's point of view, at the same time a testing of the
constancy of a man's faith and morals. A second question arises
from the possibility of men 'tempting' God or his spirit. This
'tempting' is an irresponsible challenge to God made by unbelief;
thus the fathers once 'put God to the test in the wilderness'
(*Heb.* 3.9), and Ananias tempts the Spirit of the Lord in keeping
back some of his possessions secretly for himself (*Acts* 5.9).

Varied as this New Testament concept of temptation seems
to be, it nevertheless simply reflects the numerous themes which
appear in Old Testament and Jewish writings.[19] It is also easy to
see how the different strains all derive from a basic conception
which is well expressed in Judith's speech to the harassed leaders
of the Jews at the siege of Bethulia:

'Who are you, that have put God to the test this day, and are
setting yourselves up in the place of God among the sons of men?
You are putting the Lord Almighty to the test—but you will
never know anything. You cannot plumb the depths of the
human heart, nor find out what a man is thinking; how do you
expect to search out God, who made all these things, and find
out his mind or comprehend his thought?.... In spite of everything let us give thanks to the Lord our God, who is putting us

to the test as he did our forefathers. Remember what he did with Abraham and how he tested Isaac, and what happened to Jacob in Mesopotamia. . . . For he has not tried us with fire, as he did them, to search their hearts, nor has he taken revenge upon us, but the Lord scourges those who draw near to him, in order to admonish them' (*Judith*, 8.12-14,25-7). Here not only the life of the individual but also the history of the people from its first beginnings onwards is seen as an almost unbroken history of temptations which God has brought upon his people. We must examine the basis and the theme of this rather more closely.

4. We might call the Bible, Old and New Testaments, the 'Book of Temptations'. On its first pages stands the temptation of the first man and woman, and on its last the prophetic descriptions of the great temptation which is 'coming on the whole world, to try those who dwell on the earth' (*Rev.* 3.10). Between this beginning and this end there stretches the history of the people of God and with it the histories of individual men of God, and this single history, too, is a continuous chain of temptations which begins with Abraham and does not end with Jesus and his disciples; indeed, to speak of a divine history means to speak of the continuous series of temptations which has gone on since the world was created and will go on until it ends.

We cannot be surprised by the magnitude and extent of the concept of temptation, as it touches on the basic relationship between God and man, God and the world and peoples. Temptation presupposes the tension which exists in men and peoples and the world between their present state and their future destiny, between what they are and what they ought to be; it further presupposes that this tension is not permanent, but is resolved in the pattern of life and history which men and nations follow and have to follow in freedom and responsibility before God. As long as they are still following this pattern, the goal appointed for them by God has not been achieved and the identity between 'is' and 'ought', the identity of life and action which prevails in God's world, has not been realized; all this time they are still in the state when what should be and what should not be, what is good and what is evil among men and nations, is still not distinguished. It is left to the free and responsible action of an individual or a community to shape life or history as it should be and thus to realize the power of what ought to be to destroy the power of what ought not to be. This task, which confronts every individual, is set before all men and all peoples equally; it is also the task which God so to speak set himself when he created the world and thus put it on the way towards its consummation, an equilibrium of what is and what ought to be.

Thus man's way through temptations is at the same time the way which brings him to God and brings God to him. Whatever may meet him on this way, success or failure, happens under the guidance of God. From this point of view, temptation is simply something sent by God for which man has to be thankful: 'The Lord gave, and the Lord has taken away; blessed be the name of the Lord,' says Job at his first temptation (1.21). The psalmist prays in just the same way (139.23):

> Search me, O God, and know my heart!
> Try me and know my thoughts!
> And see if there be any wicked way in me,
> and lead me in the way everlasting.

Judith speaks to the Jews of Bethulia to the same effect (8.25-27).

So God is gracious in tempting men in two ways: first, there is the general grace of the guidance of God which protects man throughout his whole life, and then there is the special grace which leads him and strengthens him in a concrete situation of temptation. Hence the psalmist's cry (Ps. 66.8ff.),

> Bless our God, O peoples,
> let the sound of his praise be heard,
> who has kept us among the living,
> and has not let our feet slip.
> For thou, O God, hast tested us;

> *thou hast tried us as silver is tried.*
> *Thou didst bring us into the net;*
> (εἰσήγαγες εἰς τὴν παγίδα)
> *thou didst lay affliction on our loins;*
> *thou didst let men ride over our heads;*
> *we went through fire and through water;*
> *yet thou hast brought us forth to a spacious place.*

Temptation therefore is a way in which God's wisdom leads nations and men to the destiny which he has appointed for his creation, and as such a way it is a gracious act which requires the individual to give thanks and praise; for it is the loving father who tests his children, while it is the avenging God who destroys the enemy (*Wisdom* 11.10): 'For thou didst test them as a father does in warning, but thou didst examine the ungodly as a stern king does in condemnation.'

Of course in this way the concept of temptation is 'only' set in the context of a divine ordinance which directs and governs the world from its beginning to its end. But does not temptation nevertheless remain for the individual or the nation a hard battle between good and evil, in which there is not only victory through God's help but also defeat through human weakness? From the human point of view the concept of temptation seems to contain some new elements.

It is hardly necessary to stress that the well-known choice, set out in Greek moral philosophy, between the path of virtue and the path of vice has nothing to do with the idea of temptation. Anyone standing at the crossroads, like Heracles in Prodicus' fable, is not tempted; he has to choose from two possible courses of action the one which will bring him to a permanent *eudaimonia*. The person who is tempted, on the other hand, does not have a choice between two ways on which he could go; he has the unconditional duty to go the one way prescribed for him. The other way which temptingly attracts him is only apparently a way; in reality, it is a fall into the abyss. The Greek approach is inspired by philosophical wisdom, which is meant to lead man to lasting good fortune in life; the other is inspired by the experience of God's will on the part of the believer, who is bound to observe and to follow this will in all situations. Wherever the idea of temptation appears, the concept of an ungodly power which will snatch men away from God underlies it. It is foreign to the moral conception of the good and the good fortune in life which it furthers, however much the conception may speak of evil; in the realm of faith, however, this hypostatization of evil is not only possible, but even necessary, and has been realized in a particular way in the Old Testament and Jewish approach.

In Judaism, the life of the pious man is a life which leads through temptations to the goal appointed by God. Abraham, who faithfully withstood ten temptations, is the great pattern of the beginning, and the life of any individual, like the whole of this history of his people, is filled with temptations. They are the means by which God refines him, as silver is refined in the furnace. A Midrash gives the purpose of these temptations (*Gen. R.* 55 fol. 34d, in Billerbeck I, 135) thus: '*Psalm* 60.4 says, "Thou hast set up a banner (*nēs*, which the Midrash interprets once as temptation, then as exaltation) for those who fear thee, that they may be raised up for the sake of righteousness." That means, one temptation after another and one exaltation after another, to tempt them in the world and to raise them up in the world like a banner. And why? For the sake of righteousness, that is to establish the divine righteousness in the world. . . . "God tests the righteous and the unrighteous and him that loves violence his soul hates" (*Ps.* 11.5).' This meditation does not look for the reason, but simply for the purpose of temptation, and this purpose is twofold: the one who is tempted is 'raised up', and by such exaltation the divine righteousness 'is established in the world'. There is no question why such a goal is to be reached only by way of temptation; it is the will of God, who has appointed the path and the goal in this way.

If, then, the concept and the fact of temptation is necessary and real not only from the divine point of view but also for man's sake, a further idea follows in close succession. In temptation, God's grace is manifested to the faithful; it is the antecedent sign with which God guides and accompanies them as long as they pass through this world. The idea soon develops into the conception of the martyr who in suffering testifies to God's truth and in testifying to God's reality suffers. In martyrdom, the faithful man answers for God against the accusations and the hostilities of the world, however these may manifest themselves, in the wicked, in princes and authorities, or even in the devil. Because all these torment him, or cover him with shame and sorrow, they tempt him; because in his suffering the faithful one bears witness for God, and with God's help, he emerges victorious in his temptation before God. His temptation is his sanctification.

If we look at the concept of temptation from the standpoint of the 'tempting power' which comes upon man, or even from the standpoint of the evil to which he is allured, there are one or two final aspects to be noted. Temptation here is the means of seducing men from the course which God has appointed for them, and of leading them along a way which he forbids. It may be that the individual allows himself to be 'dragged' to evil actions through 'his passions' (*James* 1.14), in Jewish terms, through the evil impulse implanted in him; but it can also happen that the 'Tempter' *par excellence* seizes men and nations by craft or force and makes them obey his will. The more comprehensive the concept of temptation is made, the more clearly can be seen the conception of a religious dualism which it contains. Man and the earth are the scene and the object over which and in which the powers and the kingdoms of the devil fight with those of God and his angels. Even here, then, it is primarily the man of faith, or even the community, which is exposed to the onslaught of the devil and is in need of God's support. But over and above this, temptation comes on the earth and on men as long as they have not become the final possession of the devil. Temptation here is the occasional expression of the battle between God and false god over the possession and the domination of the world and of mankind.

The nearer the hour of decision, the harder it becomes. So it appears in all its clarity and fearfulness when the devil finally attempts to make God's world his own kingdom by presumptuous strife. Jewish and early Christian writings often speak of this eschatological event. The devil 'tempts' nations as he tempts individuals; he brings upon the world suffering and tribulation such 'as has not been from the beginning of the creation' (*Mark* 13.19). Temptation here means the revelation of Satan's power and subtlety. The dualism which always stands in the background in the matter of temptation is here made quite clear, though of course it is only that qualified dualism which incorporates all the violent usurpations of the devil into God's hidden plan and the permitted course of his eschatological work.

5. In view of what has been said, it is not difficult to describe the content of the sixth petition. It does not speak of the allurements of daily human life—either the crude ones which, according to a well-known saying, lead on a broad and smooth path to destruction, or the subtle ones in which only a passing thought tells on a man's being and actions and leads him astray from his nearness to God—and it does not speak of the manifold other inward and outward dangers which crowd on the straight and narrow path of the man who is turned towards God. Here, then, temptation is not a testing to strengthen men, for that sort of testing is God's gracious gift to men. If it were meant, the petition would have had to run, 'Lead us into temptation, as thou didst once lead Abraham into temptation.'

A petition like this would not be unheard of in the Old Testament and Jewish writings, which make man the subject who decides his own permanent destiny before God; indeed, the petition of the Psalmist says just this: 'Search me, O God, and know my heart' (139.23). Behind such an interpretation of this petition of the Lord's Prayer there is still the Old Testament idea that God tries the way of the righteous and leads to everlasting salvation the one whom he has found faithful in such trials. In this context, a man can indeed pray that the temptation may not exceed his strength; the Jewish prayer, already quoted, does so: 'Lead me not into (the hands—i.e. into the power—of) temptation,' and the French translation of the Lord's Prayer similarly runs, '*Et ne nous laissez pas succomber à la tentation*', but at the same time it is impossible to say, 'Lead us not into temptation.' That would be to pray, 'Let us not be found faithful in temptations, let us not fulfil thy will.' The idea of temptation which underlies this widespread reshaping of the petition in the Lord's Prayer is at its strongest where, in the well-known Jewish words, 'the yoke of the kingdom of heaven' is willingly accepted. The stronger and more vivid the temptation is here, the more costly it is to persevere and to remain under this yoke. But that is not a purely New Testament idea.

The petition, then, refers to something other than testing. It is not concerned with the successful withstanding of temptations, but with preservation from them. While the interpretation which has just been discussed is indissolubly bound up with the idea of a life fought and still to be fought in God's service, in the present petition even the thought of such a fight is already surrendered. The petition stands at its end; the time of testing lies so to speak behind it and the time of perfection, when the dominating feature will no longer be man's being tested and proved, but God's righteousness and holiness, lies ahead. The petition stands on the threshold leading from this age of temptation to the coming age of perfection. So it is concerned with the idea of eschatological temptation. The apocalyptic basis here is particularly clear; temptation is not the work of God, but the work of the devil, who still has the rule of the world in his hands and is not unleashing it in all its fearfulness. Those who pray are still in this world, and so they can and may ask to be spared, but they also know that they no longer stand under the dominion of the devil and therefore the power of temptation because they are the children of their Father. He can lead them so that temptation does not touch them, however powerfully and inescapably it may prevail upon earth. Praying like this, the 'children' are the victors, even if they are still surrounded by temptations; they are detached from them, they are the perfect, the elect. So this petition, like the fifth, characterizes the suppliants in a twofold, only apparently contradictory, fashion, which faithfully reflects the eschatological situation in which they stand. All the powers of evil still reign on the earth, 'all the kingdoms of the world and the glory of them' still belong to the devil, but children can already pray to their Father as though they no longer belonged to this estranged world of hostile powers and temptations; the last temptation, which is to decide and has already decided the battle between God and his adversary in favour of heaven, is imminent. God can shelter his children from it, if they so pray; over this petition, as over all the rest, is the saying, 'Ask, and it shall be given to you.'

It may perhaps be objected against this interpretation that its apocalyptic colouring does not match the countless sayings which call upon Jesus' disciples to take up the cross after him, or promise them suffering and persecution. The beginning of the Sermon on the Mount even praises those who are persecuted for righteousness' sake, and do not such sufferings form part of the temptation which is meant here? But the prophecy of suffering and the commendation of martyrdom do not contradict this petition, as is clear from the narrative of Gethsemane, the greatest instance of all: The Son of Man, who 'must suffer much' (*Mark* 8.31), is also the one who prays, 'My Father, if it be possible, let this cup pass from me,' and who tells his disciples, 'Watch and pray, that you may not enter into temptation.' For it is God who is bringing the world and mankind to their final destiny in accordance with his hidden counsel; as surely as this course of eschatological action in things great and small means tempta-tion and suffering for the community as well as for the individual, because it robs '(the) evil (one)'* of the power which it has usurped, so surely can God, with tranquil power and still greater

* See note to heading of ch. IX (Tr.).

mercy, deliver his elect from all temptations, or even preserve them from them. Understood in this way, the petition supplements the celebration of suffering; it warns against going out of the way to look for suffering and martyrdom, while at the same time laying in God's hand the suffering that is necessary and brings blessedness. Precisely by doing this it shows the dualism of temptation, which still belongs to this age and as a result brings on to the age to come.

So the concept of eschatological temptation becomes clearer; it is no longer a biographical incident or even a means of edifying and strengthening the faithful. The focal point here is no longer the individual or even a particular community, but the final encounter between God and (the) evil (one) which ushers in God's kingdom. True, the individual has to withstand it, as Jesus once withstood it, and each eschatological destiny is decided by this withstanding and overcoming, but the battle is not concerned with the individual, but with the defeat of all demonic and ungodly powers, just as in persecution it is not the individual who bears witness and suffers: in both, God's affirmation and the devil's revolt are made manifest. In this temptation, then, he upholds the destiny of men and nations with the power and weakness of his own life and suffering; by suppressing his own self he allows it to be filled with all the powers of God and his world; and his dying cry is a call of the spirit for God and his kingdom.

In the light of this, the word 'us' becomes particularly important. It designates the host of praying disciples who, as children of their Father, already stand in the consummation and on earth as those who pray and are therefore tempted. Their existence is therefore burdened with all the powers and dangers which are unleashed in the encounter between God and the powers of the Tempter; it is the scene of this battle, but in the suffering and enduring power with which other forces fight over it, it is also at the same time the strongest power, which overcomes all that is set up against God.

A new concept of temptation emerges here, closely bound

up with the Old Testament one and equally clearly distinct from it: temptation here is the attempt of the ungodly powers to obtain a final decision in the battle with God over the persons of the praying community who use the word 'we' to describe themselves. The temptation is beyond any possible human strength, because it is their task, as God's fighters and God's witnesses, to overcome the transitory time of life and history; and it is precisely in this way the testing of the fidelity of the suppliants to their Father in achieving the eschatological consummation of their existence. Because of the first element, they can pray to God not to lead them into temptation—for he has already incorporated even this last attempt in the way to eschatological fulfilment—; because of the second, the inheritors of his kingdom are those who 'have continued with me in my temptations' (*Luke* 22.28*f.*).

So temptation is related to the totality of life, the 'soul', and at the same time reaches out beyond this life; it has a place in the eschatological event in which a war is waged against God, which he has, in fact, already won. From this petition onwards, one might say, each suppliant has his tempter in himself and by his side, though of course only in that he is a suppliant, not because he is a man. He has 'his' own temptation, like his own body and his own life, he is elevated by it into a fatally isolated selfishness before God, so that all the bonds which otherwise hold him and all the supports which otherwise protect him are broken. But above the solitariness of this temptation is the community of this group who speak as 'we', for only the children of God can be so overwhelmed, so tempted, by all the powers of earth and hell, and yet stand almost in their Father's heaven, and because of this conjunction of 'God' and 'community' and 'I', all temptation is already testing and sanctification. It is therefore the eschatological community which endures temptation and asks to be spared from it, the consecrated, assailed community, which bears the fate of the world on its shoulders and is therefore tempted before the world and its supposed Lord. Perhaps the 'lead' therefore has a further special shade of meaning; if the

Aramaic 'make to enter' underlies it, then it also brings before the eyes of the suppliant the longed-for and familiar picture of 'entering the kingdom of heaven'. We might therefore paraphrase the petition: so that we may enter thy kingdom, do not make us enter the kingdom of temptation. In this way it would be clear that the sixth petition corresponds to the second, as does the fifth to the third.

IX   Deliver us from Evil*

1. The seventh petition has been handed on to us only by
Matthew, so there are no significant variations in its wording.
The only one there is, τῆς πονηρίας (evil), preserved in an
Egyptian amulet from the sixth century A.D., is clearly meant
to resolve the ambivalence of τοῦ πονηροῦ (the) evil (one).

As in the case of the third petition, the variations on the
content of the seventh petition, within the Bible and outside it,
are all the greater. There are just two passages in the New
Testament which sound like allusions to this closing phrase of
the Lord's Prayer. The Fourth Gospel has the words, 'I pray . . .
that thou shouldst keep them from (the) evil (one)' (τηρήσης
ἐκ τοῦ πονηροῦ, 17.15) in the High-Priestly Prayer, and *II Tim.*
4.18 reads, 'The Lord will rescue me from every evil work'
(ῥύσεται με ἀπὸ παντὸς ἔργου πονηροῦ). The congregational
prayer which concludes the Eucharist in the Didache (10.5) runs
similarly: 'Remember, Lord, thy Church, to deliver it from all
evil.' Not only is the petition familiar in the New Testament
(and, apparently, also as a phrase used to sum up a prayer and
bring it to an end), but the words and the thought behind them
are equally widespread in Jewish prayers. In the Eighteen
Benedictions, the sixth petition, for the forgiveness of sins,

---

* In German, the phrase 'from evil' (*vor dem Bösen*), like the Greek, can
be understood either as masculine ('the Evil One') or neuter (abstract 'evil').
The ambivalence is impossible to reproduce in English. This should be
remembered throughout the present chapter, where the rendering adopted in
ambiguous passages is (the) evil (one). (*Tr.*)

is followed by the words, 'Look upon our affliction and plead our cause, and redeem us speedily for thy name's sake.' At the end of this prayer, Rabbi Jehuda used to add, 'May it be thy will, O Lord our God, and God of our Fathers, to deliver us from the imprudent and from imprudence, from an evil man, from an evil companion,' and his words go on, 'from evil hap, from the evil impulse, from an evil neighbour, and from the destructive Satan' (*Berak.* 16b, similarly *Sanh.* 107a, *Kidd.* 81b, and *Sukk.* 52b; further material in Dalman, *Words of Jesus*, pp. 352f.).

Both these traditions, the early Christian and the Jewish, draw heavily on the language and thought of the Old Testament. It is so well known that the Psalter contains a wealth of petitions for deliverances from all distress and sin, misery and tribulation, that an enumeration of individual passages is unnecessary (cf., e.g., 25.22; 26.11; 31.8; 34.22; 69.18; 78.35,42 etc.). The nearest parallel in language and content to this petition of the Lord's Prayer is a phrase from *Ps.* 17.13, 'Deliver my life from the wicked'. It is also echoed in the precept (*Prov.* 2.11f., cf. 14.25):

> *Discretion will watch over you;*
> *understanding will guard you;*
> *delivering you from the way of evil.*

It is repeated almost word for word in Esther's prayer (4.19 (LXX)): Deliver us from the hand of the evildoer.

This series of petitions has its ultimate foundation in one of the first and most profound titles given to Yahweh. In *Gen.* 48.16, God is already called, 'He who has redeemed me from all evil', and this title is continued in a number of different forms right up to the Wisdom of Solomon (16.8): 'It is thou who deliverest from every evil.'

Although the petition is widely based on the language and thought of the Old Testament, there is, however, one small difference. In all the Old Testament parallels, the dangers from which God is the deliverer are clearly described by concept or picture. Even where we have the abstract κακά or something similar, the word 'all', which particularizes this abstract as the sum of individual 'evil' deeds or events, is never omitted. But it is this very element which distinguishes the wording of the present petition from its origins in the Old Testament and from the Jewish parallels; here we have only the abstract, 'from evil', whatever that may mean. It is therefore necessary for us to establish the exact sense of the individual words and concepts.

2. Of the numerous verbs such as ἐξαιρεῖν, ῥύεσθαι, σῴζειν, τηρεῖν, φυλάττειν, ἐλευθεροῦν, λύειν and others which, with relatively unimportant differences, describe the act of deliverance, the word ῥύεσθαι has perhaps best preserved the original colouring. It does not mean the loosing of bonds which hold a prisoner, nor, in a wider sense, the freeing of captives or those constrained in any other way, as the Latin and English versions suggest. It is associated with the idea of a way and an encounter, leading and protection, and this element is further emphasized by the contrasting verb of the sixth petition, 'Lead us not into'. God delivers 'from every trouble' (Ps. 54.7), 'from the snare of the fowler' (Ps. 91.3; 124.7), from wild beasts (Ps. 22.20f.), from 'persecutors and enemies' (Ps. 142.6; 69.14); 'discretion' preserves the faithful from 'the way of evil' (Prov. 2.11). Isa. 63.16f. laments in direct words, 'But thou, O Lord, our Father, deliver us . . . why dost thou make us err from thy ways?'

Now such a picture touches on one of the basic ideas of the Old Testament revelation and religion, the idea of a covenant which God has made with his people. It includes the fact that God has taken it upon himself to lead the people of his covenant throughout history and to guide them through all dangers to their destiny. On the other hand, the people are called on to walk willingly in God's ways and to keep from all transgression. In other words, the covenant implies that God will lead his people to all good and deliver them from all evil. It is thus easy to see why Deutero-Isaiah is particularly fond of calling God 'The deliverer from of old', for he is the God who keeps his covenant, the Lord who leads and guides his people on the journeys of their history, who therefore said to the ancestors of his people, 'Behold, I am with you and will keep you wherever you go, and will bring you back to this land; for I will not leave you' (*Gen.* 28.15). He is therefore also the 'Father' of his people, whose 'name is from of old' (*Isa* 63.16). The ideas of theocracy and the eschatological consummation, the conception of history and life as a struggle between good and evil, between faith and unbelief, the certainty of the final and eternal conquest of all evil by good—all this underlies the word 'deliver'. Just as it is now easy to understand that God 'delivers us from all sins and dangers, from affliction and from death', so too it is easy to understand the attitude of the person who prays, who can at all times turn to God with the cry 'Deliver us'. He is always one who is led, who is not sure of his destination or of the way to it, and he stumbles or wanders from the path; the way which lies before him is threatened by all the dangers between heaven and earth, and man's power to go God's way is weak and halting. But the weakness and the danger simply reflect the might and the 'delivering' power of the one who leads his elect in grace and wisdom to their destiny, 'the Lord, your Redeemer, the holy One of Israel . . . who leads you in the way you should go' (*Isa.* 48.17).

The two prepositions ἐκ and ἀπό are associated with the verb ῥύεσθαι in the Greek Bible. Both equally point to the situation from which a person is saved. They are even used interchangeably, particularly in poetical parallelism:

Deliver my soul from the sword (ῥῦσαι ἀπὸ · · ·),
my life from the power of the dog (ἐκ χειρὸς · · ·)!
Save me from the mouth of the lion (σῶσον ἐκ · · ·),
my afflicted soul from (ἀπὸ) *the horns of the wild oxen!*
(*Ps.* 22.20f. LXX)

Despite this interchangeability, however, it is quite possible to establish different shades of meaning and usage. Where the preposition ἀπό is used, the question is one of removing the person in danger from the peril to which he threatens to succumb, and the stress lies on the one who effects this deliverance from danger. Where ἐκ is used, on the other hand, the act of deliverance is stressed more strongly than the fact of the danger, which is not only a distant threat, but also an immediate reality. Hence the subtle distinction in *II Tim.* 4.17f.: 'So I was rescued from (ἐκ) the lion's mouth. The Lord will rescue me from (ἀπό) every evil.' The same instance also shows how both prepositions can refer either to things or to living beings.

The exact meaning of the phrase 'from evil' has been much disputed from ancient times. Taken by itself, it can be understood in three ways. The first possible interpretation is 'from the evil man'; thus *Matt.* 12.35 speaks of 'the evil man' who brings forth evil from his treasure. This is a way of speaking usual in the Old Testament; occasionally Deuteronomy has, 'you shall purge the evil (man) from Israel' (17.12; 19.19; 22.21-4 etc.). But as a rule this abbreviation is unknown in the New Testament; it occurs only in one isolated passage (*I Cor.* 5.13), and that quotes the Deuteronomic precept.

A second possible way is to take the word as neuter. This gained authority in the Western Churches after it had been introduced by Augustine: *Cum dicimus: libera nos a malo, nos admonemus cogitare, nondum nos esse in eo bono ubi nullum patiemur malum.* 'Evil' here is either the work which man fears to accomplish or the state in which he is compelled to live, or, finally, the power from whose influence and grasp God is to save the person who prays. This 'evil' would also include the concept of 'ill' which is so characteristic of the modern Lutheran understanding of the last petition (but not of Luther's own thought: he only says 'from ill' in the *Kleiner Katechismus*; in the *Grosser Katechismus* he has 'from malice'). *II Tim.* 4.18, 'The Lord will rescue me from every evil', perhaps interpreted the phrase in this way like the congregational prayer in *Did.* 10.5: 'Remember, Lord, thy Church, to deliver it from all evil.' But is it purely by chance that the word 'all' has been inserted each time? It is not only a means of giving correct grammatical expression to the intended sense (which it does not completely succeed in doing); in particular, it assimilates the phrase to the Old Testament expression which we have already mentioned, 'Who delivers us from all evil'.

This raises the question why the Old Testament speaks only of 'all evil', whereas the New Testament differs at precisely this point, in saying 'from evil'. The question would not be hard to answer if the abstract 'evil' was also common in the New Testament. Of course it occurs in some passages, but only if quite definite conditions are satisfied. First, we have it in the contrasting pair 'good and evil'; thus Paul warns, 'Hate what is evil, hold fast to what is good' (*Rom.* 12.9). Secondly, the abstract is used to sum up individual evil deeds or words, but almost always only in phrases like 'say or do evil'. Even these are rare enough (*Acts* 28.21; 5.4D), and wherever they are used, the efforts to clarify them are unmistakable. So *Matt.* 5.11 has, 'When they say *all kinds of* evil against you', clearly echoing the usual Old Testament usage. Or Paul speaks in *I Thess.* 5.22 of the opposition between good (τὸ καλόν) and evil, but formulates the second clause as 'abstain from every form of evil', probably recalling the way Job is praised in the Old Testament (*Job* 1.1,8): 'Who turned away from every evil work'. So while it is grammatically possible to take 'evil' here as neuter, it is improbable, in view of the linguistic usage of the New Testament elsewhere.

A third way of understanding the expression is to relate it to the devil.[20] There is, of course, no instance of the devil being called the evil one in the Old Testament or in Jewish writings, but this differentiates New Testament usage all the more sharply. In the interpretation of the parable of the sower, Matthew explains, 'the evil one comes', Mark has, 'Satan comes' and Luke, 'the devil comes' (*Matt.* 13.19 *par.*). In *II Thess.* 3.3 Paul writes, 'But the Lord is faithful; he will strengthen you and guard you from the evil one' (perhaps referring to this passage) or, more clearly, in *Eph.* 6.16, 'quench all the flaming darts of the evil one'; the designation is even more frequent in later Christian literature. It should, however, be noted that only St. Matthew's Gospel and the Johannine writings use the expression to any significant extent. In *I John* 2. 13*f.*, 'You have overcome the evil one',

214

the reference to the devil is unmistakable. *I John* 3.12 says of Cain, 'He was of the evil one' (τοῦ πονηροῦ); the parallel, *John* 8.44, 'You are of . . . the devil' (ἐκ τοῦ διαβόλου) clearly gives the same sense. The figure of the evil one is also significantly prominent in *I John* 5.18f., 'He who was born of God keeps him, and the evil one does not touch him.' Thus the famous saying ὁ κόσμος ἐν τῷ πονηρῷ κεῖται which follows is also to be taken personally, especially as the expression κεῖται here evidently has the meaning 'be dependent'[21]; in that case, the petition in the High Priestly Prayer mentioned above is to be taken in the same sense.

Only the first of the Synoptic Gospels knows the devil simply as 'the evil one' and gives him this title; the other two merely use names which are also common in Judaism. Matthew uses the term particularly in sayings which are peculiar to his Gospel. In the saying (*Matt.* 5.37), 'Let what you say be simply "Yes" or "No"; anything more than this comes from the evil one', the phrase εἶναι ἐκ suggests origin or derivation, as was the case in the Johannine passages; it thus refers to the person of the devil. This conception seems harder in the other saying in the Sermon on the Mount (5.39), 'Do not resist the evil one', because this demand is contradicted by so much else in the New Testament. If *James* 4.7 or *I Pet.* 5.8 admonish, 'Submit yourselves to God, resist the devil', and if *Eph.* 6.11 demands, 'Put on the whole armour of God, that you may be able to stand against the wiles of the devil', is not then this saying of the Lord to be interpreted otherwise than in a personal sense? Such an argument confuses two different points of view: objectively speaking, the apostle's words enjoin what is forbidden by the Lord's words; there is a real contradiction here. But is the contradiction resolved if the expression 'evil' in the Lord's words is understood to be neuter, or made impersonal? All its force remains. Besides, such an approach adopts a wrong method and makes a linguistic error. For these very apostolic admonitions, although they may be put differently, resolve Matthew's ambivalent phrase by making it personal; where 'resisting' or 'not resisting' is mentioned, New

Testament language does not envisage an abstract principle, but a personal opponent. While the content of these sayings is so different, they agree in what they say: the enemy is the devil, 'the evil one'.

Thus the terminology of St. Matthew's Gospel elsewhere suggests that we should think of the 'evil one' in this petition. There is one objective reason which may add support to this interpretation. It is no accident that the last two petitions correspond word for word; both verbs and both prepositions describe opposite movements, one 'whither', the other 'whence'. So the two nouns are also to be taken together. Now if the sixth petition refers to eschatological temptation, the last onslaught and the final defeat of the devil, there is little doubt that the seventh petition similarly speaks personally of this 'evil one'. The devil is the power, the figure, who ushers in the last days; he is God's adversary in the battle of these days. We can no longer object that it would suffice here to speak of the principle of evil, for there are no abstractions in the pictures of the eschatological drama, but only angels and servants on one side, demons and princes on the other. The idea of such an apocalyptic event excludes that of an evil principle; instead, it requires the idea of a *personal* power, just as God is not a principle, but sends *himself* or his emissaries to battle and to judgment:

> *Behold, he is coming with the clouds,*
> *and every eye will see him,*
> *every one who pierced him;*
> *and all tribes of the earth*
> *will wail on account of him.* (Rev. 1.7)

As long as this age lasts, in which good and evil are mixed together, it can be said that evil reigns on earth, though even the Old Testament does not do this very often. The manifold kinds of 'evil' action and 'evil' happenings are seen as manifestations of the one evil which produces them almost from the background through men's hearts and hands. But the sixth petition has already removed the all-concealing veils of history, and they cannot be put back again here; now the ungodly powers act

216

without disguise and wage their war against God, with the 'evil one' as guide and leader at their head.

It is sometimes said that it does not really matter whether the phrase is taken as masculine or neuter. If we conceded this, we would have to disregard the long battle which has been waged over the interpretation of the phrase, and the deep distinction here between the exegesis of the ancient Greek Church and that of the ancient Latin Church. For since Origen, who first vindicated it, the masculine has been predominant and widespread among Greek commentators, whereas in the Latin West (with the sole exception of Tertullian) only the neuter interpretation of the word has been put forward. The prominence of this view of 'evil' as a 'thing' in the Middle Ages and in recent exegesis, though it has not completely ousted the idea of 'the evil one' as a person, is a result of Augustine's interpretation and later the kindred one by Luther. But is it really unimportant whether in this last petition we ask to be delivered from 'ill', or from the principle and the fact of evil, or from the uncanny domination of the 'evil enemy'? If it is not unimportant whether we pray to the personal God, to the Father of his children or to the principle of the good, it is no more unimportant whether we speak of the power of the devil or of the principle of evil. Of course we then have to go on to ask the significance of calling the devil simply 'the evil one'.

3. It is well known that Judaism did not develop a unitary conception of the devil, his status and his task. Numerous writings and trends in which one might expect him to be mentioned say nothing of him at all; for others, he is an inescapable factor in all questions which touch on the relationship between God, the people and the individual. Even writings of similar character and form differ here: the Apocalypse of Ezra knows nothing of him, he is mentioned only occasionally in I Enoch, while the Assumption of Moses or the Ascension of Isaiah are full of him. Again, the Testaments of the Twelve Patriarchs give their

paraenetic admonitions in constant controversy with the figure of the devil and the power of the demons, whereas the Book of Ecclesiasticus says nothing about him. Nor is there any single idea of the nature and work of the 'adversary' where he appears in religious and moral accounts. More a diffuse element than a clearly distinguishable figure, he everywhere damages and disrupts the bond which binds a man to God; he accuses him before God, seduces him to sin, he brings misfortune and destruction, he fights against God's gracious counsels. Himself a rebellious angel, disquieting and confusing, he follows the tracks of God and of his servants like a dark shadow. The disunity and fragmentation in this picture are not, however, merely negative; they are also eminently positive. For the more strongly faith in one God, who directs the destiny of his people and his world in righteousness, is maintained through all experiences, the less men's thoughts are forced out of this world to seek their last refuge and resting place in a world to come, and the more dispensable becomes the thought and the more tenuous the form of the devil.

In striking difference from these Jewish beginnings, the Gospels often speak of the devil as of a well-known and familiar figure. The very names which are given to him already show the change: Judaism has numerous proper names for the figure of the devil, Mastema, Beliar, Beelzebul, Azazel, Sammael; even Satan and its derivative Mastema are regarded as proper names, though they mean only the 'accuser' and, in a wider sense, 'the adversary'. These proper names show that their bearer belongs to a group or type of beings—whether angels or demons—the individual members of which are distinguished by their names. In the Gospels, on the other hand, the devil has no proper name, but only a nickname, which has a quite definite significance. The Pharisees use the name Beelzebul, 'the prince of the demons', of Jesus; he even takes it up once, though reservedly, 'If they have called the master of the house Beelzebul' (*Matt.* 10.25). In his defence against the Pharisees' charge that he drives out the demons through Beelzebul, he tacitly replaces this name with the difficult name Satan. This probably has the status of a proper name in Greek, but not in Aramaic, and the New Testament writings still betray that its significance is alive for them by alternating between Satan and Diabolos in the same narrative or description (*Matt.* 4.1-11; *Rev.* 2.9*f.*; 20.2*ff.*). One further element is significant for this name: elsewhere, even in the New Testament, we find descriptions of the devil which derive from accounts of a cosmogony, and speak of apocalyptic ends; thus the Revelation of St. John (20.2) calls the enemy of the last time, 'the dragon, that ancient serpent, who is the Devil and Satan', names which are particularly common in apocalyptic books. The Gospels never touch on such contexts which characterize the devil as a mythical monster, but describe him with particular titles such as 'tempter', 'accuser' (only *Rev.* 12.10), 'the enemy', 'the evil one'. These are all particular functions and tasks of this Satanic figure, and there is not one of them which does not also describe a human attitude.

The two traditional names, Diabolos and Satan, which the devil bears in the Gospels, do not imply any particular conception of him. They are used like worn coins, the image and superscription of which means little to their owners; all the more characteristic, then, is what the Gospels say of the bearer of these names. Of the functions which are ascribed to the devil in the Old Testament, that of accuser is mentioned only once in the New Testament, at *Rev.* 12.10, and here the name designates not an appointment and activity in the heavenly court granted by God, but the false accuser, who accuses the brethren 'day and night before our God'. Similarly, all the unnatural, horrific events which the devil could inaugurate are omitted; the battle which Jesus waged with him at his Temptation (which Origen said was so tremendous that all the writings in the world would be too small to describe it) is portrayed as a learned dispute between two rabbis. Instead, however, another, more terrifying, factor has emerged: the devil has become the ruler of 'all the kingdoms of the world and the glory of them'. Here is his real seat and his real kingdom, for the Gospels nowhere suggest that he has set up his throne 'in hell'. His kingdom is therefore in a strict sense 'of this world'; it is so great that it reaches to heaven whence he can 'fall like lightning' (*Luke* 10.18) and so close-knit that it can be likened to a house or a city (*Mark* 3.24f. *par.*), and the demons can be called its householders (*Matt.* 10.25). While Jewish conceptions split up the power and the kingdom of the devil into many lesser powers and envisage it as having a kind of anarchistic formlessness, an inward yet vast compactness is characteristic of the dominion of Satan here. One can hardly be wrong in seeing the gospel message of the nearness of the king-dom of God as the basis of such a transformation. This kingdom, too, is like a house into which a man enters, to eat and drink at God's table, and it is at the same time so boundless that it com-passes both heaven and earth; those who enter it are the children of their Father. Because it is coming and is already near, all the ungodly powers are assembling for a last resistance and attack under the sole leadership of the devil, to make the world finally their own. Thus the eschatological character of the time and the hour is expressed in the close-knit entity of the kingdom of Satan as though in profane caricature.

If the kingdom of the devil is thus concentrated in one great unity which, while manifesting itself in the 'kingdoms of the world', is not limited by them, it is all the more instructive that the lords whom the demons obey bear names which are only significant in their reference to mankind. Just as men tempt one another or make war on one another or act evilly towards one another, so too the devil is the tempter, the enemy, the evil one; the only difference is that while men are evil, he is *the* evil one, while men are enemies, he is *the* enemy, while they tempt each other he is *the* tempter. At the same time, he has come infinitely nearer to human nature and life in all his diabolical power, as though the world and mankind had already become his destined prey, and human life was subject to him. The names which the devil is given make quite clear that it means that the devil is the absolute embodiment of human possibilities.

Satan is occasionally called 'the enemy' in Jewish writings too. Thus *Test. Dan* 6.1f. runs: 'And beware of Satan and his spirits.

Draw near unto God and unto the angel that intercedeth for you, for he is a mediator between God and man, and for the peace of Israel he shall stand up against the kingdom of the enemy. Therefore is the enemy eager to destroy all that call upon the Lord.'

This name supersedes the Old Testament conception of Satan, the servant of God, of which the book of Job is so full, and speaks of him as the armed enemy of God's kingdom and God's rule of the world. He is the 'strong one' who lives safely in his house and keeps his 'goods' (*Matt.* 12.29); he exercises 'all his power' to 'harm' men; serpents and scorpions are in his service. Anything that comes from God or belongs to God or aspires to God is his enemy or his prey, and his power is so great that men need divine authority to be safe and strong against his attacks. Without it a man is surrendered to him unprotected, like a grain of corn which falls on the path and is trampled underfoot. And the devil's battle flares up now, with all power and violence and deceit, wherever the message of the kingdom is proclaimed; hardly has the good seed fallen on to the fruitful earth than 'the enemy comes and sows weeds among the wheat' (*Matt.* 13.25). So near does his victory already seem that anyone who challenges him and will 'plunder his goods' must enter his house from outside (*Matt.* 12.29).

Thus the devil has simply become 'the enemy', the enemy of God and his creation, and especially of men. Here the full extent of the tension in the conception of this anti-godly figure is revealed: he dominates all things and all men in the world, encompasses all human plans and acts, right down to the sub-human realm of snakes and scorpions; indeed he has a power which is at least analogous to the creative power of God and of the Son of Man. For just as one can speak of 'sons of the kingdom', so too one can speak of 'sons of the evil one'; just as the one are sown by the Son of Man, so the others are sown by the devil (*Matt.* 13.37ff.). But this worldly reality, which is so to speak handed over to the devil, is itself only a transitory thing; it rests on a deeper foundation, the only one that is sure. Under the surface of such domination and such transitoriness it is and remains God's possession, which belongs to him by the law of creation and preservation and consummation, and now becomes once more his own through the love of the 'Father'. So all attempts of the devil to snatch even this last foundation from God are doomed to failure, and from the dark, whirling waves of this 'age' there emerges, like a rock, the ultimate reality which no power can ever take from God, the reality of 'The kingdom of God is at hand!' Here the apocalyptic basis of the conception of the devil is quite tangible.

Now in view of all this, the figure of Satan can hardly be described otherwise than as a distant and powerful ruler who guides earthly events from an unapproachable distance, parading his deceit and power, but removed from men and perceptible to them only through his servants and his activity, in sorrow and in joy, in riches and in power, in fortune and in pleasure. In this way he would be a counterpart to God and his heavenly world and his servants who from a similar distance exercise power over the earthly world and guide its course in unutterable hiddenness. But the name 'the evil one', which occurs for the first time in the New Testament and in this petition brings the Lord's Prayer to an end, shows clearly that this contrary opposition has a deeper foundation. That the devil is evil is, of course, known wherever he is mentioned in Judaism (the Ascension of Isaiah calls him the 'angel of iniquity who is the prince of this world, whose name is Matanbukus' (2.4)), and so this name, too, merely repeats what men have always felt him to be. But now something which hitherto was one of his attributes is concentrated in the name which belongs exclusively to him and is thus raised to his ultimate, innermost being. His nature and his power are constituted not by his superhuman authority, which is obeyed by the motley crowd of demons and unclean spirits, nor by his violence and deceit, nor by the numberless means and intermediaries which allure and entice men, nor by his irresistibility, the swagger and tumult of his arrival, but by the simple fact that he is 'the evil one'. So instead of being a monstrous being he becomes a clearly defined and responsible person, instead of being an unimaginable power, detectable everywhere and yet visible nowhere, he becomes a manifest 'Thou', a 'Thou' who is now simply 'the evil one', just as on the contrary God is for men the 'Thou' of whom it may be said, 'One there is who is good' (*Matt.* 19.17). The devil is opposed to God as evil is to good, but it is now so to speak a personal opposition, and only at this point does the most profound contrast begin. We can now understand why this figure is especially characterized by human names, inconceivable though his satanic power may be; for whatever power he attempts to set up against God is merely the consequence of the one thing which also associates him with men, the fact that he is 'evil'.

But this very fact also dooms him to be conquered and subjected. For just as there can be no evil unrelated to good, through which it is first appointed and defined, so too ' the evil one' cannot exist without the one who alone is 'good'; precisely in his arbitrary rebellion and his violent self-conceit, in the self-glorification of his nature and his action, he is inescapably dependent upon God. So it is evident how he can on the one hand set up his own house and kingdom against God within God's creation and how nevertheless precisely this house and kingdom is doomed to destruction and decay. In his own nature and name, which has raised him to heaven above all the kingdoms of the world, he is subject to the judgment that is his end.

If the idea of the holy God has thus become the ultimate standard which elevates the idea of the devil as much as it clarifies it, his satanic kingdom too, despite its manifold ramifications, cannot divide itself in anarchic arbitrariness, but must always reflect merely the one, the 'evil one'. Wherever a demon has his unnatural existence it is Satan who rears his head and strengthens his kingdom; therefore Jesus can say with fierce acuteness, 'How can Satan cast out Satan?' (*Mark* 3.23). Just as God's kingdom is in the last resort God himself, so now Satan's kingdom is Satan himself. But it flourishes not only in the incidents in which Jesus and his time saw the hands of a great variety of demons, but precisely in the thoughts of men who set themselves against God's thoughts. It appears on men's faces and in men's words, even those who are apparently faithful and true: 'Get behind me, Satan! For you are not on the side of God, but of men' (*Mark* 8.33 *par.*). No saying makes clearer and less doubtful the nearness of men's thoughts to Satan's thoughts, a nearness which has its foundation in the personal character of the 'evil one.' So it can also come about that Jesus encounters Satan in the wilderness and the two talk together like rabbis, while at the same time this seemingly human conversation becomes the revolutionary event which destroys Satan's power and might. The fact that Satan appears in this form, that his demands are so human and yet so diabolical, shows the eschatological period of his rule and his life; he emerges from the disguise of the manifold variety of his intrigues, and becomes visible as Satan in person, and this very appearance is also the sign of the nearness of his end. Thus the title 'the evil one' is the key to the recognition of his nature and his eschatological defeat. On the one hand, the name makes all men and all the world the seat of his rule, while on the other it does away with this very seat. We may therefore say quite briefly that the name 'the evil one' is the counterpart to that eschatological revelation as a result of which men can now pray to God as their Father.

One last feature in this great picture, traditional, yet at the same time newly minted, is revealed by the designation 'the tempter'. Every act of the enemy and the evil one is summed up in his 'tempting'; *proprium Satanae officium est tentare* (Calvin on *I Thess.* 3.5). It embraces all possible ways in which he may work, from the outward oppression which makes the disciples tremble and shake, to the most subtle seduction of self-love. In this concept of temptation, the function of the 'inimical' and the 'evil' power are united in the idea of an all-embracing act which is as earthly and human as it is diabolical and ungodly. Those who 'are led into such temptation' make a strange contrast to what is given to and required of those who pray the Lord's Prayer: just as these latter children of God are both earthly men and the eschatological elect, so the others are earthly men and 'children of the evil one'; the one are the wheat sown by the Son of Man, the others are the weeds sown by the devil. Just as the action of the Son of Man is a historical action with eschato-logical force, so the action of the evil one is a satanic action with historical force; the one is 'forgiveness', the other is 'temptation', the one is a gift through word and work, the other is a 'rape' by force and deceit.

The devil, then, becomes an eschatologically present power in becoming *the* enemy and *the* evil one and *the* tempter. The existence and the imminence of the kingdom of God is mirrored in the existence of the kingdom of Satan; the existence of the Son of Man in the emergence of Satan. The linguistic sign of this presence, at the same time both eschatological and historical, is the article prefixed to his name; wherever there is enmity, temptation and evil, Satan, *the* enemy, *the* tempter, *the* evil one can be found as its cause. Thus he has become God's adversary and God's counterfeit, and it is only logical that Paul should call him the 'god of this age' and the Fourth Evangelist 'the ruler of this world'.

4. This petition of the Lord's Prayer has features which have not yet appeared in any previous petition: it is formed word for word in antithetic and yet climactic parallelism to the sixth petition:

> Lead us not into temptation,
> But deliver us from (the) evil (one).

Thus the concept of (the) evil (one) corresponds to that of temptation; just as the predicates ('lead into' corresponds with 'snatch away from') include a heightening which is often intro-duced by a 'but', so too there is a heightening in the two nouns. But it is only there if 'evil' means 'the power whose proper office it is to tempt'. Even if we were now to understand 'evil' in a neuter sense, we would no longer be moving in the realm of abstract principles, but in that of forces and ideas of meta-physical substantiality which are not to be derived from the moral concept of good and evil, but represent the uniqueness of religious thought. Now it is a characteristic of biblical thought to imagine these ultimate forces as personal beings (a last reflection of the personality of God), and it is characteristic of the Gospel approach to see Satan at work as though with present personal power in the eschatological time which they describe. Thus the similarity in sentence construction in the one petition confirms the idea of eschatological temptation, and in the other the interpretation of 'evil' as the devil. These last two petitions are therefore to be taken together as a unity; the requests contained in them do not differ—their content is the same, the one negative and the other positive. With this duality of expression the prayer comes to an impressive close.

Just as the positive element contains more than the negative when they are set side by side, so too the seventh petition in some ways says more than the sixth, which is comparable to it. First, it speaks literally of a 'snatching away', and this colourful word is illustrated by a number of sayings in the Old and New Testaments. In the Psalter, the phrase 'who delivers us', which Deutero-Isaiah had made the source of all comfort and all hope, has almost become a stereotyped attribute of God in which the indissoluble bond between God and the suppliant and the suppliant and God is made manifest: God the powerful and the merciful, man helpless and perplexed, God the leader, man led and guided, God the shield in all dangers, man always in danger. Hence Luther's comment, which comes very close to that of Augustine: 'We pray . . . that our Father in heaven will deliver us from all ill to body and soul, to goods and honour.' But here, as in all the other petitions, the imperative is in the aorist; it does not mean a constantly renewed testing through life, but a final deliverance, once and for all. This thought is often expressed in the apocalyptic hopes of Judaism: 'At that time your people shall be delivered . . . and those who are wise shall shine like the brightness of the firmament; and those who turn many to righteousness, like the stars for ever and ever' (*Dan.* 12.1-3). Or, as the Assumption of Moses has it (10.9): *et altavit te Deus et faciet*

226

te herere caelo stellarum loco habitationis eorum, et conspiges a summo et vides inimicos tuos in terra. Paul has expressed these thoughts of Jewish hope in a way which corresponds most closely to this petition and has celebrated them as facts of Christ's revelation (*Col.* 1.13); 'He has delivered us from the dominion of darkness and transferred us to the kingdom of his beloved Son.' The prayer here is for what is experienced there; 'May God deliver us from the power and the kingdom of the evil one.' The petition is terse, and contents itself with asking for the ultimate dangers to be averted; it has none of the wishes and hopes which speak of the eternal life of the suppliants in the joy and glory of their Father, as they blaze out in Jewish hope or early Christian experience. This silence, which is hardly unintentional in so well shaped a prayer, is probably to be interpreted to mean that even hopes of this kind are to be left to the Father, and that the suppliant cannot and may not roam beyond the bounds which are set for his still beclouded, earthbound gaze.

Just as the predicate of the sentence sums up all the last desires of the suppliant in the one word 'deliver!', so the attribute sums up all the last dangers in the one noun 'from evil'. It speaks first of all of external dangers, and it is permissible to think of all the attacks and oppressions with which, according to a widespread view, Satan fills the time of the end of the world and of men. But just as anything eschatological, however objective it may seem, never remains external, so too it is with these dangers; to have to direct life and heart to God under or even only 'from' the power of the evil one means to be threatened by it right down to the innermost feelings of the heart. There is, however, no mention here of the manifold forms of satanic action, but only of the unconcealed and graceless power of 'the evil one', of his final fearfulness, which derives from all his forms and takes effect in them. The person who prays sees here so to speak the naked power of Satan which confronts him, and his countenance threatening destruction, before which man perishes in terror and helplessness, and he confesses this helplessness and fallenness in the very cry, 'Deliver us from evil!'

This cry also defines the persons of the 'we' who utter it in two ways, as was the case with the previous petitions. Here the helpless need of the suppliants is described more strongly than ever before, but only here are they faced with the immediate power of the evil one. It 'confronts' them, in the strict sense of the word; their way to the end of the age leads right into his domain. They cannot escape it; they can only be delivered. The word 'from' also suggests that the suppliants have still not been overcome by the evil one, but stand apart from him precisely in their helpless prayer; they do not belong to him, but to the God and Father who delivers them from the evil one. They stand before 'the evil one' as his children, made in the image of God, yet subject to Satan, akin to God and opposed to the devil, banished in exile and yet already recognizing their home, indeed living and praying there. Once again we may say here that it is not the individual who lives and is involved in this helplessness and assurance, strength and weakness, but 'we', a community of children and suppliants, who have in their Father a 'shield and buckler' (Ps. 91.4) against all dangers, even against 'the evil one'. They are rooted in the history of this world, which is under the influence of the evil one, and at the same time removed from it, as the host of the elect which stands only by the support of its God while the history of the world passes away, and with it the kingdom of the evil one. Once again, the terseness of the petition is remarkable; for even the community does not ask for its own continuance but for God's support, not for the defeat of the evil one but for deliverance from the evil one. All ideas of an apocalyptic battle between God and Satan, all hopes of a judgment on the demonic powers and grace given to the elect, all dreams of a new heaven and a new earth (ideas which are touched on elsewhere in some of the Lord's words) are ignored here; they do not belong to a conversation between God and 'us'.

5. There has been a dispute since ancient times whether the

seventh petition originally belonged to the Lord's Prayer, because it has been handed down only by Matthew and not by Luke. Tertullian already explained (*De Fuga in Persec. 2*): *Respondet clausula interpretans quid sit 'ne nos deducas in tentationem'; hoc est enim: sed devehe a malo.* If the petition thus seems to be superfluous, this supposed superfluity is no reason for separating it from an 'original' Lord's Prayer as a later addition. For it is impossible to demonstrate that such a final 'clausula' could have been added only by the primitive community. This particular solemn duplication at the end, which in fact runs parallel to other sayings of the Lord, and is based on a rich Old Testament and Jewish tradition, could equally well be a sign of 'authenticity'. We will have more to say about this later.

The double conclusion suggests one final consideration: just as the two petitions at the end of the prayer are closely connected, so too are those at the beginning, though not perhaps so closely. Now if the fifth petition corresponds in position and content to the third, and the sixth to the second, it seems likely that here, too, we should assume a link with the first petition. Both petitions differ from the rest in being more strongly influenced by the language and thought of the Old Testament. There is also no doubt that in the Old Testament in particular the hallowing of the divine name implies the conquest of God's enemies and the deliverance of God's people (*Ecclus.* 36.4): 'As in us thou hast been sanctified before them, so in them be thou magnified before us.' There the foreign nations are the 'adversary and the enemy' (36.7); the petition in the Lord's Prayer differs from the Jewish prayer in that the historical opponents of the nation vanish, and the community of those who pray is confronted only with the one 'enemy and adversary', 'the evil one', with his hostile power. But this makes the parallel between the first and last petitions all the more impressive; the first leads to the highest being of the holy God, the last into the depths of the abyss of the evil one, and from the name of God, who is the personification of 'good', the sweep of the prayer spreads over to his supreme adversary, already overcome, the embodiment of 'evil'.

X   Thine is the Kingdom

1. In many manuscripts the Lord's Prayer ends with a three-membered doxology. This first occurs in Codex Basiliensis (E) (07 Gregory), a Byzantine type of text, and Codex Regius (L) (019 Gregory), an Egyptian type of text, but it is missing in all the earliest uncials, some of the Old Latin manuscripts, and the Vulgate. The earliest exegetes of the Lord's Prayer, from Origen via Gregory of Nyssa to Maximus the Confessor, and from Tertullian onwards, also end their commentaries with the seventh petition; in addition, the following scholion occurs in many codices: ' "For thine is the kingdom etc." up to the Amen is missing in some MSS.' It is therefore certain that this doxology did not occur in the earliest textual witnesses, and that it is not original in the First and Third Gospels.[22]

The earliest literary evidence for a doxology is in the Didache (8.2*f*.), which ends the Lord's Prayer with the words, 'For thine is the power and the glory for ever' (without an Amen), and adds, 'Pray thus three times a day.' Like this addition (it is the duty of every pious Jew to pray three times a day) the doxology derives from the practice of Jewish daily prayer—each petition of the Eighteen Benedictions ends with a brief doxology. The doxology in the Didache is still two-membered: there are also (with a single one-membered exception) two-membered conclusions to the eucharistic prayers which immediately follow the text of the Lord's Prayer. The prayers over the bread and after the Eucharist end like the Lord's Prayer, but that over the cup has the form, 'To thee be glory (honour) for ever'. But these two examples already presuppose another petition, that God will gather his *ecclesia* from the ends of the earth into his kingdom. The first to know of the brief hymn with an 'Amen' is Tatian (according to von Soden): 'For thine is the kingdom and the power and the glory for ever, Amen.' The Syriac versions also seem to have known the Lord's Prayer with a final doxology: the *Curetonian* has only 'For thine is the kingdom and the glory' and expands the simple αἰῶνας into αἰῶνας τῶν αἰώνων; *Sinaiticus* seems to have anticipated it in this. Thus we may term the doxology a gift of the Syrian Church, whence it came into general Church use.

Alongside this Syrian form, other, shorter, forms persist for a long while in other regions. Some of the Old Latin versions have the simple text *tibi virtus;* on an Egyptian amulet of the sixth century (BGU no. 954) we find, 'Thine is the glory', and for a long time the Lord's Prayer was used by the Church without a doxology. In the ancient Greek liturgies the closing doxology is still separate from the Lord's Prayer. The liturgy of St. James, like the liturgy of St. Mark, ordains that the congregation is to say the Lord's Prayer at the celebration of the Eucharist; after the expanded seventh petition, the priest first of all prays secretly; then, in a loud voice, the triumphant doxology follows and the congregation answers 'Amen'. Even today the doxology is not said in the Lutheran eucharistic liturgy, following the Roman Missal, which similarly has the Lord's Prayer without a hymnic ending. The doxology was later brought into general use by the Apostolic Constitutions (VII 24, Lagarde).

2. Since Origen's great commentary on the Lord's Prayer, this sentence has been called a 'doxology'; it thus takes its place among those stereotyped sentences which are in some way meant to praise God, and which derive from the liturgical usage of Judaism, in the temple, in the synagogue or in domestic ceremonies. It is not unimportant for us to recognize their various

characteristics, so that we can see what is special about this particular one.

We can distinguish three different forms of the doxology current in the Old Testament and in Judaism, and these again vary considerably among each other. The most important and most common one includes a verb and begins with the words, 'Blessed be (is) God (or his name etc.)'. God is usually referred to in the third person and not directly; it was only the 'men of the great synagogue', who, after the destruction of Jerusalem, ordained that the doxology should be spoken in the form, 'Blessed be thou, who . . .' Thus each petition of the Eighteen Benedictions ends with this form of doxology; there are only two late examples of it in the Old Testament, in *Ps.* 119.12 and *I Chron.* 29.10. The subject of the doxology often varies: 'His name' or 'The name of his glorious kingdom' can replace 'God' or 'Lord'. The priests responded in this form whenever the High Priest spoke the holy name in the liturgy for the Day of Atonement. According to a *baraitha* on *p. Berak.* x 14.*fol.*9c, each prayer in the temple ended, 'Blessed be the name of his holy kingdom for ever and ever', and this conclusion took the place of the more usual 'Amen'. The frequency with which an 'Amen' was also added to this doxology can be seen, say, in *Ps.* 106.48, 'Blessed be the Lord, the God of Israel, from everlasting to everlasting! And let all the people say, "Amen".' Often, though not always, a note of time is added in one of a number of forms. That most frequently used in the Greek Bible is εἰς τὸν αἰῶνα (for ever). It is so stereotyped that it even occurs on three Aramaic inscriptions in Palmyra (A.D. 55) in the form, 'Blessed be his name for ever'.[23]

An active doxology is as widespread as the passive one; it runs, briefly: 'Praise the Lord, Hallelujah.' It tends to be expanded by variations to the verb or additions to the object, but the short form is preserved alongside all the elaborations and is even kept in the original language in the New Testament, evidence that this Hallelujah was used antiphonally in the liturgy (*Rev.* 19.1-6). This invitation to praise tends to be embellished by a series of synonyms as, for example, in *Ps. 29.1f.*:

> Ascribe to the Lord glory and strength,
> Ascribe to the Lord the glory of his name.

The same purpose, a richer song of praise, is also served by the stereotyped sentences which elevate the brief imperative into the more solemn fullness of the passive doxology, as for example, in *Ps.* 118.29 (LXX):

> O give thanks to the Lord, for he is good;
> For his steadfast love endures for ever!

Both elements, the parataxis and the introduction of a reason for the praise, are not without significance for the Lord's Prayer.

An adjectival form of the doxology is often associated with the verbal form, as, for example, in *I Chron.* 16.23f.:

> Sing to the Lord, all the earth!
> Tell of his salvation from day to day . . .
> For great is the Lord, and greatly to be praised,
> and he is to be held in awe above all gods.

In the New Testament, this form is used above all in the Revelation of St. John (4.11): 'Worthy art thou to receive glory and honour and power.' The Old Testament version is not unimportant, because it, too, often occurs with a ὅτι clause: the New Testament one is equally so because it, too, has a series of synonyms.

The most significant form of the doxology for us is the one where the noun is used. This again has numerous variations. An acclamatory form, which puts the word of praise first, and the subject of the praise second, occurs at the beginning of the angel's salutation (*Luke* 2.14) and in the martyrs' praise (*Rev.* 7.10): 'Salvation belongs to our God who sits upon the throne, and to the Lamb!' There is no evidence of it in the Old Testament and in Jewish writings, which highlights its presence in the earliest Christian literature all the more.

Another form, consisting of four elements, is more important: first comes the designation of God, in the dative; then mention of the praise itself, either in one word or in several, in the nominative, then a note of time, and finally a concluding 'Amen'. It is a characteristic of this form that either the series of nominatives is multiplied or the note of time is considerably elaborated. There are already the beginnings of this form in the Old Testament, e.g. in *Ps.* 29.1; 96.7; 104.31; *I Chron.* 16.27; only in Judaism does it seem to have become more common and more popular. There is a first example of what has often been taken as the model for our doxology only in *I Chron.* 29.10*f.*; before the whole people, David gives thanks with the words, 'Blessed art thou, O Lord, the God of Israel our Father (so LXX), for ever and ever. Thine, O Lord, is the greatness, and the power, and the glory, and the victory, and the majesty.' *Targum Jer.* i *Ex.* 15.18 gives this version of the thanksgiving with which Moses' song of victory ends: 'His is the kingdom (*malkūtā*) for ever; his it is and remains for all eternity.' *Targ. Jer.* 10.7 has, 'Thine is the kingdom' (*malkūtā*), and the Hebrew prayer *'Alēnū* ends with the words, 'Thine is the kingdom, and from eternity to eternity thou art in glory'. So with frequent variations of detail this doxology occurs abundantly in the New Testament and in the Apostolic Fathers. Its most simple form, which, in accordance with Aramaic usage, never has a copula, is that of Paul: 'To him be glory for ever, Amen.' (*Rom.* 11.36, also with a relative pronoun at the beginning, *Gal.* 1.5; *II Tim.* 4.18; *Heb.* 13.21; *Did.* 9.2,3; *I Clem.* 20.2; 38.4; 43.6; 45.7; 50.7). It is mostly addressed to God, but also to Christ, as, say, in *II Tim.* 4.18; *II Pet.* 3.18; *Rev.* 1.6; *Mart. Pol.* 21.1; often Christ is the one through whom the praise is given, as in *Rom.* 16.27; *Jude* 25; *Did.* 9.4; *I Clem.* 58.12; 61.3; 64; 65; sometimes it already has a trinitarian form, the oldest examples of which are *Mart. Pol.* 14.2; 20.2. This simple thanksgiving is only attested on Christian soil; the more elaborate form, which was more frequent in Judaism, is developed above all in the Revelation of St. John (5.13; 7.12) and *I Clem.* 64.

This doxology in noun form is usually followed by an Amen, a clear sign that it was not a stereotyped liturgical formula but a living and independent part of the service. It will have been spoken or sung by the cantor, and the congregation will have made the praise its own in the final 'Amen'. There is, however, the possibility of another division: in the heavenly liturgies of the Revelation of St. John, 'every creature in heaven and on earth and under the earth and in the sea, and all therein, said, "To him who sits upon the throne and to the Lamb be blessing and honour and glory and might for ever and ever". And the four living creatures said, "Amen", and the elders fell down and worshipped' (5.13f.). Such instances seem to reflect the liturgy of the synagogue, and it is likely that this doxology has the same origin.

Perhaps it is even possible to define its origin more exactly. No later or even contemporaneous Primitive Christian doxology puts the address to God first, in the genitive; they all have it in the dative. This was perhaps usual particularly in Aramaic speaking regions. Thus the LXX already renders *Ps.* 3.8, 'Of the Lord (is) deliverance', in the Psalms of Solomon (11.9) we have, 'Of the Lord is mercy upon Israel for ever and ever' (similarly 9.11 and 12.6), and this is particularly frequent in the Aramaic doxologies of the Targums. True, the Revelation of St. John also has at its climax the joyful recognition (11.15), 'The kingdom of the world has become the kingdom of our Lord and of his Christ' (similarly 12.10), but it is also clear that here all the joy over the fulfilment of eschatological hopes is expressed in the verb. There are no other examples, so we may assume that this derives from an Aramaic-speaking environment. On the other hand, however, the 'is', however much it may be accentuated now, is unusual in Aramaic doxologies; it can only be regarded as an elaboration which bears strong marks of Greek terminology. So we must look for the origin of this doxology in a district where both languages were spoken, and this direction is also supported by the testimony of the earliest examples, which broadly point to Syria. We will soon come across still further evidence.

3. At first sight, it must seem surprising that our doxology begins with the word 'for'. Does not a doxology need *to be given* an explanation, rather than *to give one*? The question shows first of all that this sentence is not meant to be, and cannot be an explicit doxology; what is said there provides a reason and a support for the petitions of the Lord's Prayer. It is concerned with the person who is praised, and not with the way in which he is praised. Everything that has been prayed for lies in God's hand, and he has the power to accomplish it, for 'thine is the kingdom'. In this way, a bridge is built between prayer and praise, but it only shows why the praise has been inserted and not why it should give a reason for the prayer, for this bridge is itself the first thing to supply a reason. But is there any need for such a connection? The last petition with which the sentence is connected in syntax by the 'for' seems to contain a clear occasion for prayer of this kind. The despairing plea for deliverance is answered by the thanksgiving that all power and glory is not of the evil one, but of God. Therefore Chrysostom already says, 'If the kingdom is his, no one need fear, for the adversary is nothing and he takes the glory for himself.'

Some words of St. Paul also seem to support this association of clauses. In Gal. 1.4f., Paul expresses the same thought: 'To deliver us from the present evil age, according to the will of our God and Father', and immediately continues, 'to whom be the glory for ever and ever, Amen.' Similarly, *II Tim.* 4.18 runs: 'The Lord will rescue me from every evil and save me for his heavenly kingdom. To him be the glory for ever and ever. Amen.' But these passages also show that while the thanksgiving is closely and almost necessarily connected with the petition for deliverance, there is no expression of the ideas which connect the two; they explain the fact, but not the reason. Perhaps we ought not to look for a particular point of reference for this γάρ; it occurs not only here, at the end of the Lord's Prayer, but also in the eucharistic prayers of the Didache (9.4; 10.5), and often at the end of Jewish prayers, where a 'Praise him' or a 'Praised be he' is to be supplied almost as a matter of course. Thus the Hebrew '*Alēnū* prayer, which has already been mentioned, ends with the words, 'For thine is the kingdom'. We might even suppose that the Aramaic *dī* would correspond to the Greek γάρ; its function is not only explanatory, but also affirmative, i.e. 'Yes, truly'. This would be a further indication that this doxology, too, derives from an Aramaic environment.

A doxology characteristically begins its description of God in a joyful and impressive mood, 'Thine is the kingdom!', and it is characteristic of the Lord's Prayer that despite the frequency with which it has spoken of what belongs to God and what is his due it has nowhere shown signs of this mood. The emphasis evokes a contrast: the kingdom is not the evil one's but 'thine alone', and the contrast is the thought that these other powers still prevent and limit God's sole power. Here is a first subtle difference between praise and prayer. The petitions of the Lord's Prayer are full of the fact that before God's infinite superiority and 'our' hiddenness in him all resistance has already been overcome. True, there are still sins, temptation, the evil one, but God forgives sins, preserves from temptation and delivers from the evil one; all these rebellious powers are merely the material in which the Father's action is revealed, but because of this they are no longer of independent significance, so that it would become necessary to contrast God's kingdom and power and glory with them. Where God is exalted in a *soli Deo gloria*, the suppliant is still surrounded by the powers of this world, so that his only refuge is with the one who can deliver him from these powers. At the same time, however, the eschatological assurance of the first three petitions has vanished. There is here, one might say, a purely Old Testament idea, in which there is as yet no sign of a New Testament fulfilment.

The 'thine' which stands at the beginning of the doxology suggests a second theme. It is certainly a possessive genitive, i.e. it speaks clearly and surely of what is, and always has been, God's, and is distinguished in this way from the dative which is usual in doxologies using the noun form, which shows more plainly what God is now to make his own. The word 'is' points in the same direction; it distinguishes this doxology from the Aramaic ones, which never have a copula, and it is full of Greek linguistic sensibility. The Aramaic doxologies are composed differently, sometimes in the indicative as a statement or a proclamation, sometimes in the optative as a wish or a petition or an act of praise. The optative version is very rare in ancient times; it does not occur anywhere in the New Testament, and the first example in Christian literature is *I Clem.* 32.4. The 'is' here therefore has a special accent, repeating what has already been suggested by the 'thine': the kingdom is not the evil one's, but God's, and he remains 'king in glory' despite all attempts of the evil one to establish his own kingdom. At the same time, however, there is a new difference in the attitude of the prayer here. For this sense is indeed justified if it is meant to show the contrast between God's kingdom and the powers of the world (whether by celebrating its infinite superiority or affirming its sole reality); but what we have here is not such a testimony, but a prayer, not about the powers of the evil one but about the one God and Father.

So what does the expression 'Thine is the kingdom' mean in this conversation? In the Old Testament, the person who prays usually witnesses God's kingdom and power to the world in a doxology framed in the indicative; he knows from the fact of creation or from the history of his people that God alone has the power and glory. In the New Testament, he confesses before God, and when he bears witness, his witness is not 'Thine is the kingdom', but, 'The kingdom of God has come'. In the Old Testament this 'is' speaks of a reality which rests solely in God; in the New Testament the 'has come' also speaks of an eschatological reality which is now inaugurated.

This inner distinction becomes still clearer if we look more closely at the three nouns in the doxology. A doxology which is absorbed in the one idea of praise, however many actual words of praise there may be, will naturally understand the three nouns as the elaboration of the one concept *basileia*. The first of the nouns then speaks of God's rank and his office, the second of the characteristic which makes his kingdom possible, and the third of the nature of his royal activity; the internal relationship between the three is clearly anticipated in an Old Testament hymn (*Ps. 24.8ff.*):

> Who is the King of glory?
> The Lord, strong and mighty,
> The Lord, mighty in battle!. . . .
> The Lord of hosts, he is the King of glory!

But we have seen that the three words first appeared almost as a development of the two-membered formula of the Didache, 'power and glory', and that of the Curetonian Syriac, 'kingdom and power'; it is therefore advisable to consider the last two terms first.

Luther translated the word *doxa* as 'glory', not as 'honour', for the word 'is' suggests something which is not given to God from men, but belongs to him in himself. It is frequent for Jewish theology to speak of God's power and glory; when he reveals himself, he does so in power and glory. *Psalm 63.2* already says, 'So I have looked upon thee in the sanctuary, beholding thy power and glory.' In *Job 40.9f.*, God says to the sufferer:

> Have you an arm like God,
> and can you thunder with a voice like his?
> Deck yourself with majesty and dignity;
> clothe yourself with glory and splendour.

Psalm 145.10ff. sings,

> All thy works shall give thanks to thee, O Lord,
> and all thy saints shall bless thee!
> They shall speak of the glory of thy kingdom,
> and tell of thy power,
> to make known to the sons of men thy mighty deeds,
> and the glorious splendour of thy kingdom.

For the Wisdom of Solomon (13.3*f.*), this manifestation of the nature of God in power and glory can be seen in the works of creation, and Paul repeats this statement of a natural theology in *Rom.* 1.20*f.*: 'God's invisible nature, namely, his eternal power and deity, has been clearly perceived in the things that have been made'; in 1.23 he then interprets this as the 'glory of the immortal God'. The two words also have a close linguistic connection, for both the Hebrew *kābōd* and the Greek *doxa* have twin meanings of 'power' and 'glory'. With so traditional and widespread a view, it is clear that in the New Testament, too, 'power and glory' will often be named together and side by side. 'The Son of Man will come on the clouds of heaven with power and great glory' (*Matt.* 24.30 *par.*). In *I Cor.* 15.43, Paul writes: 'It is sown in dishonour, it is raised in glory. It is sown in weakness, it is raised in power.' So the elect should recognize 'what are the riches of his glorious inheritance in the saints, and what is the immeasurable greatness of his power in us who believe' (*Eph.* 1.18*f.*), and should pray that God will grant us 'to be strengthened with might according to the riches of his glory' (*Eph.* 3.16). Paul therefore asks that the congregation at Colossae 'may be strengthened with all power, according to his glorious might' (*Col.* 1.11). The frequent occurrence of these two terms, together with others, in the Revelation of St. John, is simply a sign of the firm foundation of this Old Testament heritage. The declaration that God reveals himself in power and glory still lives on here in its old strength; when in ch. 15 the victory song of the martyrs rings out and the temple is opened,

> the temple was filled with smoke
> from the glory of God and from his power (15.8).

So these two concepts are well attested and firmly established in the thoughts and words of both Old and New Testaments. But one difference is noticeable: wherever they appear in the New Testament, they are connected with God's eschatological revelation; here, however, this eschatological sign is missing. Elsewhere it is heavenly choirs which sing such praise, and the faithful can only hope that God will give them a share in his glory; here, on the other hand, it is precisely those that pray, oppressed with guilt, temptation and the evil one, who offer this praise to God, and the deeper idea, that God 'manifests himself in the flesh', eschatologically, has vanished completely.

Here, too, a return has been made to the Old Testament background.

The word *basileia* also fits well into this group of concepts. Of course, if 'power and glory' describe the way in which God works in revealing himself, *basileia* here does not mean the order which God will bring about, or even the house and kingdom into which he will gather those who pray, but it means the function of kingly rule, the *malkūtā*, in the traditional Jewish sense. Once again, the Old Testament characteristics of this doxology are clear, and the simplest and most pertinent paraphrase of the meaning of the concept would be 'Thou art king for ever' (*Ps.* 9.7 etc.), as it frequently occurs in the Old Testament. It is obvious how this particular concept attached itself to the other two. The idea of power and glory has already been associated with that of the kingdom on a number of occasions, 'The Lord of Hosts, he is the King of Glory!' (*Ps.* 24.10). It is at the same time a firm Jewish custom not to omit a reference to the kingdom of God at the close of a prayer, though the evidence for this custom is only late. R. Johanan (died 279 A.D.) said, 'A benediction in which the kingdom of God is not mentioned is no benediction'. This expresses a profound Old Testament idea, as the special character of Old Testament religion develops in this concept of the kingdom of God. That the one God of all nations is the God of Israel and the God of their history and its own, that the people chosen by him has a clear divine commission to fulfil in this history, that the guidance of God and the history of the people develop into the idea of an all-embracing final kingdom of God—all this, growing slowly and changing often, is through all the generations of Israelite and Jewish history the firm, particular ground on which the faith and life, pride and humility, fortune and misfortune, of the people rests. All this is also the ultimate end of all history and life, and is still attested in some of the statements of the New Testament: 'It has become the kingdom of our God and of his Christ', exults St. John the Divine (11.15). But here there is no expression of the more profound message of the gospels, which elevates this *basileia* to the order appointed for believers alone through which 'Our Father in heaven' comes near in inconceivable greatness and imminence.

4. We need not say much about the last words of the doxology. It is not wholly unimportant that our Gospels have the word αἰών and the formula εἰς τὸν αἰῶνα only in the singular (the one exception, *Luke* 1.33, is an Old Testament quotation); the solemnity which the plural implies is still strange to them, and the original sense of the singular has not yet disappeared. There is no difference between the meaning of the plural formula, which is often attested after Deutero-Isaiah, and even occurs in some texts of the present doxology, and that of the singular; it means long, measureless time, and contains the idea that one age follows another in a series beyond human imagining, of which only God can conceive. Thus eternity is understood as a long sequence of time. The article seems to put a limit to this sequence, perhaps to avoid the idea of infinity, but as the formula does not have an article in Hebrew and Aramaic we should not attach any importance to the presence of a definite article. It is deeply significant that the Old Testament has included no idea of time corresponding to its idea of God, whom it elevates above all human understanding; he remains rooted in 'the ages' and thus in history as the true sphere of his work, and is thus, despite all his distance and exaltation, the God who is near to 'the ages'. The implications of the concept of eternity are summed up, filled out and completed in the idea of the eschatological 'age'. The profound opposition and the even more profound union between this eschatological time and historical time, both of which are shown by the Gospel, has not vanished without trace in this formula. God's sublimity stands above all ages, and in them his kingdom works with power and glory.

The 'Amen' which follows this formula is widespread in the Old Testament and in Judaism as an expression of the speaker's endorsement of a statement and of the obligations which he takes upon himself, and it is so common in doxologies of the

noun form that it is not surprising to find it here, especially
as there is evidence of its inclusion in the Primitive Christian
liturgy in the Revelation of St. John. As it was used not in the
temple but in the synagogue, it also confirms that this form of
praise derives from the synagogue liturgy. Another feature is
still more important; this 'Amen' always endorses what someone
else has said or confessed; the occasional conclusion of a person's
own prayers with a joyful 'Amen', as, say, in *Tobit* 8.7f., is
simply the exception that proves the rule. So the doxology has
the character of an independent liturgical hymn; someone
leads off with it, and a second person answers 'Amen'. Between
the end of the prayer and the beginning of the doxology, as
between the end of the doxology and the 'Amen', there is a
marked liturgical pause.

5. The doxology expresses a certain general understanding of
the Lord's Prayer. It is not a prayer which the individual says
in his closet; it is the prayer of the congregation at its worship.
The doxology underlines the 'we', of which the second half of
the prayer is so full, with a hymn of praise, although it never
speaks of 'us', but seems to return to the style of the first half
of the prayer, with the stress on the 'thine'. That does not
mean that this doxology could have been spoken only at a service
(we have Jewish evidence that the doxology from *I Chron.* 29
was also spoken outside the place and times of services, and by
individuals (Billerbeck I, 424)); it means that anyone who begins
this doxology, wherever he begins it, knows that he is a member
of the community which is called to serve and to praise God in
every place.

So it was a liturgical need that caused earliest Christianity
to add a doxology at the end of the Lord's Prayer. This merely
reflects a special attitude of the Primitive Christian community,
which, from its first beginnings onwards, 'breaking bread in
their homes, partook of food with glad and generous hearts,
praising God'. When we see how the Lord's Prayer is followed

by eucharistic prayers in the Didache and how these are associated with it through the same doxological sentences, we may assume that the Lord's Prayer was originally used at the celebration of the Eucharist, and that a doxology was added to it for this reason.[24] There may also be a reason intrinsic to the prayer itself for its looking back to the beginning once more before it ends. For it is always remarkable that this prayer, which begins so to speak with the innermost being of God and with awe at his holiness, should end with a mention of the 'evil one' and awe at his fearfulness. The praise of God not only overcomes the awe and the fear; it also includes whoever prays so to speak among the choir of the heavenly hosts who are always praising God, so that here too one of the most profound New Testament ideas becomes reality: everything happens 'to the glory of God the Father'. So at the close of the prayer the doxology seeks to express once again what was already implied at the beginning: Hallowed be thy name! The praise of God transcends all changes of ages and worlds, creation and consummation, and anyone who joins in it has a share in this permanence, because he is himself the voice of this praise. But at the same time there is also a difference from the first petition: the first petition was concerned to put even the hallowing and praising of God's name in his hands and on his lips and humbly to keep silent about anything that spurred the supplicant to such work. Here this deliberate silence is transcended and the praise is sung out loud, as though even God needed 'the praise which men can offer him'.

At this point, the question of the relationship between the doxology and the Lord's Prayer arises once more. It is clear that the doxology is based on the second part of the Lord's Prayer, not on the first. For just as it is characteristically different from the first petition, so too it is perhaps even more clearly different from the second, as the concern of the prayer is not that God is king for ever but that this kingdom shall come near in reality. Behind the doxology stands the question whether God really does have the power and the glory; it was a burning question in the early days of Old Testament faith, but it no longer interests the second petition, which is concerned with something else, whether the time for the coming of God's kingdom is now fulfilled. The same is true of the third petition, for which it is more important that God's holy will should unite heaven and earth than that his heavenly glory should manifest itself so to speak over the earth. Despite all this, the doxology does not realize that in these first petitions those who pray can and may ask God for what he alone disposes and what he alone decides; they speak from a nearness to God for which astonishment and joy at God's kingly power is past and for which God's holy love has become the true basis of human understanding. The doxology sees only the dangers of debts, temptation and evil with which the suppliant is surrounded, and because of them it praises the only foundation which remains for weak and helpless humankind, God's kingdom and his power and his glory. But it does not see that those who pray here are not only the oppressed but also the children of grace, not only sinners before God but also children of God. And the one who has given them this grace is not just the manifest King and Lord, but 'Our Father who art in heaven'. The doxology says nothing about this fatherhood, God's love and his mercy, which transcends all his power and his glory and is the only real basis for it; it comes down from the eschatological heights on which the suppliant, like a second Moses, talks under the cloud with God, and returns to the historical ground on which, like the people, it sees only the smoke of God's power and glory.

With this approach, however, the doxology has stressed another element all the more strongly; it has seen that nothing but the power of God can be a 'shield and buckler' against the powers of this world. In celebrating this power, it celebrates at the same time the unshakeable guarantee of the existence of the community which makes the prayer. The greater the praise of this power which protects and holds together the elect in the history of this world, the firmer the link of the community to this power and among its members. This is the doxology of the growing Church which prepares for its own bitter destiny, and no longer the praise of the praying community, for which the things of this world have vanished before the eschatological nearness of the Father, and for which all that matters is its eschatological destiny and the Father's eschatological holiness.

XI The Lucan Forms of the Lord's Prayer

1. There are only minor variants in the wording of the Lord's Prayer in Matthew, and in Luke, too, the text of the prayer is reasonably well established. It is a well known fact that already Tatian, and later the *koine* recension, have the full Matthaean wording in *Luke* 11; a shorter version, peculiar to Luke, is attested only by the most ancient and most important manuscripts of the Alexandrine (H) and Western groups (w).[25] Their text has only minor differences. As with Matthew, some mss. have the usual aorist form ἐλθέτω in the second petition, others the strong form ἐλθάτω. In the fourth and fifth petitions, the Matthaean text has caused some confusion among the textual evidence. Here too ἀφίεμεν alternates with ἀφίομεν; the phrase παντὶ ὀφείλοντι sometimes has an article, sometimes does not. The phrase with the article may be an echo of the πᾶν τὸ ὀφειλόμενον of *Matt.* 18.34.

The addition of an ἐφ'ἡμᾶς (to us) at the end of the first or the beginning of the second petition in Codex D is remarkable; from here it has found its way into the usage of the Western churches. The addition is usually regarded as an obvious elaboration of the content, or even as a result of the influence of the so-called Marcionite second petition, in which a 'to us' was quite in place. Neither view is quite satisfactory; if the elaboration was so obvious, especially as it could find support in the Lord's words in *Luke* 11.20, it is hard to see why it is found only in this one manuscript, and the same question arises if there is an echo of the Marcionite version here, especially as the variant is evidently

247

older than Marcion. We should also remember that there is important evidence for the Lord's Prayer, as for the account of the Last Supper, not only in the manuscripts, but also in the liturgical usage of the various churches. According to the manuscript evidence, the 'to us' is probably a later addition, but it may conceal an ancient form of the second petition. The point must be discussed in more detail later.

More important than these manuscript variants are the differences between the Lucan and the Matthaean wording which were already mentioned briefly at the beginning of this book. If to begin with we ignore the fact that in Luke the address simply runs 'Father,' without the additional 'our' and 'who art in heaven', and that the third and seventh petitions are missing, only the text of the first, second and sixth petitions is quite identical. The fourth and fifth petitions differ in some small, but not unimportant, features. First, Luke's fourth petition has the present δίδου instead of Matthew's aorist δός. There may be a linguistic reason for the difference, the two being variant renderings of the Aramaic p^eal form hab, but as the same form is also to be presupposed in all the other petitions, and as, moreover, Luke has rendered it consistently in them by the aorist imperative, the present form here is all the more striking. There seems, however, to be a connection between this difference and another one in the same petition; Matthew has 'today', Luke 'daily' (τὸ καθ' ἡμέραν), which gives the present an iterative sense. The Matthaean expression points to an Aramaic yōm hādēn; the Lucan text, on the other hand, indicates not a $b^ekōl$ yōm, as the Syriac versions have, but a $b^eyōmā$. We seem to be able to detect different traditions here in the hypothetical text, and these at the same time bear witness to different ideas about the petition.

The differences in the fifth petition are still greater. If Matthew first wrote τὰ ὀφειλήματα and Luke altered it to ἁμαρτίας, the commoner Greek word has replaced the unfamiliar one; both renderings go back to the same Aramaic ḥayyābēn. Luke, too, presupposes this word, as in the apodosis he retains the metaphor of debts and debtors. So Matthew has given the more faithful translation here and Luke has paraphrased more freely, even at the cost of surrendering the identity of sense and expression between protasis and apodosis.

The differences in the apodosis are still greater, as every word is altered. The Matthaean ὡς καί contrasts with the Lucan καὶ γάρ; there is a similar variant between *Matt.* 20.28, 'Even as (ὥσπερ) the Son of Man came not to be served', and *Mark* 10.45, 'For the Son of Man also (καὶ γάρ) came not to be served'. In both cases we have different renderings of the Aramaic; a *kᵉdī* may have occurred there. The καί of Matthew is an addition here; there was probably no equivalent in Aramaic, and it is often put in Greek without any special significance (cf. Blass ⁹§453,1). The difference between ἡμεῖς and αὐτοί is to be explained in the same way; the subject indicated by the verb form is elaborated in different ways—either is quite possible in Greek—without being specially stressed. There is the same difference between ἀφήκαμεν and ἀφίομεν (or even ἀφίεμεν) as there is in the fourth petition between δός and δίδου; it is to be explained in the same way. The last difference is the most important one: Matthew has τοῖς ὀφειλέταις ἡμῶν, Luke, παντὶ ὀφείλοντι ἡμῖν. In both phrases we should probably presuppose an Aramaic participial form of *ḥōb*, perhaps *leḥayyābēn*; Matthew, as he often does, has rendered it with a noun which preserves the meaning and the imagery quite well, while Luke has kept the participial form, but chosen the verb ὀφείλω which, while it preserves the imagery, has to be given a meaning, 'to sin', which is not attested elsewhere. It is, in fact, impossible to obtain a clear picture from the Lucan text, because ὀφείλω also has the general sense, above all in the New Testament, of 'to be indebted', 'to owe' (see *Rom.* 13.8). The παντί in this context may be a free and emphatic rendering of the Aramaic plural, just as LXX often strengthens the plural with an additional πᾶς (e.g. *Num.* 6.6; 10.34; 14.14; *Deut.* 21.23; *Job* 41.2; *Ps.* 5.6; 9.10 etc.). But it is also possible that the phrase already ran *lᵉkol ḥōbēn* in the Aramaic version which is to be inferred

249

from the Lucan text, though this would destroy the rhythmic sequence of seven syllables which is otherwise observed. It would also indicate that the Aramaic recension of Luke already differed in some places from that of Matthew, as is shown by the fourth petition; this is the only way in which we can understand the great omissions of the third and seventh petitions. In that case we cannot determine the original wording *a priori* from the Greek text; we have rather to begin by establishing the significance of the content of these variants.

2. We will begin with the fourth petition, which is characterized by the iterative sense of the present and the expression 'day by day'. The petition is thus not simply concerned with today, but also embraces, though as vaguely as possible, the course of the coming days. The expression τὸ καθ' ἡμέραν (the article is almost without significance and at most indicates the adverbial character of the expression (Blass⁹ §160)) is delaying and almost suspended; it means less than 'every day' and more than 'this one day', so its meaning would correspond most closely to another phrase which Luke also uses, ἱκαναὶ ἡμέραι. What is meant is the interval over which an experienced man might calculate, not a series of weeks, months or even years. There is no idea of a fixed regularity, for Luke, like the *koine*, also knows the emphatic expression κατὰ πᾶσαν or καθ' ἑκάστην ἡμέραν. In this way, then, the petition looks to a brief, always foreseeable, series of days.[27]

The change in the sense produced by this alteration of the wording is nevertheless considerable. First, the tension between the 'future bread' and the 'today' of Matthew's text is relaxed. ἐπιούσιος can no longer mean 'future' here because the closing phrase 'day by day' already embraces the future course of days; it can hardly even continue to describe the eschatological, sacred character which the bread has in this petition, as in the rest of Jesus' preaching; it simply means something objective that can be grasped by human thought, say, the bread that we need, which comes to us from God. For if Luke still understood the bread as eschatological bread, it would be impossible to pray for it over a series of days. The eschatological bread is final, once for all, and before it the days which are still to come fuse into a single 'today'. But if that is so, this Lucan petition speaks of the bread that we need for the nourishment of our body. We may therefore assume that even the Lucan tradition did not understand the word ἐπιούσιος in the full sense at which it darkly hints.

Of course, this still does not explain the phrase 'day by day'. It is all the more remarkable, as Jesus elsewhere forbids concern for other days. The view that the prohibition and the prayer are related in that the prohibition forbids concern whereas the prayer lays all concern in God's hands, thereby satisfying the prohibition, is little help. In that case it would be unnecessary to speak of the bread which God is to give us daily; it would be enough that each day had its own prayer for the bread. So there is a difference here which cannot be explained for reasons of language or content; it can only be derived from a tradition other than that of Matthew. It is probably secondary in comparison with Matthew's significant 'today'; what reasons can there be for an alteration of this kind?

We might suppose that for Luke the Lord's Prayer was no longer the daily prayer of the community of disciples which was used especially at the celebration of the common meal, perhaps because this meal was no longer held daily, whereas the Lord's Prayer was to be spoken daily. In that case, those who prayed would form a looser community, and the 'we' would have to be interpreted in the sense of 'each of us', as is also required by the other understanding of ἐπιούσιος. A more strongly individualistic feature would then find its way into the petition, which hitherto had been *the* petition of the community of brothers before God. But this explanation would hardly be satisfactory by itself; it would raise a new question rather than give a definite answer. So another hypothesis seems more likely, which can perhaps clarify the problem in conjunction with the first one: to limit the prayer for bread to 'today' corresponds to the eschatological boldness of Jesus, but it is at the same time completely alien to the 'normal' piety of Judaism. There, indeed, God is praised for feeding man and beast every morning, for giving food to all living things in due season (*Ps.* 145.15*f.*). *Proverbs* 30.8 prays, 'Give me neither poverty nor riches; feed me with the food that is needful for me', and in this 'food that is needful for me' there is also the hint that God should continue to give the bread. Now the Lucan petition probably understood the word ἐπιούσιος in the sense of this Old Testament saying, as we have seen; so the 'day by day' marks a return to more familiar Jewish views. Just as a pious Jew prays to God for what he needs for his life, so 'we' pray here that God may give us daily the bread that we need. Thus it finally transpires that this 'we' means only 'each individual of us', and the idea of brotherly fellowship which is implied in the expression 'our future bread' has retreated behind the 'daily' need. Consequently the Lucan version of the fourth petition is demonstrated to be secondary in comparison with that of Matthew.

The fifth petition, too, takes up more familiar words and ideas in praying 'Forgive us our sins'. It uses the same words as some prayers in the Psalter; its hopes are on the God who, in the words of *Ex.* 34.6*f.*, 'is merciful and gracious, forgiving iniquity and transgression and sin'. This does not exclude the fact that behind these words there is also the deep view contained in the Matthaean metaphor of debts (it is expressed clearly enough in such well-known parables as that of the Prodigal Son), but it is not hinted at in the words of the protasis. The apodosis is altered still more radically; we can no longer say that both protasis and apodosis merely reflect in different ways the link between 'us' and God which is expressed in the almost non-committal 'as'. Here the apodosis is quite clearly a reason, and if it did not have this function equally clearly in the hypothetical Aramaic original, it does so in the Greek translation and thus bears witness to the oldest understanding in the circle which made the translation. Once again this giving of a reason marks a return to more usual ideas: these Lucan words contain the same ideas as some rabbinic sayings, touched on earlier, which counsel mercy towards neighbours so that God too will show himself merciful, and the teaching of Jesus Sirach, 'Forgive your neighbour the wrong he has done, and then your sins will be pardoned when you pray' (28.2).

The second alteration, however, is still more characteristic: we have ἀφίομεν and not ἀφήκαμεν as in Matthew. So the present of the apodosis is contrasted with the aorist of the protasis; the former speaks of a permanent or repeated action, the latter of something which is done once for all. True, the attempt is sometimes made to neutralize this difference by suggesting that the aorist imperative, which also occurs chiefly in Luke, can have a gnomic significance. But this view, while possible in itself, is unjustified here, as only the fourth petition has a present, whereas all the rest have aorists. The aorist must therefore have a once-for-all sense everywhere, which is stressed even more strongly by the one present. Similarly, the present 'we forgive' has occasionally been taken as a future, but this possibility is excluded by the sense, as only the achievement of the act of forgiveness and not the promise to forgive another can lay the foundation for the one prayer for forgiveness. 'First be reconciled with your brother' (*Matt.* 5.24) also applies to this petition. But in that case, what is the significance of the contrast between the aorist 'forgive' and the present 'we forgive'? First, there is a temporal difference; the aorist indicates God's eschatological act which frees those who pray from the burden of their sins once and for all, the present indicates a human act which is repeated and is to be repeated in this age, the act of the man who forgives the debtor his sins. The content of the 'as' is also defined more closely in the light of this distinction: because we forgive everyone who is indebted to us while we live in this age, we pray: 'Forgive us our sins once and for all'. This attention to the last day does not mean that, say, the eschatological expectation is no longer as urgent as in the days of Jesus (for this last day can even be tomorrow), but that the eschatological event which it ushers in is also different from what fills the life of the suppliant in this transitory age. This life, like that of the pious Jew, prepares for the approaching day of judgment when God 'will render to every man according to his works' (*Rom*. 2.6).

If this alteration already indicates the duty which each person who prays has before his God, the last makes this particularizing trait still stronger: '*Everyone* who is indebted to us'. For in speaking of the individual who 'trespasses' against 'us', it also interprets this 'us' as a sum of individuals who forgive one another whenever anyone incurs a debt. What in the fourth petition was only an uncertain supposition is expressed more clearly here; in the fourth petition it is a matter of the bread which each single one of us needs for his life; here it is the act which each individual needs for his salvation, and to which he is obliged and inclined *vis-à-vis* his debtor. We may also find this tendency hinted at in the fact that Luke expands the subject of the sentence with αὐτοί, Matthew with ἡμεῖς. The latter has included the four-fold echo of the 'we' in the petition and has thus fused the 'we' before God and 'our debtors' into a unity; in Luke it is looser. True, the patterns of thought which are expressed in Matthew have not vanished; even for Luke the 'we' are those who forgive with God's authority and who pray to God for forgiveness, but the power of forgiveness is here regarded more as a duty to forgive and has thus become the task of the individual. The abandonment of the parallelism between the protasis and the apodosis is so to speak a sign of this.

The features which we have discussed suggest that the minor linguistic differences of the Lucan petitions do not rest on purely terminological or stylistic foundations but are determined by a rather different approach to the whole prayer. We must go still more closely into the reasons for them. The Lucan Lord's Prayer does not have the finely-judged equilibrium of form and content that we find in the Matthaean version. In Matthew, there are three petitions referring to God and three to the needs of those who pray, and between these two halves there is the fourth petition as a bridge, transforming human need into divine grace.

It no longer occupies a middle position in Luke; here, only the first two petitions speak of God's concerns, and the last three express the burdens and dangers which oppress the person who prays. If we were to allow that the reading 'Thy kingdom come to us' had an original place here, the second petition, too, would refer to 'our' situation and longing, and by being isolated, the first would come still nearer to the doxological formulas which are usual in Jewish prayers. This possibility is to be considered only because it fits in well with the different attitude of the other petitions. But even if the first two petitions refer solely to God and do not touch on the human situation, there are still three petitions which speak of the distress and needs of the suppliant. Here, then, is the greater weight, the real content of the prayer. This extra emphasis on human affairs is no artificial one: what petition could correspond more closely to such a trend than Matthew's third, which Luke also knows in another place (22.42), the formulation of which, 'as in heaven, so on earth', matches what Luke intends? Therefore the omission of the third and the seventh petitions does not seem to be fortuitous or arbitrary, but to point rather to a special view and tradition which is taken over by this Lucan form. We can best recognize its peculiar characteristics if we look at the features which describe the community of those who pray.

Is it a community at all? The lines which in Matthew give it a certain close-knit unity do not appear here, at least not to the same extent. True, here too the suppliants may know themselves to be the children of their Father, but he no longer belongs so to speak to them alone; others, too, can call him 'Father', and they do so. The proprietary exclusiveness, '*Our* Father', has been done away with, and any child comes almost in his own right to his Father and prays to him for his concerns; only the 'we' in the following petitions seems to suggest that he is one child among others. The idea that the 'we' are historically or eschatologically different from others even in the present age is thus still more remote in Matthew, for it is also possible to make this prayer if the relationships and circumstances under which the suppliant lives remain unbroken. Furthermore, the 'we' are the poor, who pray for their daily bread. Luke has contrasted the Lord's Prayer with the prayer of John's disciples who have taken over the practice of fasting from their master as a necessary work, and one that pleases God (11.1 and 5.33). For them, a petition for daily bread is strange; here, the Father's love is experienced in the fact that he gives us daily bread—and this experience, which we find most often alongside God's gracious work of forgiving our sins, is thus more important than all the experiences of the 'mighty acts of God' (*Acts* 2.11) which the history of the people has known since its beginning. Then the distress of poverty and the certainty that God feeds the poor and the hungry also underlines this petition. Nevertheless, the distress is not so strong that it completely occupies the thoughts and feelings of those who pray; they know how to be content with the most modest sustenance in asking God to give them their bread daily. It is, in other words, a poverty of the faithful that is expressed in this petition.

Alongside poverty, the first and most important element that characterizes these suppliants, we find as a second element the petition for the forgiveness of sins. Sin estranges children from their Father; they could not acknowledge him if they did not know that he forgave them their sins. So two elements determine the whole of their earthly life, one physical and one spiritual, one natural and one of moral necessity; only the petitions which look towards the day of the divine consummation go beyond this. At this very point, the poverty of the faithful is given a definite purpose and an imminent end: those who pray look forward to the day when God's kingdom comes and God's name is hallowed. The only divine light on their earthly poverty is the eschatological hope which is guaranteed by the name 'Father', and the daily grace with which God feeds the hungry. In all this, the life and thought of these suppliants still remains within the limits of the traditional outlook of the poor.

Only one feature of the fifth petition seems to go further; the assurance that 'we ourselves forgive every one who is indebted to us' imposes an obligation which is closely connected with the particular characteristics of St. Luke's Gospel. In Matthew's Sermon on the Mount, Jesus' command runs: 'You, therefore, must be perfect, as your heavenly Father is perfect' (5.48); in Luke's 'Sermon on the Plain' it runs, 'Be merciful, even as your Father is merciful' (6.36). According to the fifth petition, this duty of mercy towards each debtor also guides the life and action of those who pray. It is presupposed here that their present transitory existence is exposed to many temptations and that all have to suffer under the transgression of each individual. But all these trespasses are still the actions of individuals against individuals; they include in themselves the fact that those who pray are still involved in their previous association with their people and their country, and if they do not perhaps participate directly in its life, they are still nevertheless not divorced from it, any more than Jesus, too, was divorced from the times in which he lived and worked. As those who are always merciful and yet for that reason need the mercy of God, as those who are poor, yet satisfied daily by God, they continue their tranquil earthly course, different from the rest of their people, but not separate from them; as those who are often tempted and yet forgiven, they still go on towards the imminent day when the kingdom of God will come to them and God's forgiving mercy will be their own.

In this way we can discover one last feature of this picture: the earthly day that still goes on and the already approaching day of God are still separate, as the earth is separate from the heavens; those who pray are still not the holy eschatological community which is also gathered round God's table on this very day; it still does not act towards its debtors with the eschatological grace of God, but remains more closely bound up with life on earth in duty and in favour. Its members are the called, but not yet the elect.

So, too, from the objective side it becomes clear that a different view and therefore a different community tradition from that of Matthew underlies the Lucan form of the Lord's Prayer. All

differences seem equally to derive from this one basis; it is therefore impossible to explain them on purely literary grounds; they
are primarily evidence of changes in the eschatological approach
in different groups of communities. Later, we must consider the
historical background which is thus indicated.

3. The phrase ἐφ'ἡμᾶς is inserted between the first and second
petitions in the *Codex Bezae* (D), so that linguistically it can
belong to either; the Latin text of the Codex doubtless took
it with the first petition in translating it; *Sanctificetur nomen tuum
super nos;* the usual view in Western Christianity took it with
the second petition, 'Thy kingdom come to us', as, say, in
Zwingli or in the Bishop's Book of 1537. What is the significance
of the addition?

If we include the 'to us' in the first petition, we have an
association which is attested nowhere else in the Greek Bible.
True, it speaks of sanctification in (ἐν) or before (ἐνώπιον) us
(e.g. *Ecclus.* 36.4), but never of 'to' or 'upon us'. The Hebrew
Bible can indeed use both *'al*=ἐπί=*super* or *be*=ἐν= *in* interchangeably; thus *Jer.* 6.4 (cf. also 22.7; 51.27; *Micah* 3.5) has,
'Sanctify war against her', which the Vulgate translates '*Sancti-
ficate super eam bellum*'; and in the Jewish prayer *ābīnū
malkēnū* we have, 'Sanctify thy name upon (*'al*) those who sanctify
thy name and sanctify thy name in (*be*) thy world . . . who
sanctifiest thy name in (*be*) the many.' The LXX, however,
often paraphrases such expressions, and the New Testament,
too, does not recognize the connection. The Old Testament
character is, of course, unmistakable, but we have to connect the
'to us' more closely to the subject than to the predicate of the
petition; in that case there are many parallels. 'Let us be called
by your name', runs a significant request in the prophets (*Isa.*
4.1; further *Jer.* 14.9; *Isa.* 63.16,19); it is a request to belong to
God and to stand under his royal shield: 'Thou, O Lord, art our
Father, our Redeemer from of old is thy name over us' (ἐφ'ἡμᾶς,
Isa. 63.16 LXX). We have already discovered the existence in

Primitive Christianity of such a theology of the name, whether of God or of Christ. *James* 2.7 speaks of the 'honourable name by which you are called', as does Hermas later (*Sim.* viii 6.4); this is a fulfilment of the Old Testament prophecy, 'they shall be called by my name' (*Gen.* 48.16; *Deut.* 14.23; 28.10). But just as God calls his name 'over us', so we are those who 'call upon his name' (*Acts* 15.17; Herm., *Sim.* ix 14.3). We are built in his name (*Barn.* 16.8), through it we receive faith, fear, peace, to be well-pleasing to his holy name (*I Clem.* 64), and we ourselves become bearers of his name (Herm., *Sim.* viii 10.3; ix 13.2*f.*; 15.2; 16.3; 28.5; Ign., *Ad Eph.* 7.1).

The addition thus closely combines two Old Testament ideas: God hallows his name and he calls it over us; as a result, we are hallowed by his name and can call to him. This association is all the easier because in Baptism and the Eucharist all events stand under the name of God and sanctify 'us' and glorify God. Baptism takes place 'in his name'; that is why *Acts* 22.16 has the command, 'Rise and be baptized, and wash away your sins, calling on his name.' The person baptized becomes the chosen instrument to 'carry his name' (*Acts* 9.15); because he is hallowed through God's name, God's name is hallowed in him. The same is true of the Eucharist; according to Didache 10.2, the celebration of it ends with the prayer, 'We give thanks to thee, O Holy Father, for thy holy name which thou didst make to tabernacle in our hearts.' This 'tabernacling', well known from the Johannine prologue, simply means that 'his holy name is named over us', for this is how the LXX already translates some Old Testament passages (*Deut.* 12.11; 14.23; 16.2,6,11) which speak of the sanctuary 'where his name tabernacles'. So we ourselves become the 'tabernacle of his name' (*Ps.* 74.7; cf. also *Ezek.* 43.7). What is given to those who call on his name in Baptism and the Eucharist is crowned in martyrdom, for the martyrs become pillars in the sanctuary of God on which Christ will write the name of their God and the name of the city of their God and his own new name (*Rev.* 3.12).

Such instances clearly reveal the origin and tone of the addition 'to us'. The cultic heritage of the Old Testament people of God lives on in the experience of being the holy and elect community of God. It is thus marked off from all nations and men and is set aside to be God's possession and his sanctuary; it is given a new foundation in Baptism and the Eucharist and looks in faith for the day 'when the name of our Lord Jesus may be glorified in you, and you in him' (*II Thess.* 1.12, cf. *Isa.* 66.5). This also means that the addition was not originally part of the first petition; for here we have a community which is no longer the eschatological group of Jesus' disciples at prayer, but which has already become the Church, living on earth, and 'bearing his holy name'. We may therefore say that this 'to us' arose from the liturgical use of the Lord's Prayer in Baptism and the Eucharist in a community which faithfully preserved the Old Testament heritage; this usage also seems to be attested by the Didache, when it puts the words of the prayer between instructions about Baptism and the Eucharist (ch. 7, Baptism; ch. 8, Fasting and Lord's Prayer; chs. 9.10, Eucharist).

The addition does, however, also produce a slight discrepancy which Tertullian already felt in his remarks on the first petition: *Cum dicimus: Sanctificetur nomen tuum, id petimus ut sanctificetur in nobis qui in illo sumus, simul et in ceteris, quos adhuc gratia dei exspectat, ut et huic praecepto pareamus orando pro omnibus, etiam pro inimicis nostris, ideoque suspensa enuntiatione non dicentes: sanctificetur in nobis, in omnibus dicimus.* The name of God is too all-embracing for it to be sanctified only through us. Because of these difficulties, it seems that this addition 'to us', once made, is better taken with the second petition. It seems to be more in place there as the ancient Church understood itself to be the kingdom of God on earth, and looked to the perfect kingdom, although in that case the position of this 'to us' in the sentence is striking. But some New Testament sayings may support the connection, particularly a Lucan saying of the Lord (10.8): 'Whenever you enter a town and they receive you . . . heal the sick in it and say to them, "The kingdom of God has come near to you (ἐφ' ὑμᾶς)".' Of course, even here the difference is plain:

the Lord's saying means by 'you' those who *will* believe, while the petition refers to those who *have* believed, who already have the kingdom of God in the community of brothers looking for the perfect kingdom. Because of this possession, the meaning of the petition approaches the explanation formulated by Zwingli: '*Petimus, ut ad nos veniat regnum dei, id est justitia, pax, gaudium in spiritu sancto*' (cf. *Rom*. 14.17), and because of the expectation to Augustine's (*Ad Probam*): '*Seu velimus seu nolimus, utique veniet, sed desiderium nostrum ad illum excitamus, ut nobis veniat atque nos in eo regnare mereamur.*' In both instances, however, even here we can see the later character of this 'to us'; we can understand its widespread use in Western Christianity right up to the present precisely because it fits more closely to the situation of the Church and the individual believer.

4. The manuscript tradition of the second petition raises another special problem. Accounts of the evidence have been given so often that a short survey will be sufficient here: almost all manuscripts and versions have the second petition in the usual form, which corresponds to the text of Matthew. Two minuscules, however, ms. 700 (*British Museum* 2160 Egerton from 11th c., § 133 Soden) and ms. 162 (*Cod. Vaticanus*, earlier *Barb.* iv 31, § 214 Soden), read 'Thy holy Spirit come (ms. 700 adds "upon us") and cleanse us' instead of the usual petition for the coming of the kingdom. Gregory of Nyssa presupposes the same wording in his homilies on the Lord's Prayer; he quotes the text three times and expressly remarks that it stood like this in St. Luke's Gospel. There are only small differences in the individual passages: 'The holy Spirit' stands once with, once without σου, 'to us' is once inserted, once omitted, and a third time it follows 'come'. Maximus Confessor also attests the same form of the petition; he quotes it in the wording of ms. 162. The same text is indirectly confirmed by the prayer in the *Acts of Thomas* (c. 27 Bonnet): 'Come, holy Spirit, and cleanse their reins and their heart' and another in the liturgy of Constantinople (Swain-

son, *op. cit.*, p. 109): 'Come, heavenly King, Comforter, Spirit of truth . . . and tabernacle in us and cleanse us from all stain, and save, O Gracious One, our souls!' The wording of this petition can be derived from Marcion, who, according to the slogans given by Tertullian (*Adv. Marc.* iv 26), read the petition for the Holy Spirit first, before the one for the coming of the kingdom.

On the basis of this evidence in Marcion and the Acts of Thomas there has been some talk of a gnostic Lord's Prayer which later also found its way into Church circles. But not only is this historical development hard to imagine; there is little that is 'gnostic' about this petition. Though it may agree with Marcion's theology to replace the Old Testament-like petition for the hallowing of the name with one for the coming of the Spirit, this 'new' petition was not composed by Marcion, but is far older than his Gospel. It can even be associated with a saying of the Lord which follows the giving of the Lord's Prayer in *Luke* 11.13: 'If you, then, who are evil, know how to give good gifts to your children, how much more will the heavenly Father give the holy Spirit to those who ask him?' It may be doubtful whether such a petition already stood in St. Luke's Gospel, but it can be demonstrated that the earliest Christians already knew and used it. Marcion's action in putting it at the beginning of the Lord's Prayer, before the petition for the coming of the kingdom, is arbitrary and artificial, for now the first two petitions begin in an almost impossible way with 'Come'. In the powerful and urgent repetition of the same word, which is so alien to the Lord's Prayer, we seem to have an indication of the provenance of these two petitions from different traditions. In that case the Church evidence is probably right in putting the petition for the Spirit in place of the usual one. But how did this petition arise, and how is it to be explained?

There is another indication that it was not composed by Marcion and that it is relatively ancient: its words are formed from Old Testament concepts—that is easy to demonstrate. The phrase 'Thy holy Spirit' occurs nowhere in the New Testament, which knows only the variant expressions 'the holy Spirit' (without the name of God or a corresponding pronoun) or 'the Spirit of God'.[28] True, the Psalter has, 'Take not thy holy Spirit from me' (51.11), or, 'Let thy holy (so BA, 'good' Sa R) Spirit lead me on a level path' (143.10). The Wisdom of Solomon asks (9.17): 'Who has learned thy counsel, unless thou hast sent thy holy Spirit from on high?' It is said of the prophet Daniel that he 'has the holy Spirit of God in him' (*Dan.* 4.8,9,18 *Theod.*), and *Isa.* 63.10*f.* laments: 'But they rebelled and grieved his holy Spirit.' The New Testament does not speak of a 'coming' of the Spirit either (apart from one exception to be discussed later); the Spirit is 'sent' or 'given' like a personal ambassador from God. Again, the Old Testament often speaks of the 'coming' of the Spirit: on anyone whom God chooses as a prophet 'the Spirit comes' (*Ezek.* 2.2); Ezekiel says of himself (3.22*ff.*): 'And the hand of the Lord was there upon me: and he said to me, "Arise, go forth into the plain," . . . and lo, the glory of the Lord stood there . . . and I fell on my face. And the Spirit came to me and set me upon my feet; and he spoke with me' (Similarly, too, 11.5). Trito-Isaiah also exclaims, 'The Spirit of the Lord God is upon me' (ἐπ'ἐμέ 61.1). What happens now to individuals and is only there for a special commission will one day be shared by all (*Isa.* 32.15*ff.*):

> *The Spirit will come upon us from on high,*
> *and the wilderness becomes a fruitful field . . .*
> *Then justice will dwell in the wilderness. . . .*
> *My people will abide in a peaceful habitation.*

So the day of eschatological consummation dawns with this 'coming of the Spirit'.

The second predicate of the petition, 'cleanse us', is also of Old Testament origin. In *Ps.* 51 the psalmist prays (vv. 2,10) 'Cleanse me from my sin . . . Create in me a clean heart, O God, and put a new and right Spirit within me', and there are similar petitions in *Ps.* 19.13*f.* and *Ecclus.* 38.10. The petition does not limit itself to man's earthly life, but also implies the eschatological promise, 'I will cleanse them from all the guilt of their sin'

(*Jer.* 33.8, similarly *Ezek.* 36.33; 37.23). Thus *Ps. Sol.* 18.5 asks: 'May God cleanse Israel . . . against the day of choice when he bringeth back his anointed.' So the 'cleansing' of the people or of the individual heart is one of the original works of eschatological consummation. Of course it is nowhere said in the Old Testament that the spirit of God cleanses men, but we come close enough to this idea in Jubilees 1.22: 'And the Lord said unto Moses: . . . "I will create in them a holy Spirit, and I will cleanse them".' There is also the same association in the idea of the prophetic call: God must first cleanse anyone whom he chooses to proclaim his Word. So in *Isa.* 6.5*f.* the prophet already says: 'Woe is me! For I am lost; for I am a man of unclean lips, and I dwell in the midst of a people of unclean lips,' and an angel touches his mouth with a burning coal, saying, 'Behold, your guilt is taken away, and your sin is forgiven.'

In the New Testament the concept of cleansing is attested in one or two places and is associated with either baptism or the blood of Christ (*Eph.* 5.26; *Heb.* 9.14,22; 10.2; *I John* 1.7). *I John* 1.9 once has in general terms, 'He will forgive sins and cleanse us from all unrighteousness', but elsewhere the cultic metaphor of cleansing gives way to the moral concept of forgiveness. Nor is it said in the New Testament that the Spirit cleanses us; only once is there a remote association between the two in a speech of Peter's (*Acts* 15.8*f*): 'God who knows the heart bore witness to them, giving them the holy Spirit just as he did to us; and he made no distinction between us and them, but cleansed their hearts by faith.' We could add to this one passage the expressions which speak not of cleansing but of sanctification; both concepts in some places conceal their Old Testament meaning, just as, say, *Isa.* 66.17 speaks of those who 'sanctify and purify themselves' or the Epistle to the Hebrews, compelled by its subject, speaks now of purification (9.22), now of sanctification (9.13) through the blood of the sacrifice. Even if we ignore the fact that the New Testament has divorced the idea of sanctification from that of purification, it is instructive that it usually associates the idea of sanctification with other concepts; God or Christ, the word or faith sanctify men (cf. *I Cor.* 1.2; 6.11; *Eph.* 5.26; *I Thess.* 5.23; *I Tim.* 4.5; *Acts* 26.18). Only Paul once speaks of the 'offering of the Gentiles' which he makes 'sanctified by the holy Spirit' (*Rom.* 15.16), and he obviously does this to fill the cultic imagery with the spirit of his message.

The meaning of this petition too is determined by these associations. It looks for an eschatological gift; with the coming of the holy Spirit, the day of consummation is to dawn 'for us' and thus God's former promises to his people are to be fulfilled. Then 'we' shall be the community of the perfect, the heirs of the people of God and its divine history; and our consummation will be to become the prophets of God, pure in heart and hand and mouth. So this second petition makes good sense with the first: the holy community of the messengers of God is associated with the hallowing of God's name, giving rise to a new trinity: God, Spirit and community. So the connection with Old Testament ideas is unbroken here; these 'we' are only conceivable as faithful members of their people; if God hears their petition they then receive the eschatological task which Deutero-Isaiah set the people, of being 'a light' to the Gentiles.

Such a definition of the sense of the petition raises far more difficult questions than hitherto. True, it is now clear that the petition does not derive from Marcion nor from gnostic circles, just as the other alterations in the Marcionite Lord's Prayer preclude this idea. But is a petition for the holy Spirit possible within a community which boasts that it possesses the Spirit? And if there must have been at least a certain trend in first century Christianity which represented such ideas and attitudes, where can we find more evidence to put it (and this petition) in a clear historical context? We must now make a brief investigation of these relevant historical questions.

5. It does not, of course, seem difficult to find a place for the petition for the Spirit in the life and belief of the Primitive Christian community. For if the community is sustained and

filled by the Spirit, this petition can be made only by those who are not yet members, but desire to belong to it. In that case the petition is for those who undergo Baptism, for the promise of the Spirit has been associated with this action ever since the events at Pentecost. It would then be, as Harnack put it, a prayer of initiation, i.e. a prayer through which a person first became a Christian. But the association of this part of the Lord's Prayer with the act of Baptism can hardly be right. For the petition does not speak of the way by which a person becomes a Christian but of the dawning of the time of salvation 'for us'; it is not the prayer of the individual before his baptism, but that of a community which prays it daily. Only this one petition would point to the act of baptism, and all the others would point beyond it. Finally, there is far too little evidence of it for it to be so closely and necessarily bound up with Baptism, the common custom and fundamental action of Primitive Christianity.[29]

If this verdict of Harnack's, then, is hardly a correct one, he has nevertheless indicated the example of the Ephesine Christians as a support for his thesis, and it is, of course, most fruitful and instructive. There are some 'disciples' who know only John's baptism and have the same attitude as Apollos to the Christian community, i.e. to 'the way of the Lord'; they have not received the Spirit, indeed they have not even heard that 'there is a Spirit'; only when Paul baptizes them again and lays his hands on them, 'the holy Spirit came on them; and they spoke with tongues and prophesied' (*Acts* 19.6). This is the only place in the New Testament where the phrase from the present petition occurs: elsewhere we usually find, 'They received the Spirit' (10.47), and here too we have a similar view to the one in the petition: these disciples become 'prophets', a phrase which we do not find elsewhere. Of course, their position is very obscure. Since Chrysostom, they have often been taken as a group of the disciples of John who have made only superficial contact with the Christian faith; but this view cannot be substantiated. They are called μαθηταί, and without doubt that means members of the Christian community; the only thing that distinguishes them from the picture of primitive communities known to us from elsewhere is that they know only the baptism of John and know nothing of the coming of the Spirit. The two elements are closely related; because John's baptism with water is the fundamental thing for them, they cannot say and know that the Spirit has already come and vice versa, for in the words of John the Baptist the baptism of water is to be fulfilled in the baptism of the Spirit which the 'stronger' one will accomplish at his eschatological coming. The Spirit has not therefore 'come' as long as this day of eschatological consummation has not dawned. In this same strain, there is no saying in the first two Gospels which could promise or even indicate that the Spirit was possessed by the community; the problem of the sayings about the Paraclete in the Fourth Gospel suggests the same thing. And the followers of Jesus who are depicted for us are in the same situation as these Christians of Ephesus; they too have nothing but the baptism of John, which forms the basis even for Jesus' authority, and the 'way of the Lord', even if we can only infer the two and find them expressed only in the Fourth Gospel. So the disciples at Ephesus represent a far broader stratum than we might assume from the Acts of the Apostles, and an established religious view which looks for the word of consummation in the 'coming of the Spirit'; they are so to speak the Primitive Christian community before Pentecost, and they remained so even after Pentecost.

The remarkable thing about the Lucan account is not so much the existence of these disciples, as Paul's behaviour towards them. Paul preaches the Gospel of Jesus Christ in Ephesus although there is already a Primitive Christian community there; he begins his preaching with those who 'had already believed' although it was in contradiction to his principle of only preaching where Christ had not been named. He begins this proclamation with baptism, although he was not 'sent by God to baptize, but to preach the Gospel' (*I Cor.* 1.17). These contradictions merely hint at the importance which Ephesus had for Paul and his mission as a city and as a community; it even led him to repeat the baptism of John, which the Christians had already received and which for Jesus and the first two Gospels was the sole eschatological sign from heaven, as though it were nothing, and worthless. But this was done not simply from a missionary point of view, but rather as a principle of faith. 'For Paul and Luke, Christianity was essentially a means of receiving the holy Spirit' (Kirsopp Lake, on *Acts* 19.2). In this way we can understand not only Paul's attitude, but also the picture that Luke paints of the first community at Jerusalem; it reflects not only the concrete situation, but also the ideal view which derives from faith in Jesus Christ.

As is well known, Luke had some material which could not be reconciled with that picture. He reports of the very community which received the Spirit at Pentecost that once again, as they prayed for support in their persecutions, 'The place was shaken, and they were all filled with the holy Spirit.' Similarly, the many sayings of the Lord which are handed down by all the Synoptic Gospels imply that so to speak the earthly day of Primitive Christian life was not always illuminated by the holy Spirit, seeing that these sayings promise the help of the Spirit only in the hour and state of martyrdom. It is further well known that even the connection between baptism and the gift of the Spirit is not a close one; sometimes people are baptized who have already received the Spirit, like the centurion Cornelius and his house (*Acts* 10.44); sometimes only the baptism is performed, as in the case of the Ethiopian eunuch (*Acts* 8.27-39), without the Spirit descending on the candidate, so that it is a further example of the attitude which the Ephesine Christians also adopt. We may therefore see in these instances the representatives of a Primitive Christianity of a pre-Pauline and pre-Lucan mould, for which the time of salvation dawns eschatologically with the coming of the Spirit. The nearness of its coming is guaranteed by the heavenly sign of baptism, and from this beginning the way that Jesus showed leads surely to its end. One cannot describe the attitude of faith and morals presupposed in the Gospels of St. Matthew and St. Mark in a more appropriate way.

So we seem to have found the ground on which this petition is possible and on which it is, in fact, based. Here is a Primitive Christianity which is closely bound up with the Old Testament hopes and which sees in John and Jesus those who prepare the Lord's way or his eschatological work. Closely as it is related to the innermost hopes of the people, it is little concerned about the historical existence of people and country. It carries on its mission and finds willing acceptance among the people, and perhaps this task, which seems to reflect the Deutero-Isaianic prophecy of the light for the Gentiles, brought to the lips of those who carried it on words which the prophets fulfilled earlier, and which will be realized by all true members of the eschatological people in the final age: 'May thy holy Spirit come and cleanse us!'

If the petition is thus of considerable antiquity, it seems quite possible even in the mouth of Jesus. But here the linguistic and stylistic form of the petition already tells against such an origin, as it draws on the text of the Greek Bible. Moreover, it would be hardly comprehensible within the Lord's Prayer; it does not fit the form of the petitions which is maintained elsewhere, in which there are never two parallel verbs connected with an 'and', nor does it fit the remaining contents of the prayer. What need is there to go on to ask, 'Forgive us our debts', when the second petition has already prayed, 'May thy holy Spirit cleanse us'? And even if we wish to attach a special significance to this 'cleansing', to take it for holiness, or even only to refer to the 'pure lips' of which Isaiah speaks, the tautology is only concealed, not removed; moreover, it is no longer remembered that the First Epistle of St. John still treats the two as synonymous: God is 'faithful and just, and will forgive us our sins and cleanse us from all unrighteousness'. So the petition is not part of the Lord's Prayer; it remains a later formation, and has been composed by a Primitive Christian community and tradition which, grounded on Old Testament and Jewish hopes (*Test. Judah*

24.2*f*.), sees the sign of, and the way towards, the eschatological consummation in the work of the Baptist and Jesus, and longs for the Spirit to come and cleanse it. We cannot go on to say how this expectation of the coming of the Spirit is related to the expectation of the coming of Christ—it is enough that it existed and was widespread. We can even understand how it could be closely connected with the second petition of the Lord's Prayer or could even replace it; this could follow not only from its identical beginning, 'Come', but also from its content, as 'Spirit' and 'kingdom' are already associated in Jewish prayers:

> *And after these things shall a star arise to you from Jacob in peace,*
> *And the heavens shall be opened unto him,*
> *To pour out the Spirit, (even) the blessing of the holy Father;*
> *And he shall pour out the spirit of grace upon you . . .*
> *Then shall the sceptre of my kingdom shine forth.*
>
> (*Test. Judah* 24.2*f*)

So we discover an extremely instructive state of affairs. A petition which did not originally belong to the Lord's Prayer later finds its way in, suppresses the petition which is supported by the Synoptic message, is taken over by Marcion, perhaps from a tradition in Asia Minor, and remains even in Church circles into later centuries. This position reveals that changes of wording were possible in ancient times as well as more recently, and warns us against any scheme and dogma which would dictate the conditions of its origin and its change.

XII   Conclusions

1. So far we have considered the individual clauses of the prayer one by one; now we must ask how the seven petitions fit together to make a whole. Of course the legitimacy of such a procedure is open to question; is the whole of the prayer more than the consequence and sum of the individual petitions—to put it in the words of Jacob Wettstein that we have already quoted, *tota ex formulis Hebraeorum concinnata?* Could we not add further petitions, as was done in Jewish prayers, and slowly adding one petition to another, make, say, an Eighteen Benedictions? And if we can count five petitions in Luke and seven in Matthew, is not the beginning of such a development clearly traceable? Moreover, elsewhere in the tradition of the words of Jesus, a number of speeches have been made up of individual sayings, and the same has in fact happened in the Lord's Prayer, as we can see from the fact that some fragments of the second or third or sixth or seventh petitions occur in both Matthew and Luke, and stand so to speak on the threshold of the prayer, asking to be included.

Despite such internal and external reasons, the inner and outer unity of the Lord's Prayer is not to be disputed; they do not preclude the idea of a totality, but merely assert one particular totality, that of a sum. It is, however, sufficient here to point to one fact; there is no tradition of the gradual growth of the prayer, but only of the action of Jesus in giving this prayer to his disciples. And it is given as a pattern, 'pray like this', i.e. it prohibits the bad and arbitrary freedom of adding together the

words and clauses of the Lord's Prayer as though they were interchangeable pieces, and allows only the inner freedom which,
bound up with the spirit and the totality of this prayer, allows a
man to pray in his own words to God. We have also seen that
there is some deliberate and comprehensive pattern in the external
ordering of the words and clauses. But if the form has been care-
fully arranged, with three petitions at beginning and end, and the
fourth petition in the centre, we may rightly ask whether the
content of the pattern matches its stylistic form.

It is clear that the first half of the prayer speaks of God 'in
heaven' and the second half purely of the needs and dangers of
the suppliants 'on earth', even if the third and seventh petitions
are taken as later additions. But in addition to this first arrangement there is a powerful internal connection between the individual clauses. The prayer begins with an address which already
expresses the basis and the end of all prayer quite clearly; all
holy and exalted names which stress the difference between the
person who prays and the one to whom he prays (names which
Jesus uses elsewhere, as is shown by his thanksgiving) are omitted
here; without any intermediary, the petitions speak from a
transitory 'today' into God's eternity, which is also the suppliant's 'tomorrow'. So it is hardly by chance, and not simply
because of a common Jewish custom, that the opening words of
its address have become the embodiment of this and all Christian
prayer.

The positive and negative sides of this intimacy of father and
children are developed in these first three petitions. The first
two belong closely together here, and their content is again
summed up by the third from a special standpoint. For the first
speaks of what is *God's* and the second of what is the *Lord's* and
King's; they are related to each other as is the Old Testament
name of God, Yahweh, on the revelation of which the life and
existence of the people is based, to the periphrasis which was
also common in the time of Jesus, Adonai, i.e. the Lord, under
whose leading and guidance the history of the people and the
life of the individual pass through time. The two names thus

merely show what is said and meant by the name 'Father'. So the prayer begins with what is over all being and life without any doubt or variation, with God's holy name. Here the idea of the creative Word and the created world have not yet been separated, but both mysteriously rest in God's heart. So we can understand why the idea of the kingdom, i.e. the ordering of all creation which lives and exists outside God, though never without him, appears only in second place. The verbs, too, match the inner relationship of the two concepts name and kingdom. The first one, 'hallow', takes its significance purely from God's name and nature as the act which is appropriate to both, and therefore derives from God just as much as it goes back to him. The second, 'come', designates the event which takes place through God, outside God, in his creation. In this 'come' we already have a distant reference to the men and things which have their life through God, but it is still not expressed, so that the inner circle of God's world is not yet left, and the outer circle of man's world is still not reached. The third is the first to bring us to God's creation, 'on earth as it is in heaven'; thus the setting has grown smaller, but it is occupied by the will of God which says what God is and what he does in the world, and says what the world should be and what God will do to it. So 'name', 'kingdom', and 'will', and again, 'hallow', 'come', and 'be done' have many profound associations. While all these words speak solely of the totality which moves not only between heaven and earth but also over heaven and earth, and overlooks each individual life as much as it embraces it, they also speak of the ground on which the individual who prays can rest himself and all his concerns.

In the last three petitions, God and his world are contrasted with the suppliant and his world. They, too, are constituted by three concepts which are interrelated in as many ways as the first three. Just as the first series began with what God is and what is due to his name, so too this second series begins with what man is and what he needs; what he is and has is called 'debts', what he needs is called 'forgiveness'. From this innermost nucleus, which describes the nature of man and still is only a hint

273

at God's forgiving love, the petitions expand and tell of the situation in which the suppliant stands, which is called 'temptation', and the power and figure which governs this situation and embraces it everywhere, '(the) evil (one)'. The second triad corresponds with the first in another respect: if the third petition speaks of the divine will which is done on earth as it is in heaven, the fifth speaks of the divine will which man fails to do; if the second looks at the promising nearness of the kingdom, the sixth looks at the threatening nearness of temptation; and if the last speaks in fear of (the) evil (one), the first speaks in reverence of the holy one who overcomes even the evil one. Perhaps a definite view of the course of the eschatological events, such as is found in some Jewish-Christian statements, still underlies these particular references. For what is the petition 'Forgive us our debts' but the human answer to the Baptist's and Jesus' cry 'Repent'? But with the days of repentance the eschatological event begins (*Ass. Mos.* 1.18), and it is followed by the 'hour of great temptation' by the devil (*Mark* 13.5ff., *Rev.* 3.10) and finally by the hour of deliverance from the devil (*Ass. Mos.* 10.1; *Rev.* 20.2f.).

Between these two sets of expressions in the Lord's Prayer we have the petition for bread as a transition from one world to the other; not only its language and style, but also its content associate it more closely with the second set. It limits itself to the physical life of man, and asks simply for bread, as the only thing which sustains 'us' until the 'morrow', when God's name and kingdom and will become present reality among men; the reference to the first set of expressions is clear, even if it still remains purely temporal. But this bread is also poverty, as opposed to riches, need, as opposed to sufficiency and superfluity; it stands against the background of the well-known saying, 'Blessed are you that hunger now, woe to you that are full now!' This characteristic of poverty opens up a still deeper connection: the scanty bread is not only what is needed now, until God gives the future bread, but as a present necessity it is already a sign of his eschatological grace and fullness, the one sign of his work which is already manifest here and now. 'We' could not ask for the threefold things of God if God did not give us 'our bread' which is already the future bread, even though it remains involved in today's need and poverty, as an infallible sign; nor could we fear the last three human—or even satanic—things were this gift of the bread not already the reality of the future world in the needs of today. We can now understand more closely how the fourth petition marks the transition from an 'as it is in heaven' to a 'so also on earth'.

The result is a clear, meaningful and significant totality, in which nothing is chance and arbitrary, but each individual element has its right and proper place. The differences between the Matthaean and Lucan forms of the prayer do not affect the interrelationships in any way, as Matthew's third and seventh petitions stand just where the two sets of expressions end, and they merely underline this end with a special clause. Whether we think that Matthew added the petitions or that Luke omitted them, in either case both merely stress the inner construction and connection which has been characteristic of the prayer from the beginning, and thus attest its internal and external unity.

This unity is illuminated even more clearly from yet another standpoint. Judaism had different sorts of prayer, but among the many varieties which it developed and used the thanksgiving stands supreme. According to a profound rabbinic saying, thanksgiving will not cease even when all earthly things cease. The Lord's Prayer contains no thanksgiving for gifts or acts of God which the suppliant has experienced, not even a thanksgiving for the knowledge of being God's children. Nor does it contain any lament over need and oppression, although these threaten and oppress 'us' in many ways; finally, it contains no praise of God, his infinite exaltation, his unapproachable holiness, his supreme power, or even his fatherly love. Here is no heart moved by passion or soul excited by joy or sorrow, tribulation and exaltation, such as we so often find in the Psalter; here is no loving and seeking, no acknowledging and praising. In a holy quietness, which is nevertheless determined by every power and every need between heaven and earth, it speaks objectively and naturally, in each and every thing putting its requests before God in simple trust. In the presence of God, even the personal afflictions and dangers of those who pray can be regarded in this objective way; they are almost a transitory, alien element before the one abiding thing which supports the suppliants with God's name and kingdom and will; they already stand in the presence of their Father in heaven and look down on their life, the life of the children of God at prayer, even as the community still looks up in prayer to heaven from this earth. Through such inexpressible nearness man's own concerns have been estranged from him and transferred to God, the Father to whom the petitions are made.

2. We can recognize the clear and larger context of the individual petitions and their inner unity still more plainly if we go back to the objective grounds on which the words and ideas of the Lord's Prayer are based.

There is no Jewish, and not even a Primitive Christian, prayer which does not speak of the intermediary or the means by which the person who prays puts his words and concerns before God. In the beginning of the Eighteen Benedictions, 'Blessed art thou, O Lord our God and the God of our Fathers, God of Abraham, Isaac and Jacob', the whole history of the people, guided by God and begun with the patriarchs, stands before him, and justifies his petitions. The 'today', in which he stands and prays, is simply a part of the yesterday from which he receives his rights and his support, and happy is he to be allowed and to be able to appropriate the past with the same right as his ancestors did. Here, however, the today is an already anticipated part of the morrow to come; the Lord's Prayer no longer speaks of a past and so it no longer knows any intermediaries to continue the chain to the present day; it begins with 'today' as though it were the first day of the coming age. So all historical roots of which the suppliant could otherwise boast are done away with; he no longer sees the earlier mighty acts of God, much less the misdeeds of his ancestors, although his own words merely derive from the words which God once spoke in the history of the people; he no longer recognizes a holy tradition given by God. Like the first man who lifted up his eyes to heaven, he stretches his arms out to God in prayer.

Of course, this directness of attitude seems often to be attested in the Psalter; 'Out of the deep do I call unto thee, O Lord', 'The Lord is my shepherd!' Do not such prayers speak face to face in the same way as the Lord's Prayer? But the one psalm goes on to speak of Israel, and the other of the house of the Lord, and even if they did not have such words to associate them with the here and now, they never surrender their link with the people, and through the people, with God. Perhaps there are also prayers in the Old Testament and Judaism which 'today' are so full of what God may do or has done that their words can omit all reference to intermediaries and their sorrow or their joy can be put immediately before God's countenance; for prayer needs a sign that God is near, that he hears and protects the person who prays, even if he himself often does not see it or express it. So the characteristics of a prayer are not only its immediacy, but also the kind of intermediacy which leads up to the 'today' in which it is made. The token of mediation known by the Lord's Prayer is very significant and clearly expressed: 'Give us our future bread'. So the only sign that God has hitherto given and is asked to give is this sign of 'today's' frugal bread, that God feeds the suppliant today as he has always fed him, and will not let him languish. It takes the place of all sacred tradition and previous revelation, the community and its history, the patriarchs, kings and prophets; all the richness and all the strength that the past gives is now, so to speak, included in the frugal bread that God gives us.

Like the idea of tradition, the expression of hope and promise is also lacking in this prayer. Perhaps we should put it more accurately: the whole of this prayer is hope and longing for the day of consummation. Almost all Jewish prayers speak of three things: what God has done, what he is to do now, and what he will do one day; past action is the basis for action in the present, and both present and past actions raise hope for the future. Here, however, all is focused on the imminent future, and even the one petition that speaks of 'today' puts this very 'today' in the context of the coming age and the coming world. The prayer is spoken so to speak from the intangible darkness of the near future, or, more accurately, from the knowledge that the eschatological light of God is hidden in this darkness. In the face of this future, past and present must vanish like smoke, and the directness of the approach which we have already noted is seen to be the pure and undimmed reflection of that light. But what is generally true of history and tradition, without which a small human life does not exist, is equally true of this one single existence; it looks back to no past or tradition, but only forward to a future, to God's future, and even the bitter thought of debt says more of what man always is than of what he was, or has become.

All this, however, merely outlines the circle within which the particular presuppositions of the Lord's Prayer lie. What are these presuppositions in themselves? The Lord's Prayer first has an apocalyptic basis, i.e. it is governed by a contrast of opposites, the tension between the holy God and his world, and the evil one and his world. The statement remains valid even if we regard the seventh petition as a later rounding off to the prayer. For the sixth petition teaches the same thing; if temptation is no longer grace, but anguish and terror, then the life of man, instead of being tested by God through temptations, becomes a prey for the 'evil one', and the 'evil one' becomes the still invincible Lord of all human destiny. In accordance with this apocalyptic outlook, the present and the future of this life are threatened by three dangers: all human action is a 'being in debt', all future happening is a 'being tempted', and all human experience is 'being led astray'. Nothing breaks out of this threefold ring to give human existence glory or joy, profundity or stature; even the loving disposition or the helping act towards the neighbour are no longer of use here, for all this remains a

278

'being in debt'. So man's life is no longer simply an undecided neutrality which is called to decide for God or for the evil one; nor is it the course to the goal that God has appointed, which with increasing simplicity and safety frees itself from sins and temptations; on the contrary, it is an existence hemmed in with debt and failure, and only the action of God, his forgiveness and his protection, can break the threefold ring, free this life from its bonds, and bring it to the blessed realm of God. Here, then, we have the expression of a metaphysics of two opposed worlds which, as portrayed in the contrast between the first and second halves of the prayer, forms the subject and foundation of all Jewish and Primitive Christian apocalyptic.

Nevertheless, the unmistakable differences between the usual apocalyptic outlook and this prayer must not be overlooked. All apocalyptic is also a view of history, indeed the mother of all history; it is concerned with the forces which determine not only the life of the individual but also the history of the Jewish people and the nations. The confused and devious courses and destinies of history, which take on different colours depending on the way in which they are approached, are seen by apocalyptic as straight lines: one set leads to salvation, the other to damnation, one to good, the other to evil. Even the Lord's Prayer is full of this particular opposition, but just as it knows no past, so too it has no concern for a possible meaning in history, whether it is the history of one people or foreign nations. All that matters is the 'today' which stretches out into tomorrow, or rather, the tomorrow that already draws the today to it; only the pure forces of God count, even if the threefold dangers of the 'evil one' stand against them. So one of the most profound concerns of apocalyptic is superseded on its own ground, and the power of God is contrasted in its pure, omnipresent glory and holiness with the power of the evil one. If it is the idea of the holy and fatherly nearness of God that reveals human life as the burden of a threefold curse, it is the same idea which puts the question of this life, 'Good or Evil?', far beyond all human and historical complications and raises the concept of the good to be the sole measure and the sole power of all life and happening.

One further difference distinguishes the apocalyptic foundation of the Lord's Prayer from all traditional apocalyptic. The latter usually sees heaven and earth perishing in a tremendous catastrophe, and imagines a completely new life in a new world; how else could it be if the evil one is the Lord of this world and temptation is its element? If God finally casts down Satan from the throne that he has usurped, there must be a complete reversal of the consequences of his rule which determine that human life should have sin, need, sickness and death. There is no longer any mention of such consequences here; no new heaven is spread out and no new earth blossoms, but the old earth and world still remain God's earth and God's world: 'Thy will be done on earth as it is in heaven!' If this third petition is rejected because it occurs only in Matthew, the same thing will be found in the following one. For if God's eschatological grace is revealed in the fact that he 'gives us our future bread' today, then this present feeding makes the still existing earth bright with the glory of God's perfect world. Other sayings of the Lord say the same thing, 'Behold the lilies of the field, behold the birds of the air'. The nearness of the eschatological day thus consecrates the suppliants' life on this dark earth through the bitter yet blessed frugality of the bread and fills it with its already dawning light. Because the apocalyptic context is thus preserved and yet is explained in such a way that only the power of the good is real, even the present is elevated to being the transitory, but already eschatologically determined, reality of God. Here we have the beginnings of the re-hallowing of the present transitory yet abiding course of the world, but it is then no longer the constitutive factor for the Jewish people that this world is God's creation and its land is God's promised land; the idea of the imminence of the consummation is what makes this hallowing possible. This new assurance derives from the utmost human insecurity; what was hitherto most distant has now become nearest; God, the inaccessible, who embraces all distances, has now become the Father who gives us, as children, 'our bread'.

So once again there is a unity where once there was a division; it is a unity in which the eschatological future is filled with the reality of today, and this today is already caught up in the holiness of the future. But in the Lord's Prayer this hallowing remains limited to the bread which supports the life of those who pray here and today.

One last difference consists in the fact that all the mythological colouring of apocalyptic imagery and vision is done away with in this prayer. There is not one word about the glorious coming of the kingdom which occupies all human hopes, not one thought goes beyond the bounds of 'today' into the world of the eternal tomorrow over which God's holy name alone holds sway; there is no sign of a petition which occurs so frequently else-where; 'Let us enter thy kingdom, let us live under thy name!' Again this humility springs from the assurance of the nearness of the end. What need is there of such wistful petitions and dreams if God's tomorrow is as certain to follow our today as the sun is to bring in another new day tomorrow? What need is there to dwell on the details of history from day to day if this new day is God's tomorrow? Just as the days of earthly life follow one another in an unchanging series, so too will God's coming day follow the transitory time of this life. The 'coming' already makes its impression on the 'today' and sanctifies it; the 'today' leads to the day to come and disenchants it. So this eschatological element becomes the holy, still pending, content of the present, and the today gives the eschatological element a clear, already transitory form.

All these presuppositions are barely hinted at in the Lord's Prayer and are only revealed at a closer examination; but they indicate, from an objective, historical point of view, the begin-ning of a 'new' message or the breakthrough of a 'new' revelation and recognition. They are only seen in the right light when we realize that each individual petition, indeed each individual word of the prayer, rests on the firm and never repudiated foundation of the Old Testament. Its words and its atmosphere are to be traced everywhere, not as an alien basis on which something else must be built, but as the living, fertile field on which the seed of the 'new' message grows and ripens and bears fruit. To put it in unmetaphorical language; because the Old Testament revelation is understood as a promise of what is to come, it continues almost as a matter of course in this prayer; but because it is still only promise, and not yet fulfilment, it is done away with here, and the words and sentences pursue their straight and narrow way, almost on new ground, to the final goal and the already apparent reality of the eschatological consummation. They therefore tend, as the minor Lucan deviations show, to turn back from the eschatological light of today to the 'daily' course of events and human necessities, and to be approximated to traditional aims and ideas instead of to those that are to come; the distant future which has suddenly materialized 'today' is again regarded as a distant future, or at least is no longer taken as an all-sustaining nearness, and the light of 'tomorrow' no longer shines for the suppliants as strongly and as clearly in the 'today' of poverty and debt.

Just as the historical powers which determine this world have disappeared for the Lord's Prayer, and only those remain which, though themselves curtailed, still stand in the way of the approaching eschatological day, so too the life of man, with its manifold possibilities and capabilities, also vanishes, and all that remains is what still fetters him, though with already loosened bonds, to his transitory existence. Perhaps the freedom is even greater here because while a positive element is not expressed, it is still clearly intended: 'we' are the children of 'Our Father who is in heaven'. This unqualified sentence paints the picture of the man who stands before God in a pure freedom which is no longer governed and limited by historical relationships. All the conditioning factors of his earthly life, nature and history, people and country, occupation and culture, have completely disappeared; the only tie which keeps him in this earthly existence is the bread which God gives to him and his brothers; the three factors that

282

fetter him and threaten him are the powers which obstruct the coming of the consummation. God gives the bread as a preliminary sign of his permanent reality, and the powers are already taken care of in the providence of the Father who forgives debts, preserves from temptation, and delivers from evil.

These three powers and dangers have no individual and external significance in human existence, but embrace and penetrate the whole of it. For 'debts' refer to the whole life and action of the man who lives on the earth; whatever aims he has and achieves, whatever plans he begins and whatever trouble he takes, all his achievements do not free him from the debts which he owes to God, and all his misdeeds increase the burden that oppresses him. So we cannot have the Old Testament petition, 'Lord, grant success', here, nor even that of the Benedictus (*Luke* 1.74):

> that we . . . might serve him . . .
> in holiness and righteousness before him
> all the days of our life.

Man can give God nothing, even through his humble service; he can only ask God for the forgiveness which he is to give him and remain a debtor to God. It is just the same in the case of temptation; it is based on the physical and spiritual entanglement of men in all manner of earthly conditions and restrictions. However much they allure a man or hem him in, however much he may struggle against them, they always remain more powerful, and he succumbs to them; for by himself a man is nothing; he is everything through the Father who keeps him. But above all temptations, above all the deeds that the faithful do, above the events to which they fall victim, is the triumph and rule of 'the evil one'. And this name, which is the last phrase of the Lord's Prayer, makes clear the presuppositions of the two previous petitions: the only measure that is valid is the measure of the morally good; the only reality that exists is the work of the holy God.

But in view of this conclusion, the question arises whether a man cannot and should not ask God for something other than freedom from the three dangers, whether he cannot also work for God and with God on earth, and fulfil his life in this work. Even the Lord's Prayer recognizes an action which fulfils a man completely and makes absolute demands on him; it runs, in short, 'Forgive our debtors'. Here all possible human action is summed up under a last and supreme point of view: just as it is God's nature to be generous and to forgive all our sins (*Ex.* 34.6*f*), so it is now the nature of a child of God to forgive debtors. Here, then, we find in other words the twofold commandment of love; love even towards the debtor as God exercises his love to us debtors, love therefore without end and without measure, at all hours and under all circumstances; this love is the greatest, indeed the sole, content of human action. This action never ends and is never exhausted; it, too, forms part of the task that has been set us and allows us only to pray, 'Forgive us our debts'. What man is, then, and what he does is solely this one and ever new act of forgiving love. So whatever else usually fills and can fill a human existence can be surrendered; for before this act, or, rather, before the one who makes it possible and necessary, all else has become inessential, a burden of 'debts'. Even life and death, about which the Lord's Prayer maintains a profound silence, life in the service of the Lord and death in the service of the Lord, have no significance in the face of this one task and this one act of love. The infinite eschatological nearness of the Father has made even these most intimate things distant, and has given all human life and action a new centre which illuminates it with the brightness of the eschatological day; it is this act of forgiving love. All struggle has become acceptance and all duty grace, and in grace we live as long as we are still in this today, and look for the tomorrow.

3. We might perhaps shrink from mentioning all these presuppositions, as they seem like distant abstractions in comparison with the general comprehensibility of the individual petitions, did not the Lord's Prayer itself offer a firm point for their

concentration and clarification. It speaks over and over again of 'us', and the second set of petitions in the prayer, including the fourth petition, leads us again and again to ask what we are to understand by this 'we'. So we must give a brief summary of what was said earlier.

In an external sense the question can be easily answered: these are the disciples to whom Jesus is Master and Lord, who listen to his instructions about prayer, as Matthew tells us, or ask for such instruction, as Luke says. The address of the prayer adds a second definition to this first one. 'We' are those who can call God their Father and in saying the prayer know that they are his children. These external indications offer some not unimportant perspectives which have a bearing on the whole prayer. The Lord's Prayer is not a prayer for the individual man, however his individuality may be expressed, whether in smallness or greatness, in need or happiness. There is no word for 'I' or 'mine', and thus no consideration of human solitude, but only of the community of men who ask for their bread on earth, and complain about their life before God. How could there be this solitude when any community rests in the Father, and 'we' are in turn bound through him in the same community of children? Nor is the Lord's Prayer the prayer for a people, as Old Testament petitions suggest or presuppose. It disregards all divisions and distinctions, all bonds and conditions which have their basis in time and space, as though they were unimportant; it elevates 'us' above the limits of any land and people and is at home only in the expanse of 'heaven and earth', or, more accurately, in the presence of 'Our Father who art in heaven'. Finally, the Lord's Prayer is not a prayer for a community or a Church; any particular quality of faith or revelation, historical election or eschatological promise, cult or law, disappears in the equality with which the children of God stand before their Father. What binds them in a unity is this prayer to the Father; the insecurity of this prayer is their one sure foundation.

So the praying community seems to have no clear distinguishing marks. Yet it is made up of particular men who still live on this transitory earth, with their spiritual and bodily needs. This double link, which almost disregards all human freedom of will, seems in a deeper way to correspond with the last association we noted. For if only he 'gives us our bread today', is not the very fact that our body needs nourishment then a sign of his Fatherhood? If he forgives us our debts, is not then the fact that we owe debts also a sign that we may pray to him as his children? If he does not lead us into temptation, is not then the fact that this temptation surrounds us again a sign that we belong together as Father and children? So the one who is involved in poor fare and religious need becomes the one who is involved in God, or, in more accurate terms; the fact that men join together in prayer to form a 'we' is only possible through the Father and before the Father. He is the sole ground of all their fellowship and its sole end, and the two lie, not in an immeasurable depth or at an inaccessible height, but in the immediate nearness of the here and now. Before this eschatological event, only one thing still preserves its reality in our today, the physical and spiritual bond among men, and it is already influenced by the holiness of the eschatological tomorrow. So we can understand from this standpoint, too, that the 'we' which marks a community develops from all the earthly restrictions of body and soul in which a man is involved as an individual and which in an incomparable way make up his being, and that this makes his prayer possible and real.

But how can all this be experienced otherwise than in the assurance of the individual at prayer? How can a community experience this twofold need and grace? The question opens only one new approach to the eschatological character of this 'our' community, which is expressed in the concept of children and grounded in the name of the Father. For this childhood gives to each individual only so much truth and reality as he has received from the Father; it grounds the oneness of the 'I' in an order which knows only the equality of children before their Father, and in it their fellowship with him and with each other. So everything that an individual can do, ask and give is 'our' act, 'our' petition, and 'our' gift, and all the life and work of 'our' community is represented in 'my' life and 'my' work. Between this 'we' and this 'I' there is an indissoluble relationship. The individual is only what he is in the community of the children of God, i.e. before the Father, and this community is only what the individual is through the Father.

This correlation is expressed in many ways. The need that only the individual can experience, the physical need of hunger and the spiritual need of indebtedness, is precisely 'our' need, and in being that it is also 'our' grace given by the Father. The smaller so to speak the human sphere which the 'I' needs as its inalienable possession, the greater is the sphere of grace that 'we' receive from the Father, and the more inward the community which binds 'us'. We can now understand why man's life is virtually reduced to the needs of body and soul, as this reflects all the more clearly the love of the Father who 'gives us our bread', and the bread, which 'I' alone need, is truly 'our bread'. For 'we' now stand in a peculiar intermediate position between the glory of what is to come and today's need and distress; it transforms our isolation into the fellowship of children before the Father and reflects this fellowship on to our isolation. This intermediate position loosens all earthly and historical ties and changes those that still remain, bodily need and moral necessity, in the mirror of God's permanent eschatological grace. An unmistakable Johannine feature is thus expressed in the picture of 'our' community: we still live in this world, but we are no longer of it; for it has been overcome, with its threefold powers of debt and temptation and the evil one.

So a new and infinite freedom has been won for 'us', and it is expressed in two ways. Of all the possibilities of human will and action, only two remain, 'to pray' and 'to forgive our debtors'. The praying constitutes the fellowship in which we live with the Father and the brethren; it means that no outward need is so great and no inward need is so deep that it cannot be transformed through prayer to the Father into an abundance of his grace and love. It also suggests the other need, which can be called the one true need, from which the sources of this fatherly love flow. With this prayer the 'as we forgive our debtors' is indissolubly associated. For if our life as that of children of men and of God is based on and sustained by nothing more than the action of the Father for which we pray, 'the forgiveness of our debts', all possibilities and necessities of this newly given life are concentrated in this one thing, 'to forgive our debtors'. Along with the tacit omnipotence of the Father's love, we once again find the sanctifying power of his work as the sole reality of 'our' still human existence. But over and above this *ora et ama*, as we might briefly describe the principle of 'our' fellowship, there is a new factor: 'we' are now the place and the means, as the divine act of forgiveness happens through our hands and hearts; 'we' are only this place and this means, but we are it wholly and completely, for otherwise we would not be the children of our Father in heaven: oppressed by debts and threatened by temptation, we are the place of love which forgives debts, without measure and without reason, just as the forgiving love of the Father is without measure and reason. We stand in a centre which embraces no historical categories but makes a basis for new ones; for 'to our debtors' we are the intermediaries between the 'still today' and the 'already tomorrow' which makes eschatological fullness the ultimate ground of human reality, and historical reality the transparent picture of that fullness.

But if we are such intermediaries between 'God and our debtors', God and the world, the question arises once again of the means for this work of divine immediacy. A comparison with the Old Testament people of God is soon called for; is this people not similarly an intermediary between God and the nations, 'a guide to the blind, a light to those who are in darkness, a corrector of the foolish, a teacher of children' (*Rom.* 2.19f.)? The parallel is plain, indeed it is necessary, if the eschatological novelty of this Lord's Prayer is simply the fulfilment of an ancient revelation of God. But in that case the differences should not be overlooked; not one of all the manifold gifts and tasks for which the Jewish people boasts that it has been chosen is mentioned here.

The actions that are mentioned here, prayer and love, are in Judaism bound up with particular institutions, with the Law, the fulfilment of which opens the way to God, and the cult, whose sacrifice also blots out all debts. We can now understand why all such associations underlie this 'we' only as insubstantial phantoms; for they would again tie the power of eschatological forgiveness to historical institutions which for the children of God have already been overcome by the eschatological nearness of the Father. We can also understand the urgency and emphasis with which this 'as we forgive our debtors' is made the sole sign of the eschatological fellowship in which we stand before the Father. We can perhaps also infer from this actual relationship one minor historical feature which characterizes the fellowship of those who pray. In the situation of the disciples of Jesus this renunciation of all historical links and this one eschatological association in prayer and forgiveness means that while they still live in an historical association which regulates its external life with commandments and duties, they are also inwardly, i.e. eschatologically, distinct from this association, and its concerns and foundations. They are still in no separate community, they are still so to speak scattered among people and countries, because they are gathered only through the Father to be his children; we can see how this sort of picture of the disciples emerges from a number of sayings of the Lord in the Synoptic Gospels and from all the sayings of the Fourth Gospel. But in that case the question whether these suppliants have not been given what this eschatological calling guarantees arises once again, all the more urgently.

The question is synonymous with another one, namely how the certainty of the eschatological tomorrow is guaranteed if the community of those who pray exists only in and through this certainty, and to this comprehensive question all the Gospels give only one answer; this guarantee depends on the figure of the Master, who preaches the coming of the kingdom of God, works from this kingdom of God, and gives this prayer to his disciples. Because he preaches and works in this way, he is the still-hidden Lord of his kingdom; because he works and preaches on earth with his disciples, he looks forward with them to the coming eschatological consummation and uses in his prayers the same address 'Father' as this prayer of his disciples. This produces a deeper connection which is at the same time both historical and eschatological: 'Because "we" are the children of God, we are also at the same time the disciples of Jesus; because we are his disciples, we are also the children of our Father in heaven.'

This twofold definition suggests one last feature which characterizes our fellowship. If God shows himself to be our Father by giving us our daily bread and forgiving our debts, that means at the same time that he has begun the work of eschatological consummation: in calling us, he is perfecting the world. So 'we' are the nucleus of that community which represents God's eternal world, like the angels, who even now are accomplishing the work of consummation. How else could we 'forgive our debtors' and so achieve with them the Father's eschatological plan? So we can understand from a new point of view why the world of debt and temptation and abandonment to the evil one is contrasted by the first three petitions with God's name and kingdom and will. For all this is no longer simply God's affair, which he carries to its goal regardless of the destiny of humankind; it is also the affair of the children of God, who in this thrice threatened and already partly fallen world have already received as their provisional share and heritage what they ask of the former thrice promised world. But in that case, the way in which these concerns of God are mentioned first is all the more instructive, the silence about all that these concerns of God mean for men and the children of God is all the deeper, and the infinite degree of fear and trust with which 'we' stand as children before the Father, whose will alone prevails, whose kingdom he alone brings in and whose name he alone hallows, is all the clearer. So the Lord's Prayer becomes a significant unity in which all questions between and about heaven and earth and all

THE LITERARY PROBLEM

realities of heaven and earth rest as in an eschatologically balanced equilibrium.

4. But the prayer of Jesus is still involved in a number of external questions which seem to endanger even what meaning we have discovered. We have it in two different forms; in view of the significance of each word of the prayer, should we not expect it to have been transmitted from the beginning in a fixed and unalterable form? If we possess a longer and a shorter version of the Lord's Prayer, must we not then conclude that there was an original form which was then expanded more and more by various additions? The original form would be the prayer as Jesus himself spoke it for the first time, and the different forms would be expansions by different communities or individual evangelists.

Adolf von Harnack drew this conclusion in his famous study of the Eucharist; by eliminating all the variants of the tradition as later additions, he obtains the following 'original form', which he then regards as the original prayer of Jesus:

> Father
> Our daily bread give us today,
> And forgive us our debts,
> As we forgive our debtors,
> And lead us not into temptation.

Both the methods and the result of this investigation are uncertain and suspect. We possess hardly a word of Jesus that has not come down to us in different forms when more than one evangelist has transmitted it; the Beatitudes, the parable of the seed, the thanksgiving are all well-known instances of this. We may therefore say (and we could find detailed support in every saying) that there never were these so-called primitive forms. We have the sayings of Jesus only in the different reflections which have been made by a variety of traditions and Gospels from Mark to John. Through the reflections, distorted in numerous ways, we can see the ideas which were expressed on particular occasions, but we cannot discover exact, original words in which they were expressed. In the literal historical sense this is a result of the uncertainty which is associated with any form of oral tradition, but there is also a richness of light and colouring, of features and motives, which allows us to guess at the greater richness and the close-knit, concentrated power of the sayings of Jesus as they once rang out, and which only the echoes preserve for us. The concept of the 'original form' has its place in the context of written literature; here we have the life of a developing language and the fidelity of the many branches of an oral tradition. Suppose, however, that there was once an original form even of the Lord's Prayer, the literary critical method that eliminates variants as later material and only allows the constants to be 'genuine' cannot lead to this hypothetical goal, as it is based on the assumption, which is to some extent justified in *literature*, that the very constancy of the wording guarantees the authenticity of the saying. But this method does not take account of the possibility that the important and decisive elements are those which are elaborated and varied by an oral tradition; something that everyone could understand would seem so obvious to the tradition that it would hand it on so to speak without any variation, whereas it would put what seemed strange and valuable in continually new forms.

An example of such change is given in the words of the Old Testament quoted in the Gospels; although their wording is relatively fixed, they nevertheless occur in a number of variant forms. We might perhaps compare the saying of Deutero-Isaiah (42.1): 'Behold my servant whom I uphold, my chosen in whom my soul delights.' Matthew alone transmits it in two different versions (12.18 and 3.17=17.5); he also knows two forms of the same saying of the Lord (e.g. 5.32; 19.9), and Luke sometimes adds a third (e.g. 16.18). We may draw the conclusion from such examples that variations in the wording need not mean uncertainty and 'inauthenticity'. Where the opposite is presumed, fixed literary sources are again presupposed, and faith is put in a concept of literary fidelity which was foreign to the Primitive

Christian tradition. The question is not that of the accuracy of a past wording but of the value and power of a present influence. Whether this value and power are kept by making an alteration or retaining the original is a question which has to be given a fresh answer in the case of each individual saying in the tradition.

These basic considerations only suggest the limits within which an attempt to find the 'original' Lord's Prayer still seems possible; we must add some objective reasons which make the idea of such an 'original' form historically impossible. Both the Matthaean and Lucan forms of the prayer are close-knit wholes. One is in a familiar Old Testament rhythmical pattern of five lines each of 2 x 2 stresses, the other in the common Aramaic form of 7 lines each of 7 syllables; the fixity of the form indicates that the differences do not go back to the literary motives of those who recorded the traditions but to actual differences in the traditions themselves. Now if the form of the sentences still seems to leave room for some uncertainty, the content shows that a different outlook and piety is expressed in each variation. Here too, it is not a matter of literary arbitrariness, but of actual necessity. These observations compel us to the conclusion that the Lord's Prayer was from the beginning received and handed down in two forms. So we may hardly ask in what form Jesus gave the prayer to his disciples, because such a question runs contrary to the tradition on which it is based; and if we still insist on putting it, the only answers are possibilities which cannot be substantiated further, either that we cannot know of any 'original' form or that Jesus, or even the primitive community, used one or other form as occasion required. The vagueness of such answers shows that we are departing from the undoubted certainty of the tradition we have and refusing the equally undoubted uncertainty of unfounded questions and answers.

Of course, if we take it that the Lord's Prayer existed in a longer and a shorter version, at first sight we seem to be faced with greater historical difficulties. Can we assume that in the Primitive Christian tradition there were at least two different trends, and therefore two different communities to hand them down? But we can trace this very duality at a number of places both in the Synoptic tradition and, to a certain degree, also in Luke's Acts of the Apostles. There were two traditions of the appearances of the Risen One; some are put in Jerusalem, others in Galilee. There were similarly two traditions about the outline of the life of Jesus; in one, Jerusalem was the climax and the end of his ministry, in the other, Galilee remained the true centre. Similarly, there were two traditions about the Eucharist; one was rooted in the last meal which Jesus held with his disciples in Jerusalem, the other in the miraculous feeding by the Sea of Galilee. There were two traditions about Jesus' attitude to the temple and the cult; for one, that of Matthew, Mark and John, Jesus is opposed to them and superseded them, for the other, that of Luke, he is their supreme preserver. If there were also two traditions of the Lord's Prayer, it seems likely that here too we should see the same duality of a Galilaean and a Jerusalem tradition; and there are a number of positive historical indications of this.

We concluded earlier from the rhythmic form of the Matthaean and Lucan traditions that the version of the Lord's Prayer in the First Gospel was in Galilaean dialect, that in the Third in the common West-Aramaic language. We cannot of course regard this conclusion as indisputable, because it does not rest on a given text, but only on a hypothetical one, but other signs point in the same direction. First of all, the Gospel according to St. Matthew, like the varied tradition which it has adopted even down to individual details, has its views and its piety completely rooted in the Galilaean tradition, just as St. Luke's Gospel is rooted in that of Jerusalem. Not only do the different outlines of the life of Jesus show this; it is stated at the beginning of the First Gospel, when, on the occasion of Jesus' return and entry to Capernaum, the words of Isaiah are seen to be fulfilled (4.15f.):

> The land of Zebulun and the land of Naphthali . . .
> Galilee of the Gentiles—

294

the people who sat in darkness
have seen a great light.

It seems possible to confirm the same thing on objective grounds:
it is a feature of the picture of the first Jerusalem community
as drawn by Acts that the apostles seek by words and works,
'to turn every one of you from your misdeeds' (3.26), and their
mission-cry runs, 'Repent, and be baptized every one of you'
(2.38). The individualizing type of piety is unmistakably
expressed in such sentences, and this very feature appears in the
Lucan form of the Lord's Prayer. The strength with which the
idea of the eschatological community of disciples predominates
in Matthew cannot be shown in any better way than by the
mission command which is analogous to the Lucan words:
'Make disciples of all nations'. So what only the individual
can be and can fulfil is to be done from now on by the eleven—
'to call all people'; in Luke the words ring out in Jerusalem,
in Matthew the command comes from a mountain in Galilee.

All these indications suggest a ready explanation at the twofold form of the Lord's Prayer. It derives from the twofold
origin of Primitive Christianity and its traditions; all the
peculiarities of language and content through which the two
forms differ are found again in the larger picture of the primitive
communities of Galilee or Jerusalem. There is thus also a
historical reason for not looking for an 'original' form of the
Lord's Prayer, and we must content ourselves with its twofold
form, one in Matthew from Galilee, and the other in Luke from
Jerusalem. The way in which the Galilaean version of the prayer
became decisive for Christendom also sheds some light on the
relationship of these two traditions and their tendencies, both
of which still know themselves to be the one community of their
Lord and Master; here, to put it briefly and crudely, Galilee
triumphed over Jerusalem; elsewhere throughout the history
of Primitive Christianity, Jerusalem slowly and more and more
strongly gained the upper hand over Galilee. And if the Lucan
form generally shows its later origin through its minor variations

of language, we must also assume that the two forms of the Lord's Prayer were shaped in the first years of the common life of the two trends and traditions, when Galilee was the true homeland of the Gospel and its disciples.

5. The Lord's Prayer is so familiar a possession of Christianity, and has found acceptance and welcome so far beyond its boundaries, that we often fail to perceive its historical significance. And yet this is easy to grasp if we take a brief look at the other religions of the world; in each one, we can find a characteristic form in which its inward and outward attitude is mirrored: Persian religion has its hymns, Buddhism its meditations, Islam its shouts of war and faith, the Old Testament its Decalogue and in addition, perhaps, the psalm; only the Christian religion has a prayer, the Lord's Prayer, to express with crystalline clarity what it is 'before God and man'. What is the basis of this peculiarity, and what is its significance?

Prayer is, of course, a common and necessary custom, indeed the centre and nucleus of all religions; it is to a special degree also a characteristic of Israel and Judaism, whose psalter has also become the prayer book of the Christian Churches. Nevertheless, the Lord's Prayer retains its solitary and unique position; it is grounded on the fact that the Gospel of Jesus is and proclaims, in a new and simple sense, a religion of prayer. True, in all religions, and especially that of the Old Testament, the word of divine revelation demands the human answer of prayer; but here prayer is the only possible and the only necessary answer, because here God's eschatological revelation draws near and takes place. It puts to silence all the manifold, reverberating voices of man, and alone has the power to speak and act. So there is no more work and struggle, no more fighting and effort in the service of God, but all action is gathered up in prayer, which is the one timid yet trusting echo of God's revealed action. 'Watch and pray', then, is the solution which Jesus gave his disciples for this eschatological time.

Two things are involved in prayer as the answer to God's eschatological word: sorrow at the end of all historical existence and joy at the beginning of the eschatological event, or, in the language of the New Testament, 'the fear and worship of God' (e.g. *Rev.* 14.7). This twofold characteristic, which seeks in God only what man should really be and finds in men only what God would take of his earthly possessions, is witnessed to most clearly by the Lord's Prayer itself. For it is hardly fortuitous that it answers a request which carries in itself the foundation of all faith and all revelation, and occurs only like this in the New Testament, 'Lord, teach us to pray'. So this answer reaches right up to the hallowed heights of the Father and right down to the abyss of the 'evil one'; so it has its limits (if they may be called limits) set wider than any other prayer, and so too it has found the firm place from which it can pray in confidence, the abiding nearness to the Father which is at the same time exposed to transitory danger from the 'evil one'. As a result, it has made not only prayer in general, but also this particular prayer the one and all-embracing, all-demanding, all-giving mark of the disciples.

Not only is it deeply significant that a prayer has become an historical characteristic of the Christian faith and was made so by Jesus; it is also important that this one prayer can be summed up in the words 'Our Father'. For in every sentence and in every word it teaches that a final and ultimate revelation of God— not some purpose of his historical guidance, but the purpose of his eschatological counsel, not a revelation of other things but a revelation of God's own being, his Fatherhood—is the permanent and inalienable ground of life and faith. The one address, 'Our Father,' implies for Primitive Christian faith fidelity on the side of God and assurance and need on the side of man, communion with God and a bond with the Master, loving fellowship with the brethren and forgiving love to 'our debtors'. If Tertullian called the Lord's Prayer a *breviarium totius evangelii*, this address is the *breviarium breviarii*.

But Tertullian's remark also applies in a quite concrete

historical sense. The Lord's Prayer indicates a Gospel of Jesus which is richer and more integrated than any written Gospel has ever expounded it. Here we have in a single concentration what is separated in our Gospels, and here the totality of their pro- clamation is made part of a greater whole. Thus the theme of the Fourth Gospel, 'I have proclaimed thy name to them' (17.26), has become the basis of the first petition, and the subject of the Synoptic Gospels, 'The kingdom of heaven is at hand' (*Mark* 1.15 *par.*) is touched on and presupposed in the second petition. Both elements, however, are taken up here into the greater idea of eschatological Fatherhood which, while occurring to different degrees in all the Gospels, is in one of them made the all-embracing and all-sustaining ground of life and proclamation. Here, however, the idea permeates the whole prayer; it is the basis of the stilling of our physical and eschatological hunger by God, of his forgiving our debts and keeping us from temptations; all this he grants us, and in turns bids us forgive our debtors and pray to 'Our Father'.

This rich variety of old and new ideas, which is a unity here, but scattered in the Gospels, cannot be proved by literary methods from the character of the prayer or on objective grounds from the faith of the primitive community; it can only be understood as the origin from which the various traditions of our Gospels have derived, like water out of one spring, afterwards flowing in different directions. In other words, the Lord's Prayer is evidence of an historical and objective mean in the preaching of Jesus between the Synoptic and Johannine traditions, between the Synoptic Gospels and that of St. John. Its words and form are closer to the one and its spirit and content closer to the other, but in addition it has an original unity which distinguishes it from both, which is centred in a secret, inner fullness which promises any number of developments. This helps us to realize how much our Gospels have limited the great heritage that they have been given and how much more they have preserved, and it shows the inexhaustible, glittering fullness of light, the kaleidoscopic reflection of which is the greatness and at the same time the limitation of our Gospels. So the Lord's Prayer is not just the perfect prayer which cannot be equalled by any other religion, and which is therefore the prayer of Christianity; it is also a clear and powerful witness to the historical work and preaching of Jesus.

Appendix

Notes

Literature

Index

Appendix : The Eighteen Benedictions

The translation of the Benedictions printed here is that of *The Authorized Daily Prayer Book*, edited by the Rev. S. Singer (Ninth edition, London, Eyre & Spottiswoode, 1912, pp. 44-54). A convenient account of their origin and use (and of the retention of the title, despite the addition of a further Benediction in Jewish worship) may be found in the article *Shemoneh 'Esreh*, in vol. XI of the *Jewish Encyclopedia* (London-New York, 1905) 270-82.

I. Blessed art thou, O Lord our God and God of our fathers, God of Abraham, God of Isaac, and God of Jacob, the great, mighty and revered God, the most high God, who bestowest lovingkindnesses, and possessest all things; who rememberest the pious deeds of the patriarchs, and in love wilt bring a redeemer to their children's children for thy name's sake. O King, Helper, Saviour and Shield. Blessed art thou, O Lord, the Shield of Abraham.

II. Thou, O Lord, art mighty for ever, thou quickenest the dead, thou art mighty to save. Thou sustainest the living with lovingkindness, quickenest the dead with great mercy, supportest the falling, healest the sick, loosest the bound, and keepest thy faith to them that sleep in the dust. Who is like unto thee, Lord of mighty acts, and who resembleth thee, O King, who killest and quickenest, and causest salvation to spring forth? Yea, faithful art thou to quicken the dead. Blessed art thou, O Lord, who quickenest the dead.

III. Thou art holy, and thy name is holy, and holy beings praise thee daily. (Selah) Blessed art thou, O Lord, the holy God.

IV. Thou favourest man with knowledge, and teachest mortals understanding. O favour us with knowledge, understanding and discernment from thee. Blessed art thou, O Lord, gracious Giver of knowledge.

V. Cause us to return, O our Father, unto thy Law; draw us near, O our King, unto thy service, and bring us back in perfect repentance unto thy presence. Blessed art thou, O Lord, who delightest in repentance.

VI. Forgive us, O our Father, for we have sinned; pardon us, O our King, for we have transgressed; for thou dost pardon and forgive. Blessed art thou, O Lord, who art gracious, and dost abundantly forgive.

VII. Look upon our affliction and plead our cause, and redeem us speedily for thy name's sake; for thou art a mighty Redeemer. Blessed art thou, O Lord, the Redeemer of Israel.

VIII. Heal us, O Lord, and we shall be healed; save us and we shall be saved; for thou art our praise. Vouchsafe a perfect healing to all our wounds; for thou, almighty King, art a faithful and merciful Physician. Blessed art thou, O Lord, who healest the sick of thy people Israel.

IX. Bless this year unto us, O Lord our God, together with every kind of the produce thereof, for our welfare; give a blessing upon the face of the earth. O satisfy us with thy goodness, and bless our year like other good years. Blessed art thou, O Lord, who blessest the years.

X. Sound the great horn for our freedom; lift up the ensign to gather our exiles, and gather us from the four corners of the earth. Blessed art thou, O Lord, who gatherest the banished ones of thy people Israel.

XI. Restore our judges as at the first, and our counsellors as at the beginning; remove from us grief and suffering; reign thou over us, O Lord, thou alone, in lovingkindness and tender mercy, and justify us in judgment. Blessed art thou, O Lord, the King who lovest righteousness and judgment.

XII. And for slanderers let there be no hope, and let all wickedness perish as in a moment; let all thine enemies be speedily cut off, and the dominion of arrogance do thou uproot and crush, cast down and humble speedily in our days. Blessed art thou, O Lord, who breakest the enemies and humblest the arrogant.

XIII. Towards the righteous and the pious, towards the elders of thy people the house of Israel, towards the remnant of their scribes, towards the proselytes of righteousness, and towards us also may thy tender mercies be stirred, O Lord our God; grant a good reward unto all who faithfully trust in thy name; set our portion with them for ever, so that we may not be put to shame; for we have trusted in thee. Blessed art thou, O Lord, the stay and trust of the righteous.

XIV. And to Jerusalem, thy city, return in mercy, and dwell therein as thou hast spoken; rebuild it soon in our days as an everlasting building, and speedily set up therein the throne of David. Blessed art thou, O Lord, who rebuildest Jerusalem.

XV. Speedily cause the offspring of David, thy servant, to flourish, and let his horn be exalted by thy salvation, because we wait for thy salvation all the day. Blessed art thou, O Lord, who causest the horn of salvation to flourish.

XVI. Hear our voice, O Lord our God; spare us and have mercy upon us, and accept our prayer in mercy and favour; for thou art a God who hearkenest unto prayers and supplications: from thy presence, O our King, turn us not

303

empty away; for thou hearkenest in mercy to the prayer of thy people Israel. Blessed art thou, O Lord, who hearkenest unto prayer.

XVII. Accept, O Lord our God, thy people Israel and their prayer; restore the service to the oracle of thy house; receive in love and favour both the fire-offerings of Israel and their prayer; and may the service of thy people Israel be ever acceptable unto thee. And let our eyes behold thy return in mercy to Zion. Blessed art thou, O Lord, who restorest thy divine presence unto Zion.

XVIII. We give thanks unto thee, for thou art the Lord our God and the God of our fathers for ever and ever; thou art the Rock of our lives, the Shield of our salvation through every generation. We will give thanks unto thee and declare thy praise for our lives which are committed unto thy hand, and for our souls which are in thy charge, and for thy miracles, which are daily with us, and for thy wonders and thy benefits, which are wrought at all times, evening, morn and noon. O thou who art all-good, whose mercies fail not; thou, merciful Being, whose lovingkindnesses never cease, we have ever hoped in thee. For all these things thy name, O our King, shall be continually blessed and exalted for ever and ever. And everything that liveth shall give thanks unto thee for ever, and shall praise thy name in truth, O God, our salvation and our help. Blessed art thou, O Lord, whose name is All-good, and unto whom it is becoming to give thanks.

XIX. Grant peace, welfare, blessing, grace, lovingkindness and mercy unto us and unto all Israel, thy people. Bless us, O our Father, even all of us together, with the light of thy countenance; for by the light of thy countenance thou hast given us, O Lord our God, the Law of life, lovingkindness and righteousness, blessing, mercy, life and peace; and may it be good in thy sight to bless thy people Israel at all times and in every hour with thy peace. Grant abundant peace unto Israel thy people for ever; for thou art the sovereign Lord of all peace; and may it be good in thy sight to bless thy people Israel at all times and in every hour with thy peace. Blessed art thou, O Lord, who blessest thy people Israel with peace.

Notes

1. For the problem of the name 'Father' being applied to God, see: R. Gyllenberg, *Studia Orientalia* I, 51-60; A. L. Williams, ' "My Father" in the Jewish thought of the First Century', HTR 30, 1931, 42-7; and especially W. Baudissin, *Kyrios als Gottesname im Judentum und seine Stelle in der Religionsgeschichte*, III 309-57. For the name and concept in primitive religions: K. T. Preuss, *Glauben und Mystik im Schatten des höchsten Wesens;* some details also in W. Grundmann, *Die Gotteskindschaft in der Geschichte Jesu*, 1938. Some evidence for the idea of the Father may be briefly collected here from Greek and Roman authors:

(a) Greek poets and philosophers: Homer, *Iliad* iv 235; v 33; xiii 631; *Odyssey* xiii 128; xx 112; Hesiod, *Theogony* 457; Pindar, *Nem.* viii 27; ix 31; *frag.* 57; Aeschylus, *Septem* 111; Sophocles, *Trach.* 275; *Oed. Col.* 1268; Euripides, *Hel.* 1441f.; *Troad.* 1298; Cleanthes, *Hymn to Zeus* 35; Callimachus, *Hymn to Zeus* 94; Critias, in H. Diels, *Fragmente der Vorsokratiker*[5] II 383,6; Plato, *Tim.* 28c, 41a, 42e; Aristotle, *Pol.* i 12.

(b) Hellenistic writers: Diodorus Siculus v 72,2 (see the quotation above); Plutarch, *Pelopidas* 21.5; *Alexander* 27.11; *Moralia* 167d; Epictetus, *Diss.* i 3.1; 6.40; 9.7; 19.12; iii 24.15f.; *Mithrasliturgie*, ed. A. Dieterich, 6.12; *Papyri Graecae Magicae* (Die Griechische Zauberpapyri) iv 1181ff., ed. K. Preisendanz.

(c) Hellenistic-Jewish writers: Josephus, *Ant.* i 20; ii 152; vii 380 etc.; Philo, *De Spec. Leg.* i 318; ii 30, 165; *Leg. Alleg.* i 18; *Quod Det. Potiori Insid. Sol.* 147; *Quod Deus Sit Immut.* 30; *De Post. Caini* 175; *De Vit. Contemp.* 68; *De Sobr.* 56; *De Confus. Ling.* 63, 145-7.

(d) Roman authors: Ennius, *Ann.* 580ff.; Cicero, *De Nat. Deor.* ii 64; Vergil, *Aeneid* iii 251; Ovid, *Fasti* ii 132, and especially Seneca, *De Benef.* ii 29.4f.; *Epist.* 107.11. Servius observes on Vergil, *Georg.* ii 4; *Pater licet generale sit omnium deorum, tamen proprie Libero semper cohaeret;* similarly Lactantius, *Instit.* iv 311ff.

2. For the name 'Father' in Judaism see: W. Bousset, *Religion des Judentums*[3]

377*ff.*; G. F. Moore, *Judaism* II 201-11. Some of the passages are: *Tobit* 13.4; 3 *Macc.* 2.21; 5.7; 6.4; 6.8; *Wisdom* 11.18; *Ecclus.* 23.1, 4; 51.10; *Orac. Sib.* iii 550; *Jubilees* 1.24f., 28; 19.29; *Test. Jud.* 24.2; *Test. Levi* 17.2. Rabbinic evidence in Billerbeck I 392-6 and Moore, *loc. cit.*

3. On this see J. B. Bernardin, 'A New Testament Triad', JBL 57, 1938, 273-9.

4. In the Pauline epistles we find:

(a) The absolute 'Father' (with or without the article): *Rom.* 6.4; 8.15; 1 *Cor.* 8.6; 15.24; *Gal.* 1.1; 4.6; *Phil.* 2.11; *Col.* 1.12; 3.17; 1 *Thess.* 1.1; see also 2 *Cor.* 1.3.

(b) 'Father of our Lord Jesus Christ' or the like: *Rom.* 15.6; 2 *Cor.* 1.3; 11.31; *Col.* 1.3.

(c) 'God, our Father' only in the formal and traditional opening greetings.

(d) 'Our God and Father': *Gal.* 1.4; *Phil.* 4.20; 1 *Thess.* 1.3; 3.11,13; 2 *Thess.* 2.16.

We never find a simple 'our Father' or even 'my Father'. The tendency is still clearer in the other New Testament writings: Acts knows 'the Father' only in the mouth of the Risen Lord (1.4,7). The Epistle to the Ephesians has only 'God our Father' in the introductory greeting, elsewhere there is just 'Father of the Lord' (1.17; 3.14) or 'the Father', without addition (2.18; 5.20; 6.23; cf. also 1.17); the Pastorals have the name 'Father' only in the initial greetings and twice omit the 'our' here (2 *Tim.* 1.2; *Titus* 1.4); the Epistle to the Hebrews speaks only once of the 'Father of spirits' (12.9). The Epistle of James knows only 'Father' without any addition (1.27; 3.9; cf. also 1.17), as do the two Epistles of Peter (1 *Peter* 1.2,17; 2 *Peter* 1.17; 3.4); and once, where a genitive is added, it is 'of the Lord' (1 *Peter* 1.3). The same picture, finally, results from the Johannine writings: Revelation and the Gospel limit the name to the 'Father of Christ' and the Epistles know only 'the Father' (see a concordance s.v.). The only exception is *John* 20.17, an ancient and already traditional saying. So the personal pronoun 'our' with the word 'Father' vanishes more and more, the more frequently the word 'Lord' is added, a word which was missing in the earliest period (*Phil.* 2.11). In this change we can see the change from the community of disciples to the growing Church.

5. For the first petition see A. Fridrichsen, *Teologisk Tidskrift* 8, 1917, 1-16; Lyder Brun, *Harnack-Ehrung* 1921, 22-31; R. Asting, *Die Heiligkeit im Urchristentum* 1930, 75-85; O. Procksch in TWNT I 113.

6. In the OT see, for example, *Prov.* 18.6; similarly *Micah* 6.6; *Neh.* 13.2

etc; in the NT, *Matt.* 16.28; 21.31. See too: J. Wellhausen, *Einleitung in die drei ersten Evangelien*², 24 and J. Héring, *Le Royaume de Dieu et sa venue*, 91.

7. Chrysostom explains briefly (in Matt. *Homil.* xix 4, PG 57, 279): τὸ ἁγιασθήτω τοῦτό ἐστι δοξασθήτω, similarly Theodoret on *Isa.* 49.7. Meister Eckhart still says, equally briefly: *sanctificetur id est glorificetur nomen tuum* (following Cassian, *Collatio* IX 18.3, CSEL XIII 266; *Opera Latina* I ed. R. Klibansky, 6). In the Rabbinic writings *hiqdîš* is often equivalent to *berākā*, in Arabic *taqdîš* is the technical term for praising God, and in later Greek ἁγιάζειν is synonymous with εὐλογεῖν, cf. Du Cange, *Gloss. Gr. Med.*, s.v.

8. The formulation comes from Oetinger, *Wörterbuch* (first ed. 1759, second ed. 1780), s.v. 'Heiligkeit', the unrivalled ancestor of all theological word-books.

9. Some evidence for the changing forms of 'if God wills' may be enumerated briefly here: Plato, *Phaedo* 80d; *Alcib.*, 135d; *Theaet.* 151d; *Laches* 201c; *Hipp. Maj.* 286c; *Leg.* 688e, 799e; *Letters* 323c; Cleanthes in: Epictetus, *Enchir.* 53,1; Iamblichus, *Vit. Pythag.* 145 (from which the quotation in the text is taken); Ennius in: Cicero, *De Offic.* i 12,38; Plautus, *Captiv.* ii 3,94; *Poen.* iv 2,88; Sallust, *Jug.* xiv 19; Seneca, *Epist.* 74.20: *Placeat homini quidquid Deo placuit*. For examples from the papyri see: A. Deissmann, *Neue Bibelstudien* 80; from Attic comedy: Aristoph., *Plutus* 347, 405, 1188; *Ran.* 500. Instances of the related formula 'with God, with the gods': Homer, *Iliad* ix 49; xxiv 430; Pindar, *Olymp.* viii 14; *Nem.* viii 28; Aeschylus, *Choeph.* 147f.; Plato, *Prot.* 317b; *Theaet.* 151b; *Leg.* 858b; *Letters* 311d, 320bc; further material in Tycho Mommsen, *Beiträge zur Lehre von den griechischen Präpositionen* 1895. See also my article '*Syn Christo*', *Festgabe für Adolf Deissmann*, 1926, 226ff. Some examples from the papyri are: *Aegyptische Urkunden aus den Museen zu Berlin* (BGU) II 423, 18; 615, 4f.; further I 27, 11f.; 248, 11f.; 249,13; II 451, 10f. Outside the well-known passage James 4. 15, related formulas occur at *I Cor.* 4.19; 16.7,12; *Heb.* 6.3; *Acts* 18.21; then Ign., *ad Eph.*, 20.1. Literature in Lietzmann on *I Cor.* 4. 19.

10. For an explanation see M. Dibelius, 'Die dritte Bitte des Vater-unsers' *Christl. Welt*, 1940, 52f.

11. For an explanation see A. Seeberg, 'Die vierte Bitte des Vater-unsers': in R. Seeberg, *Dr. Alfred Seeberg, Worte des Gedächtnisses*, 1916, 69-82; J. Bock, *Die Brotbitte des Vater-unsers*, 1911.

12. See passages like: *Gen.* 28. 20; 47.15-17; *Ex.* 16. 15; *Deut.* 10. 18; *Judg.* 8. 5f. 15; *I Sam.* 10.4; 22.13; 30.11; *I Kings* 5.9 (23); *Isa.* 55.10; *Jer.* 44 (37).21 etc.

13. For literature, see Förster in TWNT II 587-95; J. Sickenberger, *Unser ausreichendes Brot gib uns heute*, 1914; further in Bauer, *Wörterbuch*, s.v.

14. See my article: 'Das Abendmahl in der Urgemeinde', JBL, 1937, 217-52 and my *Commentary on St. Mark* on the relevant passages. An extract has appeared in *Svensk Teologisk Kvartalskrift* 1937, 333-45: 'Om nattvarden i Nya Testamentet.'

15. A personal pronoun with the noun 'bread' or a corresponding genitive describes:
   (a) The bread that men need: *Lam.* 5.9; *Ezek.* 4.15; 5.16; 12.19; *Ps.* 101.5; *Ecclus.* 12.5; *Hosea* 2.7; *Isa.* 4.1.
   (b) The bread that belongs to anybody: *Ex.* 23.25; *Lev.* 26.5; 22.7,11,13; *Tobit* 1.10*f*; *Jer.* 5.17; it is therefore a sign of close community: *II Sam.* 12.3; *Ps.* 40.10; *Ecclus.* 20.16, and is to be shared with the hungry: *Tobit* 1.16*f.*; *Prov.* 25.21; *Ezek.* 18.16. The manna in the wilderness is called 'heavenly bread' or 'angels' bread': *Ps.* 77.20,24*f.*; 104.40, and there is one mention, by transference, of the 'bread of wisdom' (*Prov.* 9.5). In all these passages such bread is distinguished from ordinary bread and is stressed.

16. Texts after A. Ungnad, *Die Religion der Babylonier und Assyrer*, 1921, pp. 221, 226. (But see Translator's Preface.)

17. On this see Franz Steinleitner, *Die Beicht* (Diss. München 1913), passim.

18. The idea that man's life is a debt to be paid also finds expression on Greek soil after Plato, *Timaeus* 42e, especially in: Plutarch, *Consol. ad Apollon.* 10 p. 106F: 'Therefore we say that life is a debt to be repaid, which our forefathers borrowed from Fate. And as soon as the creditor demands it we must leave it and pay without regret, if we do not want to be thought ungrateful and deceitful debtors.' The same thought is also found in Epictetus, *Diss.* i 1, 32. Lucretius reproduces it in Roman literature: *De Rerum Natura* iii, 971: *vita mancipio nulli datur, omnibus usu*; similarly Seneca, *Consol. ad Polyb.* 29.4; hence too the Latin proverb *mors est naturae debitum*. Philo too attests the same thought, *De Poster. Caini* 5; *De Abrahamo* 257; *Quis Rer. Div. Haer.* 282. The difference from the concept of debt in our petition is obvious.

19. For the concept of temptation see: Axel Sommer, *Der Begriff der Versuchung im AT und Judentum*, Diss. Breslau 1935; H. J. Korn, *Peirasmos* 1936.

20 On this see esp. F. H. Chase, *The Lord's Prayer*, 1891, 71-85.

21. For this interpretation see: Sophocles, *Oed. Col.* 247*f.*; *Polyb.* VI 15, 6. The other interpretation 'find oneself' is also possible; even then the ἐν

τῷ πονηρῷ is to be understood personally, after v. 18. See Büchsel in TWNT III 654, note 3 and Bauer s.v. κεῖμαι.

22. See the further details in Tischendorf and von Soden, on *Matt.* 6.13.

23. Sobernheim, *Die Inschriften von Palmyra*, no. 34 and Schürer, SBA 1897, 200-25.

24. On this see especially A. Seeberg, 'Vaterunser und Abendmahl': *Neutestamentliche Studien für Georg Heinrici* 1914, 108-14.

25. See here too the further details in Tischendorf and von Soden, on *Luke* 11.1-4.

26. The possibility that behind the two forms the custom of the holy kiss is to be found, after the eating of the Supper (fourth petition), is an attractive, but incorrect supposition of A. Seeberg's (*op. cit.* 110). It does not take into account that there is no mention of a mutual forgiveness.

27. The phrase is quite usual in the *koine*. Some examples from inscriptions and papyri are: *Sylloge Inscriptionum Graecarum,*[3] ed. W. Dittenberger, 1915-24; P. Par. 26.13; P. Giess. 17.1; from the LXX; *Tobit* 10.7; *Susanna* 8,12; I *Macc.* 8.15; from the NT: *Matt.* 26.55 *par.*; *Luke* 16.19; *Acts* 2.46f.; 3.2; 16.5; 19.9; I *Cor.* 15.31; II *Cor.* 11.28; *Heb.* 7.27; 10.11. The article, too, is sometimes added: *Luke* 19.47; *Acts* 17.11, cf. also: Aristoph., *Hipp.* 1126; Polyb., iv 18,2; P. Oxy. 1220, 4. κατὰ πᾶσαν ἡμέραν also occurs at *Acts* 17.17, similarly Josephus, *Ant.* vi 49, καθ' ἑκάστην ἡμέραν, *Heb.* 3.13, in LXX: *Ex.* 5.8; *Esther* 2.11; *Job* 1.4; *Bel* 4,6. In *Esther* 3.4 LXX translates the Hebrew yōm wāyōm thus. The indeterminate and so to speak weak sense of the phrase is clear from these examples; it is therefore probable that in Aramaic a simple b*yōmā corresponded to it, and not a b*kol yōmā, as the Syriac versions have.

28. Only *Eph.* 4.30 has, 'Do not grieve the holy Spirit of God', but this is a quotation from *Isa.* 63.10, 'and grieved his (God's) holy Spirit', where the Massora have 'iṣṣ*bū= ἐλύπησαν, which LXX translates more sharply παρώξυναν.

29. On this see also A. Seeberg, *op. cit.* 111.

Literature

Ancient Exegesis

ORIGEN, *De Oratione*, GCS II 346–95.
GREGORY OF NYSSA, *Five homilies on the Lord's Prayer:* Migne PG 44, 1120–93.
CHRYSOSTOM, *In Matthaeum, Hom.* XIX: Migne PG 57, 278.
CYRIL OF JERUSALEM, *In Catech.* 23: Migne PG 33.
TERTULLIAN, *De Oratione*, CSEL 20, 180–207.
CYPRIAN, *De Oratione Dominica*, CSEL 3, 267–87.
AUGUSTINE, *De Sermone Domini in Monte:* PL 34.
MEISTER ECKHART, *Super Oratione Dominica, Opera latina* I, ed. R. Klibansky.
NICOLAS CUSANUS, *Die Auslegung des Vater-unsers in vier Predigten*, SB Heidelberg 1938–9, phil. hist. Klasse, 4 Abh.

Collections of Ancient Exegesis

SUICER, *Observationes sacrae*, Zurich 1665.
GERHARD TILLMANN, *Das Gebet, nach der Lehre der Heiligen dargestellt*, 1877.
H. HARTER, *Sanctorum Patrum opuscula selecta* II² 1879.
CARDINAL J. VIVES, *Expositio in orationem dominicam*, Köln 1539.

Modern Exegesis

F. H. CHASE, *The Lord's Prayer in the early Church* (Texts and Studies, ed. J. A. Robinson I, 1891).
EBERHARD NESTLE, 'The Lord's Prayer', *Encyclopaedia Biblica* III 2816–23.
EDUARD V. D. GOLTZ, *Das Gebet in der ältesten Christenheit*, 1902.
OTTO DIBELIUS, *Das Vater-unser*, 1903.
ADOLF HARNACK, *Sitzungsberichte der Preussichen Akademie der Wissenschaften zu Berlin* (phil.-hist. Klasse) (SBA) I 195–208, 1904.
The Sayings of Jesus, 1908.
J. HAUSSLEITER, 'Das Vater-unser', *Realencyklopädie für protestantische Theologie und Kirche*, ed. J. Herzog, rev. A. Hauck³ XX 431ff.
G. LÖSCHKE, *Die Vater-unser-Erklärung des Theophilus von Antiochien*, 1908.

J. HENSLER, *Das Vater-unser*, 1914.

ALFRED SEEBERG, 'Vater-unser und Abendmahl', *Neutestamentliche Studien für G. Henrici* 1914, 108-14, 'Die vierte Bitte des Vater-unsers': Reinhold Seeberg, D. *Alfred Seeberg, Worte des Gedächtnisses*, 1916, 69-82.

I. ABRAHAMS, 'The Lord's Prayer', *Studies in Pharisaism and the Gospels* II 94-108, 1923.

J. KILIAN, *Untersuchungen zur Geschichte der griechischen Vater-unser-Exegese.*

PAUL FIEBIG, *Das Vater-unser*, 1927.

GUSTAV DALMAN, *The Words of Jesus*, I². 283-365.

J. HERRMANN, 'Der alttestamentliche Urgrund des Vater-unsers', *Festschrift für Otto Procksch*, 1934.

Index

INDEX

INDEX OF GREEK WORDS DISCUSSED

INDEX OF BIBLICAL AND OTHER TEXTS

(The entries are arranged in the following order: Books of the Old Testament; Old Testament Apocrypha; New Testament; Old Testament Pseudepigrapha; Apostolic Fathers; Talmud and other Jewish non-Biblical sources.)

INDEX